Awaken Your Authentic Self

Awaken Your Authentic Self

TONY FAHKRY

THOUGHT
CATALOG
Books

BROOKLYN, NY

THOUGHT
CATALOG
Books

Copyright © 2017 by Tony Fahkry

All rights reserved. Designed by KJ Parish. Cover photography by © Melpomenem

Published by Thought Catalog Books, a division of The Thought & Expression Co., Williamsburg, Brooklyn. Founded in 2010, Thought Catalog is a website and imprint dedicated to your ideas and stories. We publish fiction and non-fiction from emerging and established writers across all genres. For general information and submissions: manuscripts@thoughtcatalog.com.

First edition, 2017

ISBN: 978-1945796401

Printed and bound in the United States.

10 9 8 7 6 5 4 3 2 1

CONTENTS

Foreword

Dennis Merritt Jones

Why have you selected this book to read? With the many thousands of books available, why, specifically, are you called to read this book? You have chosen it because there lies within you a compelling voice to which you are finally paying attention. That voice has been trying to gain your attention for a long time. In a manner of speaking you could say that this book has actually chosen you because you are now open and ready to awaken to the Truth of who you really are. Complete acceptance of your true identity is central to your life and until you embrace it there will be a piece (peace) missing from the innate wholeness from which you came. The fulfillment of a life worth living rises inherently from within as you listen to—and honor—the call of the Authentic Self you have come here to be. This is why you have chosen to read Tony's book, *Awaken Your Authentic Self*. This is your wakeup call...your time to "Be."

The Dalai Lama said it puzzled him why so many people in the West suffer low self-esteem. The media portrays a world that doesn't meet our needs but tries desperately to convey what is missing. Of course, in truth, there is nothing missing—and that is what you will discover as Tony guides you through the maze of mistaken beliefs we have inherited from the collective consciousness of humankind. We're inundated with information we think we can't live without, yet at the end of the day, we're no better because we avoid connecting with the truth of our existence.

Awaken Your Authentic Self is a book to help you reconnect with the core of your essential self. It's a move away from what popular culture espouses. Tony invites you to merge with the deepest part of your being, which knows who you are and how you should live…and perhaps most importantly, why you are here.

We're encoded with everything we need to thrive. Because we are one with Life, we came hardwired to live in wholeness, with all the tools necessary to create a life truly worth living. Yet through cultural conditioning, we tend to get spiritual amnesia, forgetting who we are and from whence we have come. As a result, we lose our place to the pull of our external environment and end up living shallow lives, from the outside-in rather than the inside-out. This comes at a cost to our self-worth as we unknowingly relinquish the rich and sacred aspects of living an authentic life.

Tony contends that when we live from the outside-in, "standing out" can become a rite of passage via the clothes one wears, hair color, body piercings, and external adornments. The downside is, the "accoutrements" of the external world can be mistaken as a show of defiance instead of a declaration of distinction. He invites you to disconnect with your external shell for a moment and go deep into your being, to merge with the larger aspect of your oneness with something greater than yourself—the wholeness of Life Itself—where the Authentic Self you are awaits your arrival.

He wants you to know that you have more power than you realize. More genius than you can imagine. More wisdom and knowledge than you can ever access. This is not a patronizing statement to seduce you into a false belief. Tony's book calls you to recognize your unlimited power by Awakening Your Authentic Self.

When you let go of the false belief that you are lacking or inadequate, in that moment you arouse your potential. Who you are today results from your beliefs, thoughts and ideas of the world. Unless you challenge how things stand, you remain pulled by your desires and urges. We need only to look at mainstream culture to see how it seduces us into a false way of life. We are drawn into a fictitious existence at the expense of our sanity and hard-earned dollars.

The knowledge contained within this book invites you to connect with the greater wisdom that is your birthright. If you've been seeking a better way of life, Tony's work is a step in that direction. His insights inspire you to know thyself at the heart of your daily existence.

I highly recommend this book and trust it will be your companion as you embark on embracing your authentic nature. Please re-read it and allow the words to penetrate through to your reality. Only then will you know your authentic nature is ever present as unconditional love.

Peace,
Dennis Merritt Jones
Award-winning author of *Your (Re)Defining Moments: Becoming Who You Were Born to Be* and *The Art of Uncertainty: How to Live In the Mystery of Life and Love It*
www.DennisMerrittJones.com

Cultivating the Authentic Self

There is talk nowadays of the need to be authentic.

The media's influence portrays a fictitious world that doesn't meet our needs. We are inundated with information of news stories we can't live without. We are no better being pulled by our external world; we lose our identity along the way.

Awaken Your Authentic Self is a book to reconnect you with your essential self. It is a move away from whom you should be as espoused by popular culture. The book invites you to reconnect with the deepest part of your being, which knows who you are and how you should live.

We are evolved from nature, which means we are encoded with the DNA to thrive. Yet through cultural conditioning and paradigms, we lose our place to the pull of our external environment. We subscribe to ideologies and beliefs of whom we should be because we want to be accepted and appreciated. This comes at a cost to our self-worth since we must give up an aspect of ourselves.

What does it mean to be authentic and how do we recognize authenticity in others? Each of us knows when someone is inauthentic and we label them as fake. If a person is dissimilar to us we consider them as phony because we don't identify with them. It is important we recognize that when judging others, we avoid dealing with our own issues.

It takes great courage to buck the trend to be yourself. I commend those who stand out with their declaration of personal power.

However, standing out has become a rite of passage where

the clothes one wears, hair color, body piercings, and decorations. It may be viewed as a show of defiance instead of a proclamation of distinction.

I do not intend to cast aspersions over one's external appearance, nor to label or judge others. I invite you to adopt the same attitude. We're doing the best we can, given our level of awareness.

There are many who yearn to be noticed while others want nothing more than to uphold the status quo. They refuse to be acknowledged as different for fear of having the spotlight cast on them. They may be terrified to show their insecurities, fearing judgment by others.

Our pain and troubles may be attributed to straying from our life purpose while succumbing to external influences. The young are inundated with a surplus of information, fueled by technological advances that allow us to stay connected via social media.

Our connections are nothing more than empty posters on an electronic billboard which remind us we belong. And yet we have an inner longing for social acceptance. It is wired into your DNA to be a part of a tribe.

You have more power than you realize. More genius than you can imagine. More wisdom and knowledge than you can ever access. This is not a patronizing statement to seduce you into a false belief. You have unlimited power although accessing that power is the basis to *Awaken Your Authentic Self.*

When you let go of the false belief you are lacking or inadequate, in that moment, you arouse your potential. Who you are today results from your beliefs, thoughts, and ideas of the world. Unless you challenge popular opinion, you will be pulled by the masses. One has only to look to mainstream culture to see the effects the media and marketing hype have on our society. We are drawn into a fictitious way of life at the expense of our sanity and money.

We are conditioned to be like everyone else. We try to stand out by decorating our external shell, hoping to be noticed as different. Yet we entertain the same thoughts and live the same lives as millions of other people while longing for a better way.

Contemplate this for a moment—when did you last entertain an ORIGINAL thought?

In his book Do the Work, author Steven Pressfield realized it wasn't until he was thirty years old when he'd pondered an original thought. Every thought before that resulted from conditioned beliefs, attitudes, and thoughts derived from society.

Consider the following points as ideal qualities to *Awaken Your Authentic Self* which we'll cover in more detail in the coming chapters.

Accept Yourself: Complete acceptance of oneself entails acknowledgment of your wholeness with your imperfections, foibles, and insecurities. You cannot disown unfavorable aspects of yourself and seek to highlight positive qualities. This might lead to narcissism.

Know Thyself: This does not entail knowing your likes or dislikes. Rather, it's a call to discover the true essence of your spiritual self. Who is the real you? What are your true motivations? What kindles your soul? What are your passions?

Discard The False Self: Many people create a false sense of self—an image of who they think they are. The mind creates a false persona epitomized by the ego to keep it alive. Regrettably, life events (tragedy or loss) may disrupt this image and unexpectedly one faces re-examining their sense of self since the illusory shadow is shattered.

Don't Associate With Thoughts: I've written in earlier books about not identifying with your thoughts. Do not allow your thoughts to impress upon you the real self. Thoughts come and go, yet the essence of who you are is unchanging and authentic.

Surrender Addictions: Many people suffer from controlling addictions to things or people. Addictions extend to habitual thoughts which occupy valuable space in the mind and body. They deprive you of energy and disconnect you from your precious self. Let go of that which does not serve you—drop it like a hot piece of coal.

Stop Seeking Validation: Let go of the need to prove yourself to others. You do not need validation from others to prove your worthiness, even from loved ones. No one or nothing can offer you the authentication you long for other than yourself. True validation comes from the core of your being.

Find Time For Silence: Find time to be alone every now and again in nature. Exercise outdoors allows you to reconnect with yourself in a tranquil setting among nature. Being outdoors harmonizes mind and body and energizes the soul.

Connect With Your Heart And Mind: You get stuck in left brain logic since you are taught to reason the world through logic alone. Experiments show that the heart's electrical impulse is 40 to 60 times greater than the brain's. The heart intuits things well before the brain has time to make sense of it.

Accept The Process Of Life: You needn't change anything 'out there' since the root cause of your troubles is always contained within. As you tend to your inner landscape, your external reality harmonizes with your inner world. As the Hermetic aphorism states, "As within, so without."

Focus On Yourself First: Nurture your inner world through self-examination and introspection. When things go wrong in life, knowing you are peaceful and safe is reassuring. It is like a ship in stormy weather—nothing can destabilize a ship when it has a strong hull. It floats through troubled waters allowing the raging storm to take it where it needs to, knowing in due course it will find refuge in safe harbor.

Relationships Are Vital Lessons: What you loathe in others you disapprove in yourself. Therefore, at a deeper level your difficult relationships are a call to heal parts of yourself which you are at war with. Embrace the lesson by allowing painful memories to move through you without becoming invested in any harmful emotions.

Connect With Purpose: Your purpose may or may not be tied to your career. Your purpose is your life's calling—your spiritual truth. It is the deeper question which we beckon of ourselves—why am I here on Earth? Why am I born during this period in time and what have I come here to become? You discover your purpose by 'doing,' not by sitting around waiting for it to land in your lap. Pursue that which fuels your soul and your purpose is realized. Purpose requires discipline, hard work, commitment, and sacrifice. People who are 'lost' have disconnected with their purpose.

To allow our Authentic Self to emerge, we must let go of programmed beliefs and thoughts that no longer sustain us. We spend the first half of life accumulating ideas, only to let go of them in the latter stages. If we wish to live a rich and authentic life, we cannot be weighed down by thoughts which do not serve our highest purpose.

Throughout this book, I am inviting you to cultivate and awaken the authentic person who lies deep within you and longs to be realized. This person has always existed, like Michelangelo carving the Carrara marble to reveal the statuesque David. Underneath the block of marble lies a sculpture waiting to be freed. The artist is the conduit to allow this form to appear.

I invite you to think of your life in the same terms. There is an authentic person waiting to be realized. Your duty is to give life to this individual.

Authenticity has a place to serve in our lives, to awaken us to the person we intend to be. It is a work in progress and may take our entire lives to merge into that person, yet it is worth the effort.

Imagine playing a character that does not represent who you are, yet someone from a screenplay. Consider getting up every day and to put on a mask to be someone you are not suited to be. For many, this is a familiar story. They reach a point in their lives, which coincides at middle age, where they realize this isn't who they aspire to be. They might declare they never liked themselves and have been playing a role to appease others, or worse still, to avoid confronting the essence of their true nature.

This is not how life should be.

We have a choice about how we wish to live. Others might

be unhappy with our life choices. But if we wish to live a fulfilling life, it serves us to cultivate authenticity in our everyday life. While I acknowledge this may sound simplistic as an analogy, it conveys the story of how authenticity emerges in nature.

Imagine for a moment a tree in a park pretending to be a rock. It doesn't shed its leaves in season, nor does it grow roots into the ground and yet seems to be a tree, while still pretending to be a rock.

The tree withers and dies because it cannot sustain life trying to be something it is not. Closer to home, when we live according to the needs of others, something within us dies, because we have not given life to the authenticity within us. Like Michelangelo's marble wanting to be freed to become a statue, we too must give birth to our own creation.

Over the coming chapters, I wish to take you on path toward realizing your Authentic Self. I have included summary points at the end of each chapter to give you an overview of the main points and chief lessons. I encourage you to reflect on the lessons instead of reading the book to finish it. If they are new to you, allow them to sink in until they have meaning and substance. This is how we gain knowledge; that is, we embody the understanding and wisdom at a cellular level so it becomes engraved in our consciousness. From that point we realize the truth of who we are.

I wish you much success and trust that by the close of this book you will understand the Authentic Self that lies deep within you.

To your continued health and happiness,
Tony Fahkry

Part 1

1

Healing Emotional Wounds

Pain Is A Portrait Into The Past

"How shall I attain Eternal Life?"

"Eternal Life is now. Come into the present."

"But I *am* in the present now, am I not?"

"No." "Why not?"

"Why not?" "Because you haven't dropped your past."

"Because you haven't dropped your past." "Why should I drop my past? Not all of it is bad."

"Why should I drop my past? Not all of it is bad."

"The past is to be dropped not because it is bad but because it is dead."

The fable from Anthony de Mello's book *One Minute Wisdom* underscores the message that pain is apparent when we invite the past into the present moment. The past is an illusion because it does not exist in the here and now. From your present moment experience, what remains is a faint memory owing to the passage of time. Suffering is eased when we reconnect to this moment and honor it as a cherished gift. Through your present awareness, you minimize the intensity of painful memories and expand your appreciation of what exists. As you cast your attention back to the present moment, earlier memories diminish through a change in awareness.

Memories have an emotional relationship to thoughts and with enough intensity grow stronger neural networks in the brain. To change those memories, rather than drop them, focus your attention on forming new ones instead. "Processing an emotion entails perceiving it, acknowledging it, being with it, and then letting the wave move through the body (as it naturally will if we don't grip it or feed it)," asserts Linda Graham in *Bouncing Back.*

While it may be obvious, the path to healing takes place when you cease to identify with the pain of the past. In doing so, you invite the healing power of love to preside over your life. Freedom is attained when we write a new script. This new story does not extinguish our memories, it creates an empowering relationship connecting the past to the present, so peace, love, and healing emerge.

To heal emotional wounds requires courage to confront the pain. Our felt sense of connection to our inner spirit is far more resilient than we imagine. I recall my stern upbringing as a child, dominated by an uncompromising father who sought to shape me into someone I was not cut out to be. Years later throughout my adult life, I formed an incomplete story relating to the events of my childhood, steeped in anger and blame.

Eventually, I created a new script by directing forgiveness and peace to the past. In that moment, I healed twenty years of pain because I was no longer willing to stay captive to the emotional wounds.

In his book *The MindBody Code,* Dr. Mario Martinez states, "One of the most important lessons here is that forgiveness is a liberation from the personal enslavement you construct when a misdeed is perpetrated against you. Rather than forgiving the perpetrator, you recover the empowerment and self-worthiness you thought had been taken away from you." Is it conceivable that what took place five, ten, or fifteen years ago may be subject to your perception of it? Perhaps you formed an unfair portrayal of events and have carried that story with you, much to your disappointment?

What if it were true?

How does it feel to hold on to these thoughts all this time?

For those having endured mental, emotional, or physical trauma the pain is undoubtedly real. However, if you wish to heal your pain-story something must give way; otherwise, you become enslaved to the past. Inner peace is fundamental to your happiness. Anger, blame, frustration, and love cannot reside in the same place. One must recede to give way to the other. "We always want to get rid of misery rather than see how it works with joy. The point isn't to cultivate one thing as opposed to another, but to relate properly to where we are," affirms Pema Chodron. At the most primitive level, pain is an invitation to examine the disharmony in our life. It is not intended to prolong suffering unless we allow ourselves to stay stuck.

So, pain invites you to heal emotional conflicts by directing your attention toward peace and love. Choice is powerful because it calls you to rewrite the past with compassion. You create a compelling future instead of being dictated by untoward events of the past. Moreover, the momentary pain of confronting the past far outweighs carrying the burden of grief into the future. "I don't let go of my thoughts—I meet them with understanding. Then they let go of me," states the American spiritual teacher Byron Katie in her acclaimed book *Loving What Is*. Pain allows you to be shaped by your experiences rather than be defined by them.

If I asked you to drop the pain, why are you beneath that?

To hold onto pain distorts our known sense of self. We become caught up in a distorted impression of who we think we are. However well-meaning our intentions, the façade is a self-constructed image which serves to protect us. You are not the sum of your life experiences. While they shape you, they do not define you any more than suggesting a person's past performance dictates their future achievements. Something the Buddha knew centuries ago that is still relevant today: "Pain is inevitable. Suffering is optional." With that, I invite you to drop the past because it is dead and ought to remain behind you. You cannot awaken your Authentic Self when replaying tired and worn-out mental scripts of the past. They serve no point in your present experience and future, so we must be willing to relinquish something old to invite the new, fresh, and expansive energy to permeate our lives.

Your Emotional Wounds Strengthen You

Despite our intense emotional wounds, the hurt will pass and scars eventually heal. To relive the pain reinforces the experience because we cling to the emotions instead of process them. If we wish to lead an Authentic Life we must nurture our emotional well-being. As time moves on so does the emotional strain, yet we needn't clutch to our pain story. We can suffer or let go of what no longer serves us. Many people mask their pain by avoiding it. They rather forget the hurt, which only reinforces it. We must love and acknowledge our darker aspects like our pain and grief. If you appreciate the sun and wish away the darkness, how would you see the stars at night? Our emotional wounds lead us to the wholeness of ourselves. It is remiss to emphasize our darkness while identifying with our light since we encompass both parts.

Pain is a powerful teacher that connects us with our inner wisdom.

Without pain, how would we recognize the enduring self that lies beneath the rubble of suffering? Without pain, we are powerless to embrace the entirety of who we are. Our emotional wounds do not imply we are flawed, yet they show our true character. They are our battle scars that we have danced with and lived to tell the tale. We communicate to others of the struggles that lie ahead, having traversed the path ourselves. Our wounds lie fragmented deep within our psyche. If we have not reconciled them, they grow stronger until we address them. They are the imposing shadow, lurking in the darkness waiting to grab hold if we grow weary. The mind's self-protection is an admirable defense to preserve our emotional well-being. It stows away the pain when you're least equipped to deal with it. Rather than persecute yourself for holding onto unpleasant memories, appreciate that your mind protects you from getting hurt further.

We can become our own healer via loving and nurturing

declarations to ourselves. This reinforces how it is now safe to face these emotions with openness to heal. Our emotional wounds call us to connect with our inner child instead of escaping when the pain intensifies. To run away from pain is the opposite of loving-kindness because we neglect to honor our emotional well-being. We must love ourselves foremost as you would a friend or loved one who is hurt. To demonstrate this commitment, consider the vows recited when two people marry: to honor one another through the good times and bad. So we ought to make the same commitment to ourselves. Irrespective of the emotions that arise, we will honor them. Our emotional wounds strengthen us because they show we have lived a purposeful life. There is a broader lesson contained within each emotional wound. If we penetrate through the pain, we realize it is a return to love as the American spiritual teacher Marianne Williamson affirms.

So when you experience pain and suffering, love yourself.

When you feel anxiety and tension, love yourself.

When you feel happiness and joy, love yourself.

This simple act of self-renewal permeates our consciousness, so regardless of the external conditions, our deepest wisdom leads us to connect with our heart. I've observed that when I embrace my emotional wounds, it opens me to a greater awareness of my soulful nature. The shell which conceals the pain is cracked open to expose the loving tenderness beneath. This is the basis for heart-centered living, in contrast to the egoist self. To heal, we must de-clutter our lives and nurture the child within, while creating a secure environment for the healing to occur.

"The transformation process evolves your consciousness from fear to love. That means you have to dissolve the fears and heal the emotional wounds that are in the way—by understanding them. And that means you have to face them, feel them, and decode them, which most of us dread," states author Penney Peirce. The saying, "Time heals all wounds" does not hold significance if we don't make the time to face them. We may store away the emotional fragments of the past, only to have them reappear at a later stage. To confront our emotional wounds means to honor ourselves foremost. No matter what emerges, we trust we will cope. Everyone is bound to experience hurt and pain in their lives. We all carry emotional pain. It's how we transform the pain to develop a deeper relationship with ourselves that leads to inner freedom.

Our wounds strengthen us because they invite us to be sensitive to our emotional life. We become inquisitive about our emotions and examine them with openness and equanimity. To be curious fosters a balanced relationship with the wholeness of who we are, rather than dismissing the emotions as untoward. As we associate with our fractured parts, we strengthen our commitment to ourselves. To accept and heal our emotional wounds, we release them to invite the power of love to occupy its space. We allow the experience to transform us into empowered beings. I am drawn to author Dennis Merritt Jones' message, "Remember, forgiveness doesn't necessarily mean forgetting. We may always have memories attached to some of our emotional wounds in much the same way we have scar tissue from a physical wound that happened long ago. That doesn't mean you have to relive the pain that caused the scar."

Our childhood wounds are exposed through adult relationships and if we do little to confront them, they can ruin our lives. Therefore, they are a gift guiding us to heal within.

Through mindfulness, we learn to be grounded in the present moment and experience any emotions that emerge. This simple act cultivates true intimacy with ourselves. So avoid holding on to your pain. There is no power gained from being a victim, other than to deflect your wounds onto others to appease your suffering. Psychotherapist and author John Prendergast, Ph.D. states, "If our heart has been closed and then begins to open, we often discover why our native sensitivity originally shut down. Old emotional wounds will surface and ask for our attention. Difficult feelings such as grief, shame, self-loathing, personal deficiency, despair, and fear can arise."

This statement reaffirms the need to love ourselves completely, no matter the emotions. Our responsibility is not to judge ourselves, but to reconcile the pain and integrate it into our experience toward oneness. It is through this oneness that we are called to cultivate the Authentic Self which lies fragmented by the mind's narrative.

Sometimes You Have To Go Through The Storm

Life can be unpredictable. No surprises there. You never know what lies around the corner waiting to test your resolve. Life's challenges are part of the human condition, and yet none are immune from the ravages of existence. They arise for reasons we cannot comprehend and leave us like a wounded pigeon with broken wings. Yet contained within this knowledge and in spite of life's upheaval, we are able to reconnect to our Authentic Self however uncompromising conditions appear. The quote by author Haruki Murakami signifies our ability to assume control of how we interpret pain and suffering, "Pain is inevitable. Suffering is optional." Through my own trials, I have come to appreciate the supreme lesson that we are ultimately not in control. With this knowledge, we surrender to universal forces to imbue us with the experiences to shape our destiny. Surrender does not mean apathy; in contrast, it means mental and emotional detachment from desired outcomes. We allow the process of life to unfold through us and in doing so trust our needs are fulfilled at the right time.

You are never presented with an experience that is the sum of your conditioning. Each challenge stretches you to grow beyond your comfort zone. Comparable with the seasons which arrive and recede, your challenges serve a purpose. Sometimes it may not be obvious for a long time, yet everything unfolds in line with a supreme order. I am neither referring to religion nor spirituality, but an intricate universal order which governs the framework of reality.

There is an ancient Sufi passage that states, "This too shall pass." Reflect on these words during your darkest hour. Pain and suffering recede to give way to a harmonious solution. Painful challenges dissolve in the same way morning fog lifts to reveal a brilliant day. Yield to your challenges by leaning into them instead of opposing them. What happens when you move into your challenges rather than run away from them? You face them head-on and build self-confidence. The storm represents your darkest hour amid the backdrop of uncertainty. Known as the dark night of the soul, the storm serves a purpose. It endows you with vital resources intended for your personal evolution.

It is by no mistake that the bigger we play, the harder we fall. Challenges can arise suddenly, yet lead us to a deeper knowledge of ourselves. Your personal growth is impeded were it not for the difficult times. Man does not rise to his best under the kindest conditions, yet in the harshest storm he discovers his true potential. Do not embrace the good times, yet savor the difficult times as well since progress is realized under testing conditions. The happiest people are those who have undergone hardship to emerge with deep wisdom to share with others. We prevail not in waiting for the storm to pass, but in proceeding through the storm. Winston Churchill said, "If you're going through hell, keep going." You see, the storm shapes your inner landscape by exposing your strengths and weaknesses. It sharpens the saw as Stephen Covey reminds us in *The Seven Habits of Highly Effective People.*

If you are feeling overwhelmed by life's challenges, get back on your feet and persist through it. Acquire the lessons, experience the pain. Awaken Your Authentic Self and your unlimited ability. We must venture beyond our comfort zone daily if we are to rouse our potential. Those who settle, burn out well before their time has come. It was George Bernard Shaw who said, "I want to be all used up before I die." Similarly, we must strive to nurture patience and self-compassion as we endure the storm. In doing so you develop a resilient sense of self. Consider your advice to a close friend or family member undergoing a similar trial.

The Buddha teaches the Four Noble Truths essential to his teachings. They apply to us if we seek to understand the nature of adversity and how to make sense of it in our lives. If we wish to penetrate the true nature of our existence, we must develop a deeper knowledge of ourselves. Suffering is the threshold into one's reality, perceived through the lens of adversity. The Four Noble Truths affirm that life is impermanent—everything is in a transitory state, even our pain and troubles.

They are espoused in the following principles:

The Truth of Suffering: Life is filled with suffering.

The Truth of the Cause of Suffering: The root cause of suffering relates to our cravings for the wrong things. Our material attachments can never meet our true needs since we always yearn for more. Everything is impermanent or in a transitory state.

The Truth of the End of Suffering: Suffering can be overcome and happiness attained if we relinquish our cravings and live each day as it comes. Bliss is attained when we let go of satisfying our personal needs in place of allowing life to flow through us.

The Truth of the Path Leading to the End of Suffering: This embodies the Noble Eightfold Path leading to the end of suffering: right view, right intention, right speech, right action, right livelihood, right effort, right mindfulness, and right concentration.

Your response to hardship is measured by your attitude and mental resilience. It is Charles Swindoll who said, "Words can never adequately convey the incredible impact of our attitude toward life. The longer I live the more convinced I've come that life is 10% what happens to us and 90% how we respond to it." Therefore, it is not life's volatility that is the cause of our hardship, yet how we interpret those events that shape our life. We have two choices in each challenge: rise to it and in doing so overcome it or retreat into despair. The latter invites more suffering and erodes our personal self. We all suffer pain in one form or another, yet the degree to which we choose to suffer remains within our control.

Finding Joy When Life Hurts Most

If you were to ask any person whether they want to wake up joyful every morning, I'm certain they would reply a resounding yes. Happiness is a key desire for cultivating authenticity, yet many people are unhappy to the degree that joy eludes them. In fact, a good deal are miserable. I don't want to offer a bleak picture, yet observe any media story and you'll soon realize how people are attracted to bad news.

One in four people on average experiences depression at some stage of their life. This number is alarming. Many more are unhappy to the point they wake up apathetic, sad, and dissatisfied with life. This is not how it should be. You are not born to live out your days depressed or sad. Happiness should not be elusive. It is for this reason personal and spiritual development experts offer methods to attain happiness in thirty days or less. It is possible to experience joy. You can be happy irrespective of your past or current situation. Happiness is a key ingredient for Awaken Your Authentic Self because it is the essence of your core nature. You have choices and how you respond to your circumstances determines your level of happiness.

It was the late Dr. Wayne Dyer who said, "Change the way you look at things and the things you look at change." While you may not feel rapture every day, you can attain joyfulness and contentment by choosing to do so. "I think of happiness as a deeply felt sense of joy and well-being, flourishing within a balanced, stable, integrated heart and mind," states Lama Surya Das in *The Big Questions: How to Find Your Own Answers to Life's Essential Mysteries.* Ask those who experience happiness about the reason for their exuberance and you will get varied responses. Yet they all agree their path to joy was borne out of painful circumstances. Many encountered dark periods in which they dug deep into their core to find joy.

"The dark night of the soul is a collapse of a perceived meaning in life…an eruption into your life of a deep sense of meaninglessness," states spiritual teacher Eckhart Tolle, who experienced prolonged periods of depression. The journey into the dark night of the soul compels people to discover an eternal river of joy once resistance is overcome. Mental and emotional blocks such as negativity, pride, materialism, greed, selfishness, fear, and anger overshadow our spiritual essence. Research professor and author Brené Brown affirms in *Rising Strong*, "There are too many people today who instead of feeling hurt are acting out their hurt; instead of acknowledging pain, they're inflicting pain on others. Rather than risking feeling disappointed, they're choosing to live disappointed."

I recall the story of a friend who lost their child in a terrifying house fire years ago. The pain suffered due to their loss engulfed the family with unending grief. They were devastated and experienced intense anguish and emptiness. Their dreams were shattered and negative emotions soon filled their lives. They could have stayed in their dark place, overwhelmed by the crushing sorrow. Many people remain in dark places for long periods. They may not have the emotional resilience to escape the pain or are too weakened to make the effort. Yet this couple dug deep within their core knowing if they did not attend to their well-being, they would cease to exist. Therapy arrived at the right time to help them conquer their anger and sadness. In time, they shared their story with others and in doing so, healed and renewed their life.

"Forgiveness does not mean condoning, pardoning, forgetting, false reconciliation, appeasement, or sentimentality. It is a practice, daily and lifelong, of cultivating our own inner peace and wisdom that allows us to see that our pain is part of the pain of all human beings universally, to reset our moral compass, and to remain compassionate even in the face of injustice, betrayal, and harm," writes Linda Graham in *Bouncing Back: Rewiring Your Brain for Maximum Resilience and Well-Being*.

Painful places cause people to re-evaluate circumstances they wouldn't normally if things are going well. You've no doubt heard people discuss how undergoing a tough period opened their eyes to valuable truths they might have missed otherwise. It is easy to get bogged down with work, family commitments, and further obligations. The routine and fast pace of life puts the brakes on pursuing activities we enjoy. Responsibilities and expectations lead us to a dark place and when we least expect it, depression consumes us in little time.

Pain in life is inevitable, but you need not stay stuck in pain. Allow it to do its work and push you to rise above it. The human spirit is resilient and capable of overcoming life's trials when put to the test. Water finds its own level and so can you. If you are struggling with pain and sadness, take time off to connect with your pain. If you believe in a higher power, call for insights and strength to overcome your struggle. Read inspirational books or join a support group. Being in the company of others helps us overcome adversity by sharing our sadness and grief. You need not go it alone.

In his book *Falling into Grace,* the American spiritual

teacher Adyashanti states, "In this moment of grace, we see that whatever might be there in our experience, from the most difficult emotional challenges to the most causeless joy, occurs within a vast space of peace, of stillness, of ultimate well-being." Life is precious and to live it joyfully is a great blessing. The path to joy comprises pain, though the essence of your pain involves *getting through* it to experience abundant joy. At your core where lies the Authentic Self, you are peace and joy.

Sense it. Embrace it. Live it. Be one with it.

The Power Of Love Will Heal Your Life

The power of love is such that it surrenders itself so its presence is known. I am reminded of the quote by author Leo Buscaglia, "Love and self are one and the discovery of either is the realization of both." The realization he speaks of is that at the core of our being we are pure unbounded love. Any thoughts we hold to the contrary distort this truth. We go to the source of our pain to heal any thoughts of separation and it is there that we discover the Authentic Self.

When we let go of resistance, what is discovered is pure love. To heal our life, we reconnect to that source. Healing signifies a return to wholeness. Through distorted beliefs, the mind reinforces an image disrupting the mind and body's natural homeostasis. It was American philosopher and psychotherapist Eugene T. Gendlin who coined the term felt sense. He was referring to an internal bodily awareness or body-sense of meaning that develops when we align with the truth.

If you perpetuate fear, your body responds by adopting the physiology of this fearful state. However, love heals and brings the body back into balance when we associate with this all-powerful energy. It was the late David R. Hawkins, M.D., Ph.D., a renowned psychiatrist and consciousness researcher who said, "If we are willing to let go of our illness, then we have to be willing to let go of the attitude that brought about the illness because disease is an expression of one's attitude and habitual way of looking at things." When you disconnect from your authentic nature, you detach from your state of ease and the body becomes dis-eased.

Dis-ease signifies disharmony in one's thoughts. Love renews and restores inner harmony because every cell in our body is attuned to this natural healing state. I liken it to returning home after being away to find your key still fits the same door lock. Healing arises the moment we align our mental and emotional frequency to coincide with love. Love is a healing agent because its energetic frequency is stronger than other emotions and is the foundation of universal order. "Your body is your subconscious mind and you can't heal it by talk alone," affirmed the neuroscientist and pharmacologist Candace Pert.

As an example of the healing power of love, the Institute of HeartMath states that your heart has an electromagnetic field 50,000 times stronger than the brain's. Ancient wisdom has known for centuries the heart is the seat of the soul. To heal means to reconnect with our soul within the embodiment of love. So at the deepest level, healing is a return to the source of our being. We disconnect from this wisdom by identifying with fear and anxiety. This creates an inaccurate mental image expressed in the body as illness and disease.

In his book *Healing and Recovery*, Dr. David Hawkins affirms, "A loving thought then heals and a negative thought creates illness. Choosing to become a loving person results in the release of endorphins by the brain which has a profound effect on the body's health and happiness." I consider the cause of illness and disease a spiritual abandonment from oneself. The body is crying out to reunite with its core self. We internalize fear in all forms nowadays to the detriment of our physiology. Over time, our body learns the language of fear by inhibiting vital biological processes.

We must love ourselves and embrace the wholeness of our being if we seek to heal our life. Consider this. How can you possibly heal when your body receives negative messages on how it looks or cannot act? To heal means to renew and by renewing we strengthen our connection to our Authentic Self. Love means accepting our current circumstances without opposition. Your opposition to what is manifests as fear. Thus, we turn our attention away from fear and embrace our core nature.

At the deepest level, our separation from our Authentic Self intensifies dis-ease in mind and body. To merge with the wholeness of our being is a call to love, as Marianne Williamson states. Self-criticism and self-hate instruct the body to turn on itself.

The power of love to heal your life is distilled in the following ideas:

- Love is a healing agent and has the power to renew.
- Fear, anxiety, anger, and other lower emotions overshadow this healing force.
- You are not broken or flawed. It is only your perception which creates this illusion.
- Embrace your wholeness and perfection.
- Transform your thoughts relating to your unworthiness and imperfections.

- As you heal your thoughts, your body discovers its inherent healing power.
- Meditate on aspects of love in your daily life.
- In essence, love is simply the absence of fear. For what is eternal is love's enduring power.

Why Self-Compassion And Self-Acceptance Are The Keys To Optimal Living

Have you ever wondered why some people seem happy and content in their own skin? In contrast, do you know people who are miserable and pessimistic? How about you? What is your predominant outlook toward life? Do you like yourself? Feel worthy? Struggle with confidence? These are questions we seldom contemplate until life overwhelms us. Yet if we don't make time for self-inquiry, we will be overcome with emotional grief when we least expect it. Two important factors for optimal living and an Authentic Life are self-acceptance and self-compassion.

From the time we are children, we face emotional abandonment of some form, leaving us with a less-than-positive mental script. We can be hard on ourselves and that unkindness permeates into other areas of our life, leading toward a destructive path. Emotional abandonment means to run away from fulfilling your emotional needs like self-love and self-acceptance. Even young children will entertain thoughts such as, "I don't like myself" and "I'm not worthy" and carry these thoughts throughout their lives. What does a young child know about forming such judgments when they're barely old enough to reason with the world?

Perhaps your emotional needs were not met as a child and you developed low self-esteem? This is a common scenario, where children believe they are unworthy well before developing a self-identity. They mature into adults only to bottle up their pain or cover it up with addictions, unhealthy relationships, hollow success, or material possessions. This poses a threat to one's emotional well-being, because living like this makes for a miserable existence and leads to depression, severe anxiety, mental health disorders, and tremendous pain.

In her book *Bouncing Back: Rewiring Your Brain for Maximum Resilience and Well-Being,* author and transformational psychotherapist Linda Graham MFT states, "True understanding and compassionate self-acceptance are especially necessary when there are parts of ourselves that are still caught in negative stories about what has happened to us—parts that still feel invisible, misunderstood, not accepted, or a failure."

Countless people with low self-worth have faced their inner struggles and learned to love themselves. They were vulnerable and faced their insecurities and disappointments to learn self-compassion and acceptance. When we dissolve these fictitious tales, we discover our Authentic Self was present all along. In fact, a part of an adult's journey often leads them to face the darkness to walk in the light. Sometimes personal growth requires walking through pain to discover a fertile oasis ahead.

"The first step we need to take on the path toward self-compassion is to embrace the most simple and basic fact that when our emotional immune systems are weak we should do everything in our power to strengthen them, not devastate them even further," affirms psychologist Guy Winch. Everyone encounters some form of pain on their life's journey. It begins in childhood and continues throughout life and none are immune to it. How you respond to your inner wounds will determine your attitude and actions throughout life.

To illustrate this point, consider the Buddhist tale of a man shot in the chest by an arrow. While the pain was immense, the Buddha pointed out how much greater the pain would have been if he was shot by a second arrow in the same spot. This lesson demonstrates that despite intense pain or suffering, when we add a second arrow of judgment about our experience, we intensify the pain. Inner wounds can lead to self-persecution. We believe "I must deserve this" or "I'll never be good enough," and this keeps us trapped in unworthiness. We can be hard on ourselves at times, not realizing it's possible to respect who we are, despite our pain. To learn self-love and self-compassion begins with appreciating our worthiness.

Author and social researcher Brené Brown states in *Rising Strong*, "When we practice self-compassion, we are compassionate toward others. Self-righteousness is just the armor of self-loathing."

You matter.

You are worthy.

You can love yourself and treat yourself with compassion.

While it's wonderful to treat others with compassion, do you treat yourself the same way?

Do you take pride in yourself?

Cut yourself slack from time to time?

Believe in yourself?

Are you aware of the inner critic that tells you otherwise?

Self-compassion does not mean feeling sorry for yourself and is not self-pity. It means developing a nurturing relationship with yourself foremost. Similarly, self-compassion is not a sign of weakness. It implies being your own guardian, best friend, and healer instead of critic. Self-compassion and self-acceptance are essential ingredients to living a fulfilling life, more so than high self-esteem. The roots of self-compassion stem from our earliest recollection of our caregiver environment. So it makes sense we learn to connect with these nurturing qualities to provide the loving-kindness we deserve. Authenticity means to honor our spiritual essence whether it be through darkness or in pain. We tend to our needs when it matters most.

Self-compassion and self-acceptance mean to eliminate expectations of oneself. It starts with the smallest gesture of loving yourself when you're angry, scared, confused, or tired. We cultivate a supportive inner dialogue instead of allowing the inner critic to take hold. We learn to embrace our worthiness. It begins by gazing into the mirror and declaring you are worthy of love. Notice the feelings and sensations that arise as you make the declaration. Some people are brought to tears while others delight in the self-affirming dialogue. Become your own best friend and soul mate. Scouring the globe for your soul mate begins at home standing in front of a mirror, confirming your complete acceptance of self: *your flaws and your assets.*

Author Linda Graham reminds us, "Self-compassion helps us recognize and use our frailties, flaws, and vulnerabilities as opportunities for proactive self-care. We especially need to practice self-compassion and self-care when our inner critic starts to pummel us with harsh, negative self-talk." No one is perfect and you're no exception. Embrace and love yourself without reservation. Life will make sense, because you will be in tune with your Authentic Self, which is Love at the core of your being.

How The Power Of Forgiveness Can Set You Free

It would be remiss of me to get this far into the chapter and not touch on forgiveness as a path to Awaken Your Authentic Self. Forgiveness does not erase the past but looks upon it with compassion. To withhold forgiveness keeps alive emotions of hurt, anger, and blame which discolor our perception of life. To forgive, we avoid ruminating on thoughts of being wronged. Rather, we trust the power of forgiveness to heal the hurt and pain. By holding on to pain and resentment, we suffer because the sorrow is intensified to keep it alive.

Despite people's perceptions that forgiveness means to forget, its motive is preserved in self-forgiveness and the role we play to co-create the circumstances. This does not mean you agreed to what transpired. Given your involvement, even as a victim, you forgive yourself regardless of the role you played. Forgiveness means to let go of hatred instead of allowing it to eat at you.

In the 2009 film *Invictus*, Nelson Mandala played by actor Morgan Freeman avows to the African National Congress in a show of defiance, "Forgiveness starts here....Forgiveness liberates the soul....It removes fear, that is why it is such a powerful weapon....The past is the past, we look to the future." Remarkably, there's a close link between negative emotions and illness, documented over the past decade by notable doctors. Toxic and destructive emotions have the potential to activate disease in the body if we don't attend to our emotional well-being.

I acknowledge it is difficult to forgive a perpetrator for wrongdoing and goes against our moral code. Yet if we consider it from a greater perspective, forgiveness is associated with our emotional welfare, not merely granting the other person pardon. "At the end of the day, forgiveness is really not for the other person's benefit at all—it's for our own. Regardless of how illogical it may seem at times, it is through unconditional forgiveness that we surrender the past to the past and enter the present, freeing ourselves to stand in the infinite Light that knows how to heal our deepest and most painful wounds," states author Dennis Merritt Jones.

I grew up in a strained relationship with my father and carried resentment toward my emotional mishandling for a long time. Yet I experienced a profound shift when I forgave him and myself. I saw the greater lesson of my experiences which were guiding me toward self-love. It was brought about through a change in awareness that undermined my limiting beliefs: "What if my relationship with my father was perfectly orchestrated to teach me self-love?" From that day, I realized there are no accidents in this purposeful universe, only our perceptions that distort the truth.

Anger and resentment keep us stuck in the past replaying disempowering emotions, instead of living in the present moment. People wish for a happier life yet are reluctant to let go of toxic emotions, believing forgiving their perpetrator erases the past. This is the furthest from the truth. "When you're wounded, especially by significant people in your life, your empowerment is challenged, and your worthiness is called into question. The vulnerability your loss of empowerment creates within you allows the wound to damage your worthiness," affirms author Mario Martinez in *The MindBody*

Code: How to Change the Beliefs that Limit Your Health, Longevity, and Success.

From a spiritual perspective, the ego feeds off fear and convinces us we were wronged. It holds onto anger and resentment to keep the pain alive. Conversely, love asserts the opposing view—forgiveness, peace, and joy. I cited a quote earlier in the chapter by Dr. Wayne Dyer who said you can be happy or you can be right, but you can't be both. We must let go of destructive emotions to discover peace and happiness because the two cannot coexist. Irrespective of the circumstances, we respond to the past with compassion, not hold onto the experiences. Confucius said: "The more you know yourself, the more you forgive yourself."

So we choose positive emotions if we wish to live a fulfilling life. Anger and resentment are a call for self-love since what we crave is to be loved and appreciated. Given our aim, we must let go of that which stands in our way, and forgiveness is the bridge that leads us there. We look into our hearts and forgive ourselves for being co-conspirators in the experience. A co-conspirator is defined as someone involved in the experience instead of consenting to it. "Rather than forgiving the perpetrator or minimizing the intensity of the misdeed, you recover the empowerment and self-worthiness you thought had been taken from you," states Mario Martinez.

We forgive that part of us that holds onto resentment and transforms any destructive emotions. In doing so we rise above fear. It was the late psychiatrist and consciousness researcher Dr. David Hawkins who showed that Fear has a lower consciousness level, in contrast to Love which registers higher. Fear registers as 100 on a logarithmic scale, while Love registers as 500. The energy of Love is calibrated higher and capable of disentangling lower emotional states. When faced with holding onto anger and resentment, forgive yourself and others. Each time you experience fear, choose forgiveness over hatred.

In doing so, we heal ourselves, which leads to inner freedom and cultivates a deeper connection with our Authentic Self. We renew our connection to the truth. A poignant quote from author Dennis Merritt Jones from his book *Your Redefining Moments* affirms, "Forgiveness is the practice that opens the window and exposes our wounds to the Light, and it is a practice that, as long as we live in a human skin, we'll have a need to employ throughout our lives."

By exposing our wounds to the Light not only do we heal our suffering, we invite Love to transform our anguish. In that act of clemency, we are reunited with the wholeness of who we are and merge with the authenticity of who we really are.

Chapter Summary

- *Pain is apparent when we invite the past into the present moment. The past is an illusion because it does not exist in the here and now.*
- *To change old memories, rather than drop them, focus your attention on forming new ones instead.*
- *Our emotional wounds lead us to the wholeness of ourselves.*
- *To heal, we must de-clutter our lives and nurture the child within while creating a secure environment for the healing to occur.*
- *Transforming pain develops a deeper relationship with ourselves and leads to inner freedom.*
- *To accept and heal our emotional wounds, we release them to invite the power of love to occupy its space.*
- *Our responsibility is not to judge ourselves, but to reconcile the pain and integrate it into our experience toward oneness.*
- *You are never presented with an experience that is the sum of your conditioning.*
- *Yield to your challenges by leaning into them instead of opposing them.*
- *You do not rise to your best under the kindest*

conditions, yet in the harshest storm you discover your true potential.

- The Four Noble Truths affirm that life is impermanent—everything is in a transitory state, even our pain and troubles.
- We all suffer pain in one form or another, yet the degree to which we choose to suffer remains within our control.
- Happiness is a key desire for cultivating authenticity, yet many people are unhappy to the degree that joy eludes them.
- Happiness is a key ingredient for Awakening Your Authentic Self because it is the essence of your core nature.
- Pain in life is inevitable, but you need not stay stuck in pain. Allow it to do its work and push you to rise above it.
- Dis-ease signifies disharmony in one's thoughts. Love renews and restores inner harmony.
- Love is a healing agent because its energetic frequency is stronger than other emotions and is the foundation of universal order.
- An adult's journey often leads them to face the darkness to walk in the light.
- Despite intense pain or suffering, when we add a second arrow of judgment about our experience, we intensify the pain.

- *Forgiveness means to let go of hatred instead of allowing it to eat at you.*

2

Discover Your True Identity

> *"People often say that this or that person has not yet found himself. But the self is not something one finds, it is something one creates."*
> —*Thomas Szasz*

Have You Lost Your Way?

A Roman general known for his valor insisted a slave follow him everywhere holding a sign that read, *Memento Mori* which translated means, "Remember that you have to die." I invite you to consider the extent of your life be measured by the significant moments instead of missed opportunities. Knowing life is short, we must seize the day to discover our Authentic Self. Events play out in our favor, despite the worries and frustrations which open us to a greater experience of ourselves. Yet without warning your existence may be cast into despair as you come to terms with changing circumstances.

Have you experienced losing your way? Remember how you

felt at the time—connect with that moment by recalling the times of uncertainty. Now cast your mind back to the present moment. Note the insignificance of the experience from this vantage point. A loss in direction is precipitated by losing sight of one's core purpose. It is straying from your Authentic Self. A feeling of emptiness is accompanied by worry and confusion as you come to terms with your situation. I can attest to this, having experienced it when I transitioned from an earlier career over a decade ago. The listless state of mind was too much to bear. My vulnerability clouded my incapacity to make sense of my state. I sought to establish my foothold in what appeared to be a bottomless pit.

Let me set your mind at rest—you can never be lost in this purposeful universe. Contained within every experience of uncertainty is the knowledge you have taken a sidestep; a holding point to reconnect with your intuitive compass. We are prone to lose our way during moments in our life, since we are not born with an internal GPS routing our passage through life. While we are endowed with inner guidance by way of emotions, depending on our level of awareness and consciousness, we are less likely to heed the signs. We are so caught up attending to the cascade of emotions which being lost invokes.

Allow me to propose a thought experiment—indulge me if you will. What if being lost turned out to be your greatest gift? Consider the following scenario. You set out in search of a dream to find you have become lost. Right when you are likely to concede defeat, you find your way and while the road is unfamiliar, it allows you to create a new path toward your destination. If you use a GPS device and take a wrong turn, as long as the right coordinates are stored, the unit seeks an alternative route to deliver you to the destination, regardless of which road you take. Life functions in the same respect. You are the vehicle while your intuition and emotional guidance serve as the GPS. If you are lost, reconnect with your Authentic Self to get back on course with your journey.

The primary aim when you lose is to concede to your current state. Second, navigate your way ahead from your current position and trust you will reach your destination. Equally, retreat into silence. When the mind is caught up in excessive thought, one cannot navigate the path forward owing to the cloud of distorted thinking. Remain still and silent until a stirring within your soul summons you to take proper action. You will know when you are ready to take the next step. A music device may cease to emit a radio frequency due to interruptions to its signal, yet it still remains a music device. Life functions on recurring themes, which means honoring the rhythms which rise and fall—sometimes we may be lost while other times our path is obvious. There is a purpose to everything, which becomes clear further down the road.

When you sense you are lost, get in touch with your inner nature. What materializes often reflects what is held within the psyche. Could being lost highlight the same concealed feelings beneath the surface? It was Carl Jung who said, "Your vision will become clear only when you can look into your own heart. Who looks outside, dreams; who looks inside, awakes." He was referring to awakening our potential. In the same way, despite popular opinion espousing the happiness movement, seeking happiness while lost is expecting the sun to shine through a raging storm. One must continue to advance through the storm so the sun finds its way through an unblemished sky.

Share your pain with others who can support you to navigate your way back. What may appear as being stuck holds your greatest gift toward victory, yet seldom does it appear that way. It was Dan Millman who said, "When we feel stuck, going nowhere—even starting to slip backward—we may actually be backing up to get a running start." In Paulo Coelho's book *The Alchemist*, Santiago the young shepherd boy traverses the globe in search of his personal legend, only to find it was present at home all along. Had he not embarked upon the journey, he may not have gained the valuable wisdom and insights along the way. He may have overlooked the connections made and the lessons which shaped his life

Your mental frame of reference is paramount when you've lost your way. Not every person's character is shaped by success, yet failure musters personal growth in every person. The person we become at our lowest point flames our inner spirit. Andrew Matthews, author of *How Life Works*, reminds us, "When we think everything is going wrong, it usually isn't. We just can't see the whole picture." Knowing our time is limited beckons us to stop clutching for answers that do not exist. It is acceptable to be lost at moments of our life, given that man spends a lifetime cultivating his way on earth. Nothing good can arise out of fearing for the worst or expecting a future to arrive as expected. Remain resolute that the breadth of your life is measured by the memorable moments, instead of a loss in direction. For contained within each period of uncertainty lies the opportunity to unearth your hidden potential.

Discover Your True Identity

What is lost can never be found and what is found can never be forgotten. So echoes the quest to realize your true identity. I remain convinced you do not discover your identity inasmuch as evolve into it. As you discard the image of the formed self, you allow the Authentic Self to emerge. According to author

Neale Donald Walsch, "Your soul is who you are. Your body and your mind are what you use to experience who you are in the Realm of the Relative."

A strong identity is upheld by the capacity to realize your life purpose and live it. Those who stray from their purpose lose their identity and strive to assign meaning to their life. People in intimate relationships refer to similar feelings of losing their identity. These examples highlight the cause of attaching one's identity to action—i.e., being, doing, and having does not define identity. The ego adds a layer to the formed self to keep it safe while safeguarding its position in the world. What if you failed to realize your purpose or if your relationship dissolved—what is your identity then? This is a common experience for those who endure a similar fate. It begs the question—Who am I? If I am not my [insert title here], then who am I? Allow me to convince you that a title does not make up your identity; it imposes a mental construct of it. A relationship does not define you, it complements you—it draws out the best in you. If the relationship ends, it does not mean a part of you is lost. The relationship revealed aspects of your identity by adding a piece to the puzzle.

The perceived self is a façade owing to your past conditioning.

Reflect on that for a moment.

Who are you if not for the sum of your past, i.e., family, schooling, friends, and life experiences? Who is the person you call "I" after all? Allow me to cite a personal example. Over a decade ago I formed an image of being a successful fashion designer working abroad. My father was a tailor and mother trained as a dressmaker. Meanwhile, I gained a B.A. in Fashion Design at university and fulfilled my dream to work in Europe prior to my realization. Yet the image of a successful designer was an identity I created to convince myself that a tailor's son would make it big. Yet many years later when my father passed away, I recall that image perish along with him. I abandoned the identity of the successful designer since it was not what I wanted after all.

We must venture beyond who we think we are to allow the Authentic Self to reflect our identity. We should dare to step outside our comfort zone, to peer through an alternate reality if we wish to discover who we really are. Your true identity may be found somewhere between your imagined self and outside your comfort zone. It was Bruce Hood, author of *The Self Illusion: Who Do You Think You Are?* who stated, "Who we are is a story of our self—a constructed narrative that our brain creates." While it may appear clinical to consider your self-image representative of your brain activity, I am inclined to believe this to be true on an inclusive level.

It begs the question: Why do we form an identity? It is known as individuation, a Jungian term which refers to transformation of the psyche by uniting the personal and collective unconscious into consciousness. It is the awareness of oneself to discover your true identity. Erik Erikson, a developmental psychologist, proposed we undergo eight stages to psychosocial development throughout our life. Self-identity then is seen to be an evolving process over the course of your lifetime. In keeping with this understanding, make it a priority to discover your essential self to avoid living an inauthentic life. Once realized, strive to live according to those values and principles by embodying them at the deepest level. Be wary of associating conduct with identity given its inaccurate measure of character. Behavior is fluid and changes as you grow and evolve.

True identity is formed through self-awareness of conditioned thoughts and beliefs. At this lev are in alignment with your true identity. You held beliefs by choosing to retain thoughts that ı your deepest self and discarding others. As your life circ stances change, you integrate those experiences into your identity. To strengthen one's self-identity is commensurate with acting according to your formed image. Your self-esteem is reinforced when you uphold this image. As you look past inherited cultural identities, e.g., tough, emotional, sensitive, brave, etc., you discover your own identity. Cultural identities diminish over time while the Authentic Self is timeless and not bound by labels. The Authentic Self is often obscured beneath the veil of an imagined self which thrives due to the reinforced image of self.

Acknowledge your limitations while working within your perceived boundaries by directing your attention toward your passions and interests. You let go of outdated beliefs to make room for actions that emanate from your Authentic Self. To discover one's identity becomes a journey of self-exploration. You might venture from one extreme to the other while finding your true identity lies somewhere in between. Hence, once you have determined your values, abide by them. Whenever you violate your values, you weaken your sense of self.

To discover your true identity, surrender the formed image of self while allowing the Authentic Self to emerge. The Authentic Self cannot be weakened or destroyed since it remains the essence of your being at the core level. Similarly, discard ideas, beliefs, and destructive emotions which no longer serve you. Release them so your essential nature merges to replace the formed identity which you have given power to.

ce found, your true identity can never be lost since it has
een present all along. It merely impersonates itself as the ego
to help you find your place in the world.

How To Embrace Your Real Identity

To embrace our true identity, we must rise above our known
existence and associate with our core self. It was the African
American author and philosopher Howard Thurman who
declared, "There is something in every one of you that waits
and listens for the sound of the genuine in yourself. It is the
only true guide you will ever have. And if you cannot hear it,
you will all of your life spend your days on the ends of strings
that somebody else pulls." That something Thurman speaks of
is the silent whisper of our soul crying out for us to merge with
it. However, we must become silent long enough to recognize
its voice. We repeatedly drown out the call of our inner wisdom
by obscuring it with disempowering thoughts.

It is apparent many people hide behind a fictitious persona
to please others. Uncertainty arises when others no longer
identify with us and so we form our entire personality around
pleasing them. We should welcome our individuality since our
identity is fluid and undergoes many transformations as we
develop. It's unwise to forsake your negative qualities in favor
of positive ones since you're already complete with your still-
evolving character. If we discard the negative facets of ourselves
how can we devote attention toward our personal transformation? Our Authentic Self often takes a backseat to build a
public persona which we try hopelessly to defend. Yet behind

closed doors, we are like a theater actor who looks forward to coming off stage.

Your identity evolves throughout your life. Comparable to a house, once a stable identity is constructed, there's little to bring about its collapse. "Our identity is the sum of our memories, but it turns out that memories are fluid, modified by context and sometimes simply confabulated. This means we cannot trust them and our sense of self is compromised. Note how this leaves us with a glaring paradox—without a sense of self, memories have no meaning, and yet the self is a product of our memories," states author Bruce Hood. Beyond embracing our true identity remains the desire to embody our core self which is bestowed in peace, love, and harmony. This is your default nature and if we stray from this ideal, we invite disharmony into our lives.

Similarly, to entertain disempowering thoughts such as victimhood, anger, fear, and hate, we detach from our Authentic Self. This is because we disconnect from our true identity which lies beneath the surface of the constructed self. This authentic Self is obscured because we forget our way among the countless thoughts related to our identity. Author of *Emotional First Aid*, Guy Winch states our self-worth is influenced by our identity: "When our self-esteem is chronically low, feeling unworthy becomes part of our identity, something with which we feel comfortable, a way of being to which we become accustomed."

It's crucial to recognize your identity is not determined by how you make a living, but rather who you are and who you grow into. Speak to any individual made redundant following years of work and they'll convey the clear void missing in their life. This is linked to identifying with their job instead of their underlying nature. They identify with their occupation and are lost when they no longer have that to look forward to. It's as complex and as straightforward as this. If your occupation no longer reinforces your identity, who are you beneath that? Once more author Bruce Hood makes an argument that our identity affects our self-worth: "The need for identity is so strong that when prisoners or institutionalized individuals are stripped of their possessions, they will confer value on items that would otherwise be considered as worthless."

Moreover, our successes and disappointments don't govern our identity; they add a piece to the puzzle. To recognize our true identity, we surrender fixed labels, cultural paradigms, and opinions of who we are. Only then can we form an identity devoid of limiting beliefs. Our concept of self regulates our identity to reinforce negative or empowering qualities. Where attention is concentrated becomes our focal point. To associate our identity with our self-worth when it's reliant on satisfying others is destructive in the long run. What if others change their opinions of us? Without warning, if we're to appease them, we must change our identity once again to satisfy them. The downfall is that we're not being authentic in nurturing who we are.

You are not the sum of your mistakes, yet if you allow them to define you they will consume you. It was St. Thomas who wrote, "If you bring forth what is within you, what you bring forth will save you. If you do not, it will destroy you." However, if you appreciate that your prior mistakes helped you awaken your Authentic Self, you build a bridge to show your true identity. Similarly, many people give up their identity when they begin a new relationship. There's a sense of agreement as partners seek to live as one instead of divided. Here, we abandon facets of our identity to please our partner because we fear we might lose them. Consequently, individuals struggle to recover their identity once the relationship breaks down. The answer lies in being unapologetically you in every situation. This means people will reject us while others welcome us. This is considered the best display of who we ought to lean toward.

Honor yourself and take pleasure in your individuality, realizing you are a work in progress. You will continue to evolve until the moment you no longer inhabit your physical body. Don't go to war with yourself or oppose aspects which you disapprove; instead, incorporate them into the wholeness of your being. Only then will you dare to embrace your true identity beneath the rubble of the divided self.

Accept Your Imperfections

To embrace your imperfections, first let go of identifying yourself as inadequate and embody the wholeness of your being. Consider the accompanying narrative of how our imperfections can be channeled correctly:

A water bearer had two large pots, each hung on the ends of a pole which he carried across his neck. One pot had a crack in it while the other was perfect and consistently delivered a whole portion of water.

One day, at the end of the long walk from the stream to his house, the cracked pot arrived half full. This continued daily for two years, with the bearer bringing home one and a half pots of water.

The perfect pot was proud of its accomplishments. But the

cracked pot was embarrassed by its imperfection since it fulfilled only a fraction of what it was designed for.

After two years of what it regarded as disappointment, it spoke to the water bearer one day by the river. "I'm ashamed of myself because this crack in my side causes water to leak all the way back to your house."

The bearer replied, "Did you notice that there were flowers only on your side of the path, but not on the other pot's side? That's because I've always known about your flaw. I sowed flower seeds on your side of the path and every day on our walk back to the house, you watered them.

"For two years I've picked these beautiful flowers to decorate the table. Without you being the way you are, I wouldn't have this beauty to decorate the house."

What you regard as limitations are good fortune clothed as hardship, yet when applied correctly can transform your life. Accept yourself completely, knowing you possess a combination of qualities. Instead of bringing attention to your weaknesses, view them as gifts to transform into the wholeness of your being. It's pointless striving to become someone you're not. To maintain a façade over time is exhausting and strips you of your Authentic Self. We are not attracted to others because of their virtues; their wholeness of character is what resonates with us most. Consider being in a room of attractive people and notice the tendency to fixate on your own faults. It's human nature to measure ourselves against others, though we need not subjugate our self-worth. "In fact, it is the favorable comparisons that we draw against others not in our group that help to define who we are. This is how we formulate our identity—by focusing on what we are not. The trouble is that by focusing on others, we miss our own imperfections," states author Bruce Hood. To accept your imperfections, cease trying to satisfy others. The more you aim to please, the less people are inclined to identify with you, because people-pleasing is a powerless state.

There are several leading actors and successful entrepreneurs with notable imperfections which they used to their advantage. Consider Arnold Schwarzenegger's heavy accent which didn't discourage him from becoming Hollywood's most prominent star. Similarly, Richard Branson's dyslexia had little hindrance when he was establishing his thriving billion-dollar Virgin empire. While I acknowledge the following wisdom is often given out, it is underutilized owing to its simplicity. The power of gratitude can help us to realize the wholeness of our character. A blemish on an apple does not make it inedible but gives it further appeal. Equally, vulnerability allows us to embrace our imperfections because we communicate the same intention to others. It shows our humanness, given perfection is an unattainable ambition if we wish to lead an authentic life. Without doubt, what you look for, you are certain to encounter.

We must be mindful of our shortcomings yet still bring our greatest work to life. As a further example, the actor Sylvester Stallone was once advised that his slurred speech would pose an obstacle to becoming an onscreen actor. Nevertheless, he channeled that objection to create a streak of successful films playing the lead character Rocky Balboa, the impoverished boxer hailing from the slums of Philadelphia. I appreciate the message from psychotherapist and author David Richo who affirms, "Error and errancy are not tragedies. They are ingredients of and directions to discovery. They show us paths that humble us, startle us, and point us to new horizons. They do not have to lead to regret or shame. We say yes to our imperfection and accept our mistakes."

So welcome your imperfections and stop regarding them as an impediment. Delight in them while affecting the lives of others. At some point in our life, we subscribe to a distorted image that portrays people as perfect. Perhaps the media plays a role, yet this image is far removed from reality. We must let go of striving for perfection and accept our true identity. We are complex beings and our physical appearance is one facet of our being. If we fixate on our imperfections while downplaying other aspects, we overlook the wholeness of who we are. Consider viewing a masterpiece painting close up. Your attention is drawn to the bold brushstrokes that appear distracting to the eye. Yet when you step back and view the painting from afar, you realize the beauty and complexity of those brushstrokes outline the entire picture.

See yourself as a masterpiece beyond your shortcomings, replete with bold brushstrokes that complete the whole person. Transformational psychotherapist Linda Graham states in her book, *Bouncing Back: Rewiring Your Brain for Maximum Resilience and Well-Being*, "Include an appreciation of your own wholeness and your goodness, all your strengths, all your weaknesses, including the ones your inner critic is currently harping on. Include your friend's love and acceptance of you, exactly as you are, with all of your human imperfections, and their understanding of all the events that created your way of being and your particular flavor of the universally human inner critic."

Our imperfections call us to exercise self-compassion with our inner critic. Don't abandon yourself when the inner critic judges your imperfections. Instead of waging war, see it as an opportunity to love and accept the disapproving part of you. With concentrated attention, we reframe our inner dialogue to be more affirming. We must honor our feelings and use it to examine what inflames our emotions. In this manner, we transform our inner dialogue to reaffirm our wholeness instead of focusing on our separateness.

You are born to be real, not perfect.

There is no personal growth in a utopian world and the last time I checked, we are a great way off heaven, nirvana, or paradise. We must quietly evolve into the highest version of ourselves. Perfection is not the answer if we aspire to attain inner peace. It will lead us further astray because we'll continuously strive to change aspects of ourselves we're unhappy with. Gratitude, however, opens the doorway to acceptance and a heart-centered focus. Your imperfections are based on an illusory perception that highlights one facet of your being.

You must welcome them so the wholeness of who you are is realized. After all, it was Martin Luther King, Jr. who declared, "Take the first step in faith. You don't have to see the whole staircase, just take the first step."

Remember Who You Really Are

Author and teacher Jeff Foster calls us to reaffirm our attentiveness to the present moment in the following passage: "Remembering who you really are is a subtle shift of attention from a tense present to the present tense." There is an aliveness to being grounded in the here and now; we slip out of the intriguing dream of the past to appreciate this moment. If the past serves as accumulated memories, there can be no depth to our experience of it from our present state of awareness. Yet if we are alive in the present moment, life materializes in that instance. The aliveness of our present experience transcends any distant memory we hold onto. It is through this connection of the now that we unlock the gateway to a deeper relationship with our spiritual self.

Many people are oblivious to life's deeper purpose. Just like mice in a lab experiment, they merely survive to the next meal before their time runs out, lamenting how life passed them by. Yet it need not be this way. You have a choice to overcome any limitations that are self-imposed or otherwise.

Consider your response to the following:

What is your life story about?

Why are you attracting these life experiences?

What are the lessons contained within those moments?

These are questions we must consider to pay closer attention to our purpose. What themes and struggles have followed you over time to create the canvas of your life? Every experience is unique to you because it compels you to evolve; otherwise you stay stagnant. While it may sound like New Age cliché at a click, the wisdom you seek is contained within you. This is the same intelligence which directs blood supply to your beating heart and regulates the intricate division of cells. We disassociate from our thinking mind into the quiet space within to connect with that wisdom. You may call it home; others liken it to returning to a comfortable, yet reassuring presence they never left. However you experience it, you are the expression of universal intelligence constantly shifting. You were conceived out of love, irrespective of the conditions that supported your birth.

Jeff Foster reminds us, "Remembering who you really are

stops you living in suspense, longing for your next holiday, tired of life and waiting for retirement, and makes every day a holiday—a holy day. Which it always was, of course." I remember with fondness catching the train to school each morning in my pre-teenage years. I saw office workers clutching the daily newspaper under their arms, expecting the day ahead. Coincidentally, during my ride home I observed those people grappling the same newspaper under their arms, appearing jagged and worn, having been read cover to cover. The paper was symbolic of how they felt working in a dreary job: worn-out and listless.

I invite you to stop for a moment in your day to be alive—I mean really be alive in your surroundings. Notice your breathing, your heartbeat, your thoughts which arise and fall to produce the accompanying emotions. This is life functioning as the individual you call "I." It is no surprise that you are the director and star in your life's story. While you have a minor influence over how the plot unfolds, you have the power to direct the course of your destiny nevertheless, instead of being stuck in your current circumstances. As a powerful co-creator and through the power of your mind, you set this intention to coincide with your heart's desire.

"Question: Since you are here to remember who you are, why have you forgotten? Answer: Perhaps you have lived another's dream and not your own," states author Rusty Berkus in *To Heal Again*. What if this life is a dream, a very real dream? What if you were to awake from this dream to realize you haven't really lived or worse still, just survived? I am reminded of the uplifting Samuel Taylor Coleridge poem which invites us to acknowledge our power to create a wonderful world, "What if you slept? And what if, in your sleep, you went to heaven and there plucked a strange and beautiful flower? And what if, when you awoke, you had the flower in your hand? Ah, what then?"

To honor our inner wisdom is the core of our spiritual evolution. We reconnect with our authentic nature by honoring the values which point us toward our true self. As we abide by these values, we awaken our genius, our potential, and the willingness to see through the lingering fog of confusion. We never disconnect from our source of knowing; rather we lose our way back to it. There is a salient undercurrent which simmers beneath the surface of mankind. This mysterious energy is unassuming and yet is known when you meet somebody who leaves a lasting impression on you. Some are fortunate to connect with this spiritual energy during their lifetime while at the same time accomplishing their deepest desires. For others who stray from their spiritual self, it heralds the path back home.

"However, every moment is an invitation to remember, that although the waves of consciousness may rise and crash, in the Ocean's depths lives the deep peace and silence of yourself. Silence, and knowing," affirms Jeff Foster. I encourage you to surrender labels, ideas, and beliefs of who you think you are. This is a formed image that keeps you safe in the world. You don't need this persona any more than you need reading glasses when your eyesight is 20/20. Life leads you to discover this unyielding Self by guiding you to honor the foundations of your unlimited potential. To remember who you really are requires a subtle shift from struggle, worry, and anxiety to being surrounded by the richness of the present moment. Who we are is contained within those pockets of tiny moments, interspersed throughout our life. If we are not completely aware of them, they pass us by at the drop of a hat.

Love Is Who You Really Are

Your complete acceptance of your identity is central to your existence. For every interaction stems from the recognition of your true self. The Dalai Lama said it puzzled him why so many people in the West suffer from low self-esteem and lack of acceptance. We have everything we need to thrive, yet are tormented for honoring our spiritual self. Self-love is a soft concept for many since our upbringing emphasizes serving the needs of others. To nurture ourselves first is selfish, so individuals indulge in altruistic service to the detriment of meeting their own needs.

To cite a personal example, I spent countless years locked in a futile struggle to approve of myself. This was compounded by an inflexible parent whom I could not please. As a result, I turned to intense physical activity as an outlet to vent my discontentment. I took part in grueling sporting pursuits to punish myself. My inner dialogue summoned me to go harder until I was overcome with exhaustion or I collapsed in pain. Undeniably, the inner voice was the same one echoed by my parent, and I had adopted it as my own. Yet underneath, my body was crying out to be loved and nurtured. The constant pain reinforced my childhood conditioning until I could take no more—something had to give.

Thankfully, exercise nowadays encompasses low-intensity movement and has evolved to embrace the self-love I uphold. While I'm a work in progress as many others, I am at peace with myself having endured the contrasting state. The path to self-love is slow and gradual, requiring patience and commitment to create an empowering inner dialogue. "Here's the real secret; underneath all of the 'problems' you carry around is just one belief: I am not good enough," affirms Louise Hay in *Loving Yourself To Great Health.*

Self-love is expressed to the degree we are vulnerable. By exposing our cracks, we give ourselves permission to be authentic and thus attract like-minded individuals. Contained within that vulnerability is the need to love ourselves again. Countless books and articles espouse loving yourself foremost for others to love you. While I acknowledge this as helpful advice, it should not be your sole reason. Your duty is to honor yourself primarily because within your DNA is the disposition for self-nurturing. To accept ourselves as whole means to embody our strengths and limitations—our shadow self. To disown your dark side means going to war with yourself, a move away from self-love. Shame, disgust, and self-disapproval are feelings we impose upon ourselves. You are not born harboring such thoughts. It is perpetuated when you find evidence to support it. Loving who you really are starts with the smallest act of self-renewal and self-compassion. It is the recognition you are already worthy, irrespective of your limiting beliefs. Author Dennis Merritt Jones states, "Who you really are is not subject to transition because the true Self is formless and changeless."

You are *perfectly imperfect.*

The dichotomy of that statement affirms that your imperfections make you perfect. Therefore, embrace the wholeness of your being from your place of awareness. Know that you personify goodness by your mere presence. Use your imperfections to engrave upon your character that which you aspire to be. While an overused analogy, the diamond formed through heat and pressure is akin to that which takes place within you. Your trials are nourishment for your soul. Your imperfections are nature's gifts to impress upon your being. Reframe from assuming you are broken, since that merely capitulates to your woes. "As soon as you believe that a label you've put on yourself is true, you've limited something that is literally limitless, you've limited who you are into nothing more than a thought," avows spiritual teacher Adyashanti.

Loving who you really are denotes the impenetrable self that lies beneath the voice of the ego. This reaffirming voice cannot be obscured since it does not affix itself to labels relating to your self-worth. It is as eternal as your spiritual nature and your primary aim is to make peace with the inner critic. What assurances do you have that the inner critic is not the real you? Look to your feelings as a guidepost. The inner critic strives to make you inferior. This is clear when provoked; you respond in anger to uphold this image. The Authentic Self does not revile you, nor does it hide behind a veil of deceit. To differentiate these voices, we realize the inner critic is nothing more than a learned script often recited.

By confronting pain, we summon our intent to move through it. Pain is a portrait to the past to the degree that suffering means referencing the past by bringing it into the present. As you abandon your pain story, you recognize you are not your feelings or thoughts, but something you have tied yourself to. In any moment you suffer, direct your attention inward by asking: "What is going on inside me right now?" Stay attentive to the sensations which arise: a thought or an impulse. Move toward them with modest attentiveness instead of running away from them. The act of embracing your feelings is a show of self-love because you are nurturing your emotional well-being. It is a prompt reminder to quote Sufi mystic Rumi who said, "Your task is not to seek for Love, but merely to seek and find all the barriers within yourself that you have built up against it." Ultimately, loving who you really are entails tearing down the barriers that stand in the way of your spiritual essence.

Chapter Summary

- *You do not discover your identity inasmuch as you evolve into it.*
- *The perceived self is a façade owing to your past conditioning.*
- *Your true identity may be found somewhere between your imagined self and outside your comfort zone.*
- *Self-identity, then, is seen to be an evolving process over the course of your lifetime.*
- *True identity is formed through self-awareness, by letting go of conditioned thoughts and beliefs.*
- *To discover one's identity becomes a journey of self-exploration. You might venture from one extreme to the other while finding your true identity lies somewhere in between.*
- *Whenever you violate your values, you weaken your sense of self.*
- *The Authentic Self cannot be weakened or destroyed since it remains the essence of your being at the core level.*
- *Don't go to war with yourself or oppose aspects which you disapprove of; instead, incorporate them into the wholeness of your being.*
- *It's pointless striving to become someone you're*

not. *To maintain a façade over time is exhausting and strips you of your Authentic Self.*

- *Perfection is an unattainable ambition if we wish to lead an authentic life.*
- *See yourself as a masterpiece beyond your shortcomings, replete with bold brushstrokes that complete the whole person.*
- *You are born to be real, not perfect.*
- *Gratitude opens the doorway to acceptance and a heart-centered focus.*
- *To honor our inner wisdom is the core of our spiritual evolution. We reconnect with our authentic nature by honoring the values which point us toward our true self.*
- *Surrender labels, ideas, and beliefs of who you think you are. This is a formed image that keeps you safe in the world.*
- *Self-love is expressed to the degree we are vulnerable.*
- *To accept ourselves as whole means to embody our strengths and limitations—our shadow self.*
- *Loving who you really are starts with the smallest act of self-renewal and self-compassion.*
- *To abandon your pain story, you recognize you are not your feelings or thoughts, but something you have tied yourself to.*

3

Embrace Who You Are

> *"The most splendid achievement of all is the constant striving to surpass yourself and to be worthy of your own approval."*
> —Denis Waitley

Why You Are Already Worthy

Worthiness is a measure of what you're willing to receive. At the deepest level, self-worth relates to our sense of entitlement. Self-worth means to embrace our true self, whose essence is pure love. You are worthy because your thoughts related to your self-worth do not make up the real you. These are composed storylines that don't show who you are beneath the surface. They're made-up narratives, gained from well-intentioned people and were never yours to begin with. I appreciate it may be difficult to comprehend, yet you will realize that your unworthiness is an invented script not worthy of consideration. "The most dangerous stories we make up are the narratives that diminish our inherent worthiness. We must reclaim the truth about our lovability, divinity, and creativity," affirms author Brené Brown in *Rising Strong*.

To claim our worthiness, we must acknowledge our faults and insecurities, while knowing these are one facet of our being. Your worthiness is a call to honor your whole self and not focus on the disempowering aspects. I recall working in an upmarket men's shoe store as a young adult and discovering the imperfections in leather shoes. Customers flocked in droves to buy shoes with slight flaws, attributed to the animals grazing against barbed wire fences or trees. This exhibited the hide's true character replete with natural blemishes. Equally, your scars and imperfections are not something to cower from, yet to embrace as the wholeness of your being. Author Paulo Coelho states, "Take pride in your scars, they speak more loudly than the sword that caused them." No one is perfect, not even the most enlightened being. Our earthly existence means to evolve into the person we wish to become. This means our insecurities and negative attributes have the potential to be transformed into endowing characteristics.

Low self-worth is evident in others when they're paid a compliment. Some will offer thanks while others dismiss it because they're unable to receive praise. This small gesture alone communicates the individual's capacity to receive. Moreover, our ability to receive and give love determines our self-worth. If we're unaccustomed to receive abundance, whether as compliments, love, compassion, kindness, or otherwise, we limit our ability to enhance our self-worth. "We increase our worthiness when we embrace the conditions that enhance self-esteem," states Dr. Mario E. Martinez in *The MindBody Code: How to Change the Beliefs that Limit Your Health, Longevity, and Success.* Beyond achieving our dreams or attaining success, our greatest triumph results from embracing our worthiness. You are worthy because you are the representation of abundance. Your genetic expression, talents, and gifts are the highest form of abundance. It rests on you whether you embrace these gifts and use them rightfully. In the same way, you enrich your self-worth by acknowledging your worthiness to receive. I invite you to let go of limiting beliefs that claim you are unworthy. Such thoughts are not conducive and impair your personal growth. Instead, we replace them with empowering thoughts.

We must upgrade our thoughts, similar to updating computer software so it runs efficiently without a virus impacting its performance. While I appreciate the computer analogy is a simple metaphor, it highlights that when we let go of undesirable beliefs, we create a fulfilling life devoid of stories that no longer serve us. Author Brené Brown affirms once more, "One of the truisms of wholehearted living is you either walk into your story and own your truth, or you live outside of your story, hustling for your worthiness." To accept your worthiness, let go of playing the victim and forgive yourself and others. Every experience, whether good or bad, has brought you to this point in time, so that even the words on this page are orchestrated to guide your personal transformation. Rest assured, you needn't accumulate more thoughts to validate your self-worth. Instead, let go of who you think you are to allow your Authentic Self to be known. For change to occur, we must accept our current circumstances without conditions.

Consider a car restorer who buys a dilapidated vehicle to refurbish. His thoughts are fixed on the car's final transformation rather than its current condition. I invite you to adopt the same consideration and accept every facet of your life with conviction. I'm not asking you to take pleasure in your current circumstances; however, accept reality to create the life you deserve. You are worthy of love because the conditions that contributed to your conception were conceived out of love. Until a certain age you rarely questioned your self-worth. With the passage of time you assumed other people's opinions and understood them as your own. To own your worthiness, make it a priority to embrace every facet of your being. Avoid focusing on your negative qualities, yet appreciate they are an evolving facet of your being. There'll come a time when you'll look back and see how pointless it was to focus on your negative characteristics.

I often overhear people declare how they'll feel worthy once they have [insert thing, person, or way of life here]. You'll never be worthy even with a surplus of money or love if you carry your unworthiness around like a handbag. Unworthiness is a virus that infects our spirit and stifles our potential. We must remove the virus by seeing it as an obscuring veil of deceit that robs us of our authenticity. A passage from Brené Brown's book *Rising Strong* captures the spirit of embracing our worthiness. "I define wholehearted living as engaging in our lives from a place of worthiness. It means cultivating the courage, compassion, and connection to wake up in the morning and think, *No matter what gets done and how much is left undone, I am enough.*" After all, beneath the suffering you are worthy because you are already enough by your presence alone.

To embrace who you are you must be willing to become a higher vision of yourself by stepping into your own power, not cowering from it. We must seek to create a vision of the person you wish to become and what life would look like at this level. As you move closer to the vision, there will be times it may seem difficult to achieve. The idea of living up to a vision created out of the stillness of your thoughts may seem too much to contemplate. Giving up may cross your mind since you have no reference point to gauge your transition. Yet each step one takes to advance in the direction of living their dream, the universe multiplies a counter move in the same direction. As you make much needed changes in your life, you will not wish to return to the life once lived. As you confidently move forward, you embark on a journey of self-discovery and inner awakening. A joy which knows no limitations will begin to stir within, awakening you to the splendor of your Authentic Self. If you contemplate this journey of self-discovery, simply turn inward and connect with your inner wisdom. It is natural to question how life will unfold as you set about your journey. If there is feeling of joy and harmony, trust that you are being guided and supported by a benevolent universe. I wish to remind you of your greatness and genius via the following quote by Rumi:

"You were born with potential. You were born with goodness and trust. You were born with ideals and dreams. You were born with greatness. You were born with wings. You are not meant for crawling, so don't. You have wings. Learn to use them and fly." Knowing this, I invite you to feel a growing sense of empowerment and motivation to make live the life you have always imagined.

The Power Of Potential

It was Steven Pressfield who acknowledged, "The song we're composing already exists in potential. Our work is to find it." Every man yearns to express his potential through his life and work. The dictionary defines potential as: *latent qualities or abilities that may be developed and lead to future success or usefulness.* If we wish to lead an authentic life, we must be willing to embrace our potential to create that life in earnest. Potential evokes the impression of an idle car, roaring with possibility before hurtling down the road. It is the car's engine and driver that decide the car's speed. Yet without someone to take control of the vehicle, there is little potential to speak of. I recall taking an elective subject in automotive design at university. The lecturer, a former automotive designer, spoke of how the badge ornament on the Ford Mustang, the galloping wild horse, came to be. The final design evokes a sense of movement and potential, so that even while stationary, the car conveys the image of movement.

Regrettably, many people are held back by limiting beliefs, fears, and doubts related to their potential. Left unchecked, these destructive energies perpetuate into a contracted self-worth. Whatever you buy into long enough and with enough conviction forms your reality. We recognize potential within ourselves foremost when we abide by our highest distinction. In doing so, it summons our dormant strengths and commitment toward greatness. Consequently, the power of potential is the idle horse ready to gallop. Potential necessitates discipline, attention, and commitment to bring it to life. "I saw the angel in the marble and carved until I set him free," declared Michelangelo. Potential is harnessed when you give yourself to the process. The greatest minds in history began life with little potential. Abraham Lincoln's learning difficulties as a young man is an example of one who transformed potential into achievement.

To cultivate potential, we hold steadfast to move in the right direction without becoming fixed on the path which leads us there. Potential must be obvious to the individual and is accompanied with passion and desire. "Vision without action is merely a dream. Action without vision just passes time. Vision with action can change the world," states futurist and author Joel A. Barker. Self-awareness is a favorable virtue to understand your strengths and limitations. We must emphasize our strong points while coming to terms with our weaknesses. Make it your duty to nurture your strengths since passion and enthusiasm alone only get you so far. An indomitable will spawned by inspiration rouses potential. It is through dedicated focus toward a vision or dream that transforms desire into action since strong aspirations alone are insufficient. "The difference between those people living their potential and those who don't, is not the amount of potential itself, but the amount of permission they give themselves to live in the present," avows spiritual teacher and author Marianne Williamson.

Whatever is possible is attributed to the mind that can conceive it. The realization of our goals and dreams is constrained only by our limiting beliefs. They slow if not halt progress altogether, because the same creative intelligence that manifests our desires also gives birth to our insecurities. The power to unleash potential is overcome by rising above our obstacles instead of being defeated by them. Each time we rise above our defeats, we embrace who are by nurturing our potential. Potential is clothed in hard work, an indomitable will, commitment, and courage. To take a contrasting view, I equate lack of potential to simmering water which never boils because the heat is turned down. In recent times there's been much discussion given to the widely held opinion we use ten percent of our brain power. While acknowledged as an urban myth, I believe we are yet to tap into our other faculties such as intuition or the deeper subconscious mind to harness potential. In *The Power of Habit*, author Charles Duhigg suggests we reveal our potential by developing sound habits. Many people's failures are attributed to poor habits formed throughout their lifetime.

To nurture potential, we form a strong foundation to harness those gifts and nurture them as we evolve. I am fond of the saying, *Life doesn't know what it will become until you create it.* Similarly, author Michael Talbot who wrote *The Holographic Universe* affirms, "We are not born into the world. We are born into something that we make into the world." Potential exists in all living things and is the lifeblood of universal intelligence. To allow this intelligence to act through us brings to life that which resonates with our deepest self. The same energy which gives birth to our ambitions does so at the right time and not a moment sooner. "Everything in the Universe, including you, your soul, everyone else, and every soul, participates in a continual unfolding of potential," avows the American spiritual teacher Gary Zukav. You cannot escape your potential any more than refusing to inhale oxygen from the air surrounding you. However, how you use that potential forms the foundation for life to express herself through you. Steven Pressfield struck upon a crucial point, that all potential exists within the space-time realm. Your task is to birth that potential by giving it life through dedication, commitment, and inspired action.

The Truth Will Set You Free

The following tale symbolizes that while we desire an authentic connection to our real self, pursuing the Truth may not be the charmed existence we hope for.

"I wish to become a teacher of the Truth."

"Are you prepared to be ridiculed, ignored, and starving till you are forty-five?"

"I am. But tell me: What will happen after I am forty-five?"

"You will have grown accustomed to it."

Your Truth is the source of all wisdom—every person retains their own Truth while no two are the same. To seek the Truth means seeing past the illusory thoughts of what life should be. "We perceive the world as we are, not as it is," said Anaïs Nin. To see past the mind's self-constructed bias, we surrender thoughts which perpetuate this distortion. The Truth is relative to what you observe and what you hope to see. No two people have the same experience, given subjective reality.

It was the late Dr. David Hawkins, a renowned psychiatrist and spiritual teacher who wrote in *Truth vs. Falsehood: How to Tell the Difference*: "The human mind, by virtue of its innate structure, is blind to its limitations and innocently gullible. Everyone is the victim of the ignorance and limitation of human ego." Living in the material world means we are unable to escape the vicissitudes of sweeping changes ushered through life. From the moment of conception, we are indoctrinated with rules, beliefs, and ideas not of our choosing. I mean that in the kindest possible way—we are at the mercy of those we trust to reason the world for us.

Yet many of these beliefs remain unchallenged throughout our life. We need only interact with adults who behave in a regressed, childlike state to notice how they perceive the world through an automated lens. Therein lies our challenge to uphold our authenticity while not succumbing to external forces which try to pull us in every direction not of our choosing. Still, these same people claim to know the Truth: "Everyone secretly believes that their view of the world is correct and any other is wrong. Thereby opinion becomes promoted to 'ostensible' fact and pseudovalidity," states Hawkins.

So what is Truth at its core?

To live the Truth means to live according to your Authentic Self. To think and reason the world without other people's thoughts to dominate your mental landscape. Popular culture is lined with the herd mentality espoused through mainstream music, pop culture, political influences, and inauthentic leadership. These are ways in which our minds are subdued into a distorted illusion of what is real. In his book, Your *(Re) Defining Moments*, author Dennis Merritt Jones states, "We have to enter into unknowing to discover the truth, because there is no room for unknowing in a mind that believes it already knows the truth." We must empty our minds of inaccurate distortions to discover the Truth—a busy mind cannot gain new information when it overflows with ideas.

How do we arrive at this state of emptiness?

Everything is relative to the perceiver. For example, you do not see the sun where it is now since it has moved. You see it where it was eight and a half minutes ago, given the Earth's approximate distance from it. Subjective reality asserts other people's perception differs to yours since no two people share the same experience.

Who is right? Who upholds the Truth?

To take a different view, British-born philosopher Alan

Watts states, "To 'know' reality you cannot stand outside it and define it; you must enter into it, be it and feel it." We must go beyond the self-created illusion if we wish to penetrate the Truth while letting go of thoughts that no longer serve us.

Speak your Truth, trust your Truth and live your Truth.

Be who you came here to be, irrespective of your religious denominations or cultural beliefs—live your Truth at the deepest level. Embody it; even if you take a lifetime to discover, it will have been worth it. Refuse to be indoctrinated with someone else's Truth—those same people are prone to regurgitate knowledge and have nothing new to offer the world. Such distortions will consume you until you honor your Truth by giving it life—yield to it. While disheartening, the ego delivers a false impression of security as it consolidates its hold on you. The illusion keeps you from realizing your Authentic Self. "Truth and Reality are identical and eternally present merely waiting discovery," affirms Dr. Hawkins.

The Truth sets you free since it liberates you from a self-imposed prison disposed to minimize your potential. The wisdom of the soul is your real connection to your spiritual source—trust this connection to the Truth. Confront the Truth with compelling certainty, an open mind, and a sincere heart—then can you claim to have a command over it. Don't allow the egoic voice to drown out your inner spirit. Reason and logic will bargain to convince you the Truth is unattainable—don't argue with it. The Dutch philosopher Gerardus van der Leeuw reminds us, "The mystery of life is not a problem to be solved, but a reality to be experienced." Embody the Truth in your obligations, whether it be through your thoughts, actions, or words. The world needs more original thinkers than naysayers who conform to popular opinion. As James Blanchard Cisneros reminds us, "Once you awaken you will have no interest in judging those who sleep."

Life Begins Outside Your Comfort Zone

It was Neale Donald Walsch who quipped, "Life begins at the end of your comfort zone." He was drawing awareness to move out of our safety zone to experience the richness of life where our authenticity lies. Your comfort zone is a safety net where anxiety levels and the status quo are preserved. It is your harbor of contentment. Mankind has an inherent drive for safety, wired into his DNA to seek food, water, and shelter for survival. However, once those needs a met, apathy and listlessness set in since the mind becomes accustomed to certainty. In fact, it will go in search of it to maintain harmony and order.

Staying comfortable suits some people. The axiom *nothing ventured, nothing gained* serves to remind us that being content does not yield the success we search for. The mind has a negativity bias that any attempt to move out of our comfort zone is met with unease. This is evident when we're in a dreary job or an unfulfilled relationship. If life is chaotic we are likely to feel overwhelmed and stressed. The key is to attain balance in between, since being outside of our comfort zone can add further stress. It is normal to experience anxiety when we're uncomfortable. The body responds to perceived fear as a precautionary survival mechanism. Yet anxiety impairs our ability to gain new information because the mind cannot reason when stuck in a stressed state. It alerts us to impending danger if we move out of our comfort zone by impairing performance. Being comfortable may also be age-related. As we mature, we become set in our ways and less likely to take risks. The lure of perceived rewards may not be as appealing beyond a certain age.

The pain-pleasure principle refers to your motivation to seek gratification or avoid pain. To venture beyond your comfort zone is influenced by how you relate to pain or pleasure. "Choosing to be curious is choosing to be vulnerable because it requires us to surrender to uncertainty. It wasn't always a choice; we were born curious. But over time, we learn that curiosity, like vulnerability, can lead to hurt. As a result, we turn to self-protecting— choosing certainty over curiosity, armour over vulnerability, and knowing over learning," states Brené Brown in her recent book, *Rising Strong*. Yet taking risks is shown to enhance self-esteem and self-worth. Even if we fail, we are likely to discover a new horizon and gain wisdom related to our strengths and weaknesses. Thus, we create an internal reference point the next time we enter uncharted waters. Similarly, to push past our comfort zone can cripple and inhibit performance. We must be vigilant in safeguarding our personal interest so as not to move beyond the tipping point of stress and anxiety. It may be akin to walking a tightrope while striving for balance.

Nevertheless, optimal performance is attained outside our comfort zone. The Authentic Self thrives on reaching beyond its comfort zone, for that is where we connect with the truth of our core nature. We seldom achieve success when we're comfortable, because everything is familiar. There is little need to draw on your mental faculties when you're in the safe zone. We must commit ourselves to take bold risks if we seek to become the best version of ourselves. To move beyond your comfort zone requires smaller steps to confront your fears, while managing discomfort. We learn to become **comfortable with uncertainty** like how elite forces such as the Navy Seals are trained.

It's no surprise that personal growth becomes apparent beyond our comfort zone. In extending ourselves, we celebrate our gains as we accomplish new skills and emotional resiliency along the way. The late Stephen R. Covey reminds us in *The 7 Habits of Highly Effective People*, "It takes an enormous amount of internal security to begin with the spirit of adventure, the spirit of discovery, the spirit of creativity. Without doubt, you have to leave the comfort zone of base camp and confront an entirely new and unknown wilderness. You become a trailblazer, a pathfinder. You open new possibilities, new territories, new continents, so that others can follow."

Cultivating new thoughts leads to a rise in awareness. Our Emotional Intelligence Quotient (EQ) is reinforced when we venture beyond our comfort zone. We find our optimal anxiety zone which leads to improvements over time. This will vary according to individuals, yet the key is not to become complacent. You need not stay uncomfortable to reap the rewards. Long-term discomfort can damage your self-esteem and put the brakes on performance. Instead, focus on making small strides toward your endeavors until you profit from the experience. Mankind can withstand most circumstances. Evolution has allowed us to survive harsh conditions and engineer our biology with the tools to sustain life. That adaptability can work for or against us depending on our actions. If we stay idle, we risk rusting out, thus impairing our personal development. "However, if you were rarely exposed to growth experiences or taken outside of your comfort zone, then you may have to work harder to cultivate a positive attitude toward positive personal growth," affirms American author and speaker John C. Maxwell in *The Difference Maker: Making Your Attitude Your Greatest Asset.*

It is the fear of the unknown, not change itself, that frightens us most. We can mitigate this uncertainty by reframing it as Stephen R. Covey avows, "Create an internal 'comfort zone.' Then, when you get into the situation, it isn't foreign. It doesn't scare you." He is referring to creating an inner sanctuary when change overwhelms us. Within that space is the reassurance that what eventuates cannot disrupt what is familiar. Given life begins at the end of your comfort zone, what lies beyond your perceived security is far greater than your habituated environment. Authenticity begins by recognizing we needn't hide behind our fears to live a fulfilling life. We must assault our fears to embrace who we really are beneath the façade of an impenetrable self. Life undergoes constant change and we must celebrate the challenging journey if we strive for a more enriching life.

How To Live While You're Alive

Our time here is but a fleeting moment in eternity. Relative to your life's journey, you may hold a different perspective of what living fully entails. Those in their final moments will recount a list of regrets or failed opportunities, many of which stem from working too hard, not spending enough time with loved ones, an emphasis on material possessions and not expressing their true feelings to those who matter. What are your regrets regarding the road less traveled? Regrets are a call to take action in that part of your life. Do not wait for the right time since that time may never arrive. Why? Because time is bound by your internal state. If your inner state remains the same, you may never take action. In Mitch Albom's book *Tuesdays with Morrie*, the author recounts his time with his dying sociology professor. Morrie states the following on the impermanency of life and the need to take inspired action: "Everyone knows they're going to die," he said, "but nobody believes it. If we did, we would do things differently."

Knowing this, we can take life by the lapel and seize every opportunity while we are alive. I affirm that we need not compose an elaborate bucket list, nor undertake extravagant experiences hoping to discover the essence of life in those encounters. To live while you are alive begins at the smallest level and expands far reaching, like a pebble dropped into a pond so that its ripples are felt by those around you. It begins at the level of the Authentic Self by making peace with your inner world. Perpetual internal conflicts mean going to war with that part of yourself. What you oppose within, you oppose in others. As you make peace with your fears, doubts and anxieties you transform them into higher emotional states.

Freedom and inner peace are gained from this purposeful intention. Do not go to your grave having allowed your emotions to dominate your existence. There is much to be attained by transforming disempowering emotions into the wholeness of your being. Author and philosopher Julian Baggini writes in his book, *Freedom Regained: The Possibility of Free Will*, "The springs of our actions do not appear to be our conscious thoughts, desires and intentions but unconscious processes in the brain, ones which often set actions in process before we are even aware of anything." Viewed from this context, your actions originate from the unconscious will and stem from your beliefs, thoughts, and observations spanning your lifetime. Can you truly claim your thoughts are unique to you or are they the product of your conditioning?

Consider your response to the following question: What does it mean to be in tune with your emotions? To know your emotions at the deepest level, not dismiss them as fleeting experiences. What emotions arise when complimented by a stranger? What is the smell of a spring morning? Or the sense of falling in love for the first time? Connect with these emotions by allowing yourself to go into them. Only then can you claim you have fully lived. Equally, don't dull or anesthetize your emotions with drugs, alcohol, or toxic foods. Your body is a wondrous chemical facility capable of producing hormones and sensations it perceives from its environment. Nowadays a potion or pill is readily available to dull every mood at the drop of the hat, yet it does nothing to dissuade you from perceiving your way through life.

We must strive to attain self-mastery if we wish to live an authentic life. Self-mastery at the deepest level is the knowledge of one's core self beyond the superficial façade of your likes and dislikes. I consider these the paint on the exterior surface of a house, yet it tells me nothing of the foundations of the house. To know yourself entails connecting with your core self which resides at the soul level. A measure of this wisdom is echoed by your willingness to assume responsibility for your life. Embrace a better version of yourself by connecting with the deeper wisdom within you—the wiser self. Draw on that wisdom to help you navigate the torrents of life. Author and psychotherapist Linda Graham states in her book *Bounding Back: Rewiring Your Brain for Maximum Resilience and Well-Being*, "The wiser self can be seen as an imaginary guide who embodies all the positive qualities—such as wisdom, courage, resilience, and patience—that you see yourself growing into."

This begs the question: What matters to you? Explore your answer to this and sure enough there lies the essence of your existence. I urge you to go deep into it to explore what mystery lays waiting for you. Life does not know what it will become until you step into it with an open mind. Pursue what makes you come alive—what are your passions, interests, joys? Follow them, fall in love with them. Savor them and let your spirit come alive through them. Find your flow within them. Explore your talents, gifts, and genius. Dr. Wayne Dyer said, "Don't die with your music still in you." You were born to prevail, to let your light shine. To withhold it due to past suffering or apathy creates a deep void which yearns to be filled. This advice does not take away from your struggles since they are part of the journey contained within this material realm. A life well lived is not been in vain, yet it fertilizes the seed for others to know the way.

Chapter Summary

- *You are worthy because your thoughts that relate to your self-worth do not make up the real you. These are composed storylines that don't show who you are beneath the surface.*
- *Our ability to receive and give love determines our self-worth.*
- *To accept your worthiness, let go of playing the victim and forgive yourself and others.*
- *To own your worthiness, make it a priority to embrace every facet of your being. Avoid focusing on your negative qualities, yet appreciate they are an evolving facet of your being.*
- *Whatever you buy into long enough and with enough conviction forms your reality.*
- *The power to unleash potential is overcome by rising above our obstacles instead of being defeated by them. Each time we rise above our defeats, we embrace who are by nurturing our potential.*
- *To live the Truth means to live according to your Authentic Self. To think and reason the world without other people's thoughts to dominate your mental landscape.*

- *Speak your Truth, trust your Truth, and live your Truth.*
- *Embody your Truth; even if you take a lifetime to discover it, it will have been worth it.*
- *The mind has a negativity bias that any attempt to move out of our comfort zone is met with unease.*
- *The Authentic Self thrives on reaching beyond its comfort zone, for that is where we connect with the truth of our core nature.*
- *Learn to become* **comfortable with uncertainty.**
- *Assault your fears to embrace who you really are beneath the façade of an impenetrable self.*
- *Perpetual internal conflicts mean going to war with that part of yourself. What you oppose within, you oppose in others.*
- *Your actions originate from the unconscious will and stem from your beliefs, thoughts, and observations spanning your lifetime.*
- *We must strive to attain self-mastery if we wish to live an authentic life.*
- *Embrace a better version of yourself by connecting with the deeper wisdom within you—the wiser self.*
- *Life does not know what it will become until you step into it with an open mind.*

4

The Importance Of Self-Trust

"As soon as you trust yourself, you will know how to live."
—Johann Wolfgang von Goethe

The Most Powerful Ways To Develop Self-Trust

To develop self-trust, stop seeking the opinions of others and recognize the guidance within you. Self-trust is harnessed when we follow our sacred wisdom instead of looking outside ourselves to provide inner peace. We develop self-trust by honoring our emotions instead of hiding behind them. As you honor your feelings, you develop trust in your capacity to deal with what arises. Equally, we must distance ourselves from people who undermine our self-trust. Some people push your pain buttons because it pleases them to see you suffer. While they can help us to identify our disowned parts, we are better to distance ourselves from them rather than become embroiled in their deceitful ways.

Self-trust is developed by nurturing our innermost

thoughts. While we cannot control external circumstances, we become curious as to what is going on inside us instead of retaliating in anger. "As we learn to recognize and understand the body's subtle sensations, and then act on them, our self-trust will grow tremendously. To me it is rather amazing that the body has this innate sense of the truth as if the body is hardwired for it," states psychotherapist John Prendergast, Ph.D. The subtleties of the human body point to what is going on beneath the surface, so we become attuned to the minor fluctuations and our true needs.

It's vital we honor our commitment to ourselves, whether it be in the goals we set or pursuing our dreams. To dishonor them diminishes our self-trust because we fail to follow through on our plans. To foster self-trust involves developing a compassionate dialogue with ourselves. In times of turmoil, we should cultivate compassionate thoughts rather than be ruled by the unfolding drama. We plant the seed of equanimity and nurture it with kindness so it grows strong. Self-trust arises when we make time to honor the child within us. This means devoting time to being with ourselves instead of declaring how busy we are in the midst of craving emotional compassion.

John Prendergast states, "As we learn to slow down, tune into our inner guidance, and act on it, our self-trust grows. We increasingly get the feel for when something resonates as being true or false for us, in or out of accord. This sense of inner resonance becomes our inner authority." Our inner authority is the pillar of a stable emotional life. We take the time to connect with our emotional well-being and attend to any disturbances that show up. How do you recognize when you need time alone? Whenever you notice internal unrest, it is a call to spend time in silence to examine the emotions.

It is no surprise our lives are hectic. We are more likely to pay attention to external events instead of meet our personal needs. We spend our waking life fixed on the world "out there" instead of within. Yet if we continue down this path we neglect our inner life, which influences how we relate to the world.

A practice I mention in my book *Reconstructing the Past to Create a Remarkable Future* involves a simple question to see how we relate to the world.

"How am I doing?"

This simple question allows us to distinguish what is going on inside us instead of dismissing the emotional disturbances as unjustified. Eckhart Tolle states that whenever emotional chaos is apparent, we invite an earlier Pain-Body experience into the present moment. This is obvious when others trigger our Pain-Body, such as being cut off in traffic or someone taking our line in the queue while shopping. If we don't take the time to examine what is going on beneath the surface, we react instead of interact with our core emotions. "Most of us have not tried just sitting in and through a feeling experience. We have not trusted ourselves enough to let our feelings take their full course. So we never find out that a feeling is not so tough on us as we imagine it will be. We miss out on how much better we feel when we let go instead of hold back. Nothing is so hard to handle as the fear of facing it," affirms author David Richo. Building self-trust does not mean we will always say or do the right thing. Irrespective of our words or actions, whatever arises is there to guide our personal evolution.

A well-known practice for developing self-trust is to be mindful of your body moments before you react to external events. So with someone taking your place in the shopping queue, move into your body and note any tension or tightness.

Become curious toward these sensations and observe them nonjudgmentally. For example, you might be aware of a constricting sensation in your chest moments before retaliating with the person who took your place in the queue at the supermarket. Be with the emotion and simply notice it without an agenda. Silently repeat the phrase, "I'm aware of you" or as Daniel Goleman suggests, label the emotion. So we affirm to ourselves, *anger or fear* instead of act on it. This simple action puts the brakes on deferring our emotions and draws our awareness to what is going on inside us. In this way we become aware and awake, instead of unconscious to the emotional drivers in our life.

We develop self-trust by honoring every facet of our being irrespective of whether we approve or disapprove of that part of us. For example, those with diminished self-esteem might criticize themselves for reacting angrily to a situation. In contrast, those with an empowered self-esteem see it as an opportunity to become inquisitive and a teaching point from which to grow. To develop self-trust is to listen to our heart's guidance rather than be dictated by the incessant thoughts. Our thoughts are saboteurs since they cannot be trusted. Given their volatility from moment to moment, we cannot rely on them to make sense of our environment. For example, at the end of a working day your thoughts are scattered, while mid-morning after you've had a cup of coffee they're less likely to be reactive.

However, the heart is not influenced by fluctuating mood changes. There is a stillness that longs for you to connect with, even during your darkest hour. Practice moving your awareness into your heart in the midst of the commotion and observe the silence. Be with the sensations that arise and meet them with openness. You'll soon realize the habitual and stressful thoughts melt away, leaving a sea of expansiveness that permeates your mind and body. Self-trust is an invitation to develop a relationship with your core self which is the seat of the Authentic Self. We learn to become our own best friend and appreciate the interplay between our thoughts and emotions, instead of remaining unconscious to them. In doing so, we learn to trust the guidance from our deepest wisdom. Ultimately, if we continue to place our trust in others' opinions, we will disengage from our sense of authority and diminish our self-confidence over time.

Why Timing Is Everything

Given the developing self-trust is an integral component of harnessing our Authentic Self, timing is that compelling force apparent when chance and coincidence collide. Author Dan Millman states in *Living on Purpose*, "I learned that we can do anything, but we can't do everything…at least not at the same time. So think of your priorities not in terms of what activities you do, but when you do them. Timing is everything." It is observed in universal order and the seasons which arrive and recede. The ocean tides are influenced according to the moon's gravity and the planets' orbit according to the sun's gravity. Recognized by Carl Jung, synchronistic events relate to *meaningful coincidences* that occur with no causal relationship yet are related. When you have a pressing question in your mind and a book falls off the shelf which contains the answer, or the phone rings from a friend who you were just thinking of, these are examples of synchronicity. How do timing and synchronicity play their role within the cosmos? The wise man learns to collaborate with this occurrence, just as a farmer sows his seeds expecting the coming harvest.

In *The Power to Navigate* Life, I alluded to timing as the art of allowing: "Rather than becoming attached to your own agenda, that governs the timing of how things should play out in your life; you come from a place of allowing which is seeded in infinite possibilities." What works one season may be unsuitable the next. We adjust by working with the forces of life instead of opposing them. In his acclaimed book *Outliers*, Malcolm Gladwell illustrates how timing plays a role in chance opportunities. He cites the births of young men and their demographic fortune as significant factors in determining their success.

Is there a connection between timing, fate, and destiny?

Consider Amy Neftzger's perspective in her book *The Ferryman*: "The problem with Fate is that no matter how many times you call out to her, she has her own timing that's irrelevant to whatever anyone else happens to be doing." Why do particular goals transpire with little effort, compared with earlier attempts? Certainly, timing plays a role. To make better use of timing is to be in touch with intuition. Most people use conscious thought alone to make major life decisions. Read any biography on successful CEOs, and it's clear they profited from using intuition to make astute business decisions.

What does this mean to you?

Appreciate that universal forces are at play in the backdrop of your life that lead to your personal growth. Often plans don't work out as expected because timing commands that something better has yet to arrive. Viewed in this light, timing serves to guide your passage through life. Decisions correspond to the flow of universal energy instead of opposing *what is*. It is natural that people associate timing with meeting their life partner. In several instances, the individual may have experienced relationship misfortune leading to the successful connection. Timing serves a role to uphold cohesive order and orchestrates the natural flow of events. Actions fall into place because of universal timing and when combined with synchronicity, they bring those events into your awareness to seize your attention. Author Robert Greene states in *The 48 Laws of Power*, "Time depends on perception, which can be wilfully altered. This is vital in mastering the art of timing."

How can we make better use of timing in our lives?

For starters, appreciate the natural rhythm of life. We needn't push for things to happen; instead we should recognize circumstances seldom follow an ordered pattern. Your emotions guide your actions in harmony with the natural flow of events. For example, if you resist conditions beyond your control, timing may be a barrier. To labor ahead obscured by the truth is unfavorable to achieving a positive outcome.

Our thoughts are subject to timing.

It may be difficult to grasp ideas at a certain time, while later with a raise in awareness the learnings are reinforced with little effort. The flow of thoughts dictates that some days are tempered while other days are erratic. "One can't live mindfully without being enmeshed in psychological processes that are around us," affirms Philip G. Zimbardo in the book *The Time Paradox*. Thus, timing gives rise to changes in the psychological process which affect us. It bodes well to cooperate with the natural forces of life by linking time, coincidence, and opportunity to favorable outcomes. Ordered chaos can be a powerful phenomenon so that events unfold in our favor. If we stay grounded, we trust life to serve our needs beyond our limited knowing. My greatest life experiences happened when I least expected them, through random chaos. What seemed erratic from my first impression was my mind's perception of the event. As I suspend judgment, I let go of how these events should materialize and allow universal timing to play her role in establishing my reality. My task is to keep my thoughts and emotions in check without succumbing to what unfolds. Dan Millman's quote invites us to perform all our activities in line with timing since it is the glue which binds the cosmos and the natural flow of events. It is the key that unlocks the door to authenticity. We trust that what needs to take place will do so of its own accord free from our stress-driven thoughts.

The Power Of Mindful Action

Deliberate action emanates from an awakened mind and pure heart—the Authentic Self. Mindful action unfolds when we are present in the moment, not elsewhere absorbed in runaway thoughts. Our actions stem from being aware and awake to our greater purpose and not victims to our innate desires. It is easy to succumb to numbing thoughts because they are buried deep within our psyche. We are only aware of them once we have carried out the deed. Mindful action involves bringing your whole self into the present moment, engaged with life as it unfolds. Its power lies in its practice and application. The more we are mindful of our actions, the less pain and suffering we encounter. Jon Kabat-Zinn, the founder of Mindfulness Based Stress Reduction, states the aim of mindfulness is **to act with clarity and intent.** Mindful action calls us to be prepared instead of having a divided focus. We become absorbed in the flow experience of life and bring our thoughts into the present moment with openness and honesty. "Callous actions are caused by callous minds," states author Nicholas Epley in *Mindwise*.

To avoid heartless action, we practice mindful thinking to pay attention in a particular way, on purpose, in the present moment, and non-judgmentally. For some, it may take a lifetime of anxiety, pain, and suffering to realize who they are. Yet through mindful action we connect with our deepest, Authentic Self, so our actions result from thoughtfulness. We harmonize with our inner intelligence and trust the intuitive guidance that appears, rather than dismiss it as unrelated. We realize underneath the façade, we are already wise and not at the mercy of our thoughts and emotions.

Likewise, mindful action helps us deal with stress and anxiety because we are no longer governed by them. Instead, we use those disempowering states as motivation toward wholehearted living. Stress and anxiety serve no role within the body's landscape since we are now mindful of the purpose they served—unity over separation. Often, we are at the mercy of our emotional instabilities and turn to food to feel better about ourselves. While short-lived, the consequences of not attending to our emotional well-being heighten the discord between mind and body. Moreover, using food as an emotional blanket desensitizes our emotions, so we react instead of merge with our core feelings. We may experience runaway emotions while powerless to guide ourselves back to harmony.

Linda Graham MFT states, "Choose to recondition afflictive emotions that block wise action, freeing up energy that lets you move in the world resiliently." Mindful action allows us to inhabit our body with attentiveness and act according to our core values. Similarly, the power of focus directs our thoughts so our actions are intentional and not automatic. To focus means to harness our mental faculties toward appropriate action, which arises from intrinsic motivators and not external circumstances. Our focus can be deceived by the tide of disharmony, which is disconcerting. Once we regain our composure, we shift our attention so our actions originate from mindful intent. It is no surprise life can be filled with circumstances not of our choosing. At these times, we must be careful with our thoughts and highest intentions, instead of being governed by external elements. "Indeed, we are constantly engaged in the self-construction business, on both outer and inner levels, through both thought and actions, in our ongoing effort to convince not only others but ourselves that we really exist," states Lama Surya Das.

Our actions define who we are while our words reveal who we aspire to become. We must be persistent in choosing mindful actions that resonate with harmonious thoughts. We are defined by our actions more than our words, so it stands that they be congruent with how we want to be perceived by others. This is the one true barometer of our character that speaks volumes of who we become. Mindful action leads us to observe the call of our inner spirit where the stillness of the Authentic Self resides. It is the modest counselor directing our soul's evolution. Again Lama Surya Das reminds us, "Through understanding, we can avoid looking for what we want and need in the wrong places, repeating the same actions while hoping for and even expecting different results, and seeking happiness in ways which simply perpetuate our unhappiness and suffering."

I believe we have discovered something important here. Mindful action emerges from a greater intelligence tied to a pure heart and awakened mind. To the uninitiated, an enlightened mind means a mind free of prejudices and conditions. Let us be attentive to our inner spirit by allowing it to influence our thoughts, rather than be led by the chaos of our external world. As the computer idiom goes, "garbage in, garbage out." To be mindful of our thoughts leads to deliberate action, which is the fertile ground of an awakened mind.

How To Gain Clarity On What Matters Most

Thus far we have examined that to build self-trust is a call to connect with our authentic nature. When we align with the truth of our being, self-trust emerges to enhance our connection to authenticity. The philosopher Søren Kierkegaard said that life is not a problem to be solved; it's a mystery to be experienced. Contained within that message lies a conceivable reality if we will embrace it. The principle underlying most self-help guidance is to surrender control on how circumstances play out. The need to influence conditions is an illusion since we have limited power. What if underneath our desire for control lies the need for safety? It's widely held that what we want and what we need are distinctly opposed. Upon examination, we realize our desires are obscured by past conditioning to maintain a sense of security. Yet open any news bulletin and you'll see how little control we have within the natural order of events. Jamie Smart writes in his book *Clarity: Clear Mind, Better Performance, Bigger Results,* "In your waking experience of reality, your mind continuously creates and perceives a world simultaneously....So well that you don't feel your mind doing the creating." The creating he refers to functions beneath the surface of the subconscious mind. Through the neuroscience of free will, it takes 300ms to evoke a response from your nervous system, demonstrating the updating of working memory. At 500ms we are thinking about what we saw for the first time. In the context of free will, your mind is one step ahead of your nervous system before you intend to act.

So what does this mean when gaining clarity on what matters?

The mind is notorious for pulling us in different directions, whereas our Authentic Self has no agenda to lure us into. To pierce the essence of our existence, we surrender our self-fabricated story and allow the truth to emerge beneath the rubble of misperception. Yet for many to discard their long-held beliefs is as painful as throwing money down the drain. To gain clarity we connect with our soul nature which knows the best path to take and uncover our truth along the way. The late Dr. David Hawkins spoke of finding one's truth and living it as best we can. Living your truth may oppose others and even annoy them. Yet to support a distorted view of reality because it supplicates to their needs is deleterious to our human potential. "Living an authentic life is probably the most challenging thing a human being can endeavor to undertake because it is not the way of the world, but it is the way of the heart that connects you to what is real, what is meaningful, and what is eternal," affirms author and teacher Dennis Merritt Jones in *Your Redefining Moments: Becoming Who You Were Born to Be*. I find it helpful to re-examine my purpose when I am pulled in different directions. Do I want to pursue my deepest desires or be at the mercy of others while living an inauthentic life? Ultimately, I want to live my calling, my purpose, and truth as much as life will allow me. This does not mean I won't encounter situations to test my resolve. Knowing life is a mystery to be experienced, I trust that as long as I take daily action toward my dreams, I am moving in the right direction.

It's apparent that life offers us no assurances.

Clarity is apparent the moment we direct our inner compass toward that which we long for, instead of waiting for external conditions to dictate our future. Many people believe life is done to them instead of lived through them. This subjective view of reality diminishes their personal power. Life invites us to take proper action and matches it with the right opportunities to advance us to the next stage. The Determinist view states that life functions within the container of a self-organizing system. Experience and wisdom have taught me to stay attentive to the signs and symbols which play out in my life. These signs lead me to connect with my inner wisdom and correct my course if I veer off direction.

How will I know when I veer off course?

My actions become mechanical and devoid of inspiration. I find myself stuck instead of navigating my life's purpose. Problems arise and as Albert Einstein reminds us, the same mind that creates those problems is not the same mind which solves them. "Attention is valuable because it's not just an act of focusing your mind on a single point, it is the bringing of your very essence, your soul—the most valuable thing you have—fully into the moment, to perceive with clarity," affirms author and intuitive counselor Penney Peirce. To discover what matters most means to live the questions we put forth. What you believe was once important is an incomplete perception of reality pulling you in a direction not of your choosing.

You can be pulled by your troubles or lead with your solutions.

The latter invites you to find your own North Star as author Martha Beck calls us to discover. To have life imposed upon us prevents living an authentic life. Our authenticity is the one true freedom awarded us at the moment of conception. It is a carte blanche with no conditions other than we embrace it wholeheartedly. I enjoy psychotherapist David Richo's perspective in his book *The Five Things We Cannot Change: And the Happiness We Find by Embracing Them*: "You can learn to trust that there is a sane, wise, and nurturing resource within you. In fact, the more you know what you really want, the less desperately you need it. This happens because your self-esteem, confidence, and clarity grow." With this knowing, we welcome Søren Kierkegaard's sentiments to embrace the mysteries of life through experience. Only then can we gain clarity on what matters most amid the pursuit of excellence.

Being Comfortable With Uncertainty

The Chinese proverb states, "If you want to know your past—look into your present conditions. If you want to know your future—look into your present actions." Reality is filled with uncertainty. Seldom do we have an exact picture of the path ahead, so we accept what arises with determined courage. It is natural to uphold a level of control, yet we need uncertainty to prevail since the seeds of opportunity lie in the unexpected. At a deeper level, we fear uncertainty because we lack the life skills to navigate through it. Recognized as the mind's negativity bias, we doubt our capacity to cope with the unexpected and exaggerate events to the detriment of our mental and emotional well-being. With so much talk of stress these days, we need to know what the imminent future holds in store for us. Yet the security we crave is but an illusion to lull us into a false sense of safety. Author David Rock states in *Your Brain at Work*, "The brain craves certainty. A sense of uncertainty about the future and feeling out of control both generate strong limbic system responses."

As a result your brain looks to your external environment to reinforce a known sense of balance. In primitive times our ancestors had to contend with a variety of conditions to sustain life. The threat of wild animals, adjusting to climatic conditions, fear of attack from rival tribes, and the outbreak of disease were barriers to their survival. Thankfully, life in the modern world is not as bleak, yet is replete with its own stressors which pose a hazard to our well-being. Uncertainty for the modern man is contained within intimate relationships, volatile economies, job insecurity, weather fluctuations, and health concerns. Bruce Hood affirms, "…in situations where outcomes are important, we get stressed by uncertainty and feel the need to do something so that we can have the illusion that we can control events." To retain binding command of our lives is both a blessing and curse. In one way it affirms our sense of safety, knowing we need not contend with tentative conditions. On the other hand, its misleading bias is overstated by our limited control, if any. It is no surprise that the mind is notorious for emphasizing circumstances which appear less dramatic than they are. This is known in psychology as catastrophizing, the inherent bias to perceive events within a negative context. The fear of "not knowing" what lies ahead impedes our long-term welfare. At a deeper level, fear of the future terrifies us because of the unfamiliar conditions which lie ahead. It interferes with attaining emotional freedom.

So how can we embrace the unexpected without the barrage of emotions which ensue?

How can we use uncertainty to build self-trust and cultivate the Authentic Self?

To accept uncertainty in our lives requires a change in perspective. We yield to the intrinsic forces of life instead of oppose them. However uncomfortable it may seem, we surrender to the natural order of events by leaning into our fears and insecurities. You reason with your anxieties by perceiving them with a logical mind instead of becoming embroiled in them. Otherwise, we risk activating our fight or flight nervous system every time, which senses we are in imminent danger instead of being uncomfortable. Remain present in your body when anxiety threatens your emotional well-being. Choose a proper time to examine the motivation for your anxiety.

Have there been moments in the past which caused similar anxiety?

If so, are you repeating those same feelings instead of facing them?

Fear is confronting, though we gain strength when we embrace it as a useful emotion. I remind myself often that fear is an illusion. I can reduce the volume of fear by being exposed to it moderately each time. We rarely have all the answers, which means uncertainty is as much an inner declaration that everything will turn out well in due course. It strengthens our resolve and commitment to the natural cycles of life. Change in itself is terrifying, not the conditions themselves. The key lesson is to be comfortable with uncertainty—why? Because it exists and we should avoid retreating in resignation wishing life were different. Authenticity calls us to embrace every aspect of our nature—the shadow and the light. We evolve by being exposed to uncertainty and confronting our fears; otherwise, they dominate our mental landscape and grow in intensity. To that extreme that which we oppose must be met head-on. It was the Roman Emperor Marcus Aurelius who declared, "If you are distressed by anything external, the pain is not due to the thing itself, but to your own estimate of it; and this you have the power to revoke at any moment."

Find a middle ground between living with uncertainty and maintaining a level of control, short of manipulating outcomes. Let go of tension, anxiety, and fear by embracing the unknown. Consider uncertainty a worthwhile journey toward a daring future. Uncertainty allows us to re-evaluate the past and make new choices in light of what transpires. It presents opportunities to create a compelling future based on new information. Often, our most ambitious plans emerge through the obscuring veil of uncertainty. Welcome curiosity and excitement which go with uncertainty by affirming your belief to move through it with ease. The vital lesson is to expose yourself to uncertainty by building your tolerance to it. To know the future, we must become acquainted with our present actions while embracing uncertainty. In doing so, we move toward the unknown with firm ambition to resolve the past.

Chapter Summary

- *You develop self-trust by honoring your emotions instead of hiding behind them; you develop trust in your capacity to deal with what arises.*
- *To foster self-trust involves developing a compassionate dialogue with yourself. In times of turmoil, cultivate compassionate thoughts rather than be ruled by the unfolding drama.*
- *A well-known practice for developing self-trust is to be mindful of your body moments before you react to external events.*
- *Be with the emotion and simply notice it without an agenda. Silently repeat the phrase, "I'm aware of you" or as Daniel Goleman suggests, label the emotion.*
- *To develop self-trust is to listen to your heart's guidance, rather than be dictated by incessant thoughts.*
- *Self-trust is an invitation to develop a relationship with your core self which is the seat of the Authentic Self.*
- *To make better use of timing is to be in touch with intuition.*
- *Actions fall into place because of universal timing and when combined with synchronicity,*

they bring those events into your awareness to seize your attention.

- *Appreciate the natural rhythm of life. Don't push for things to happen; instead, recognize that circumstances seldom follow an ordered pattern.*
- *Mindful action involves bringing your whole self into the present moment, engaged with life as it unfolds.*
- *Mindful action invites you to be prepared instead of having a divided focus.*
- *Through mindful action you connect with your deepest Authentic Self, so actions result from thoughtfulness.*
- *Mindful action emerges from a greater intelligence tied to a pure heart and awakened mind. An enlightened mind means a mind free of prejudices and conditions.*
- *In the context of free will, your mind is one step ahead of your nervous system before you intend to act.*
- *You can be pulled by your troubles or lead with your solutions.*
- *Your authenticity is the one true freedom awarded at the moment of conception. It is a carte blanche with no conditions other than you embrace it wholeheartedly.*
- *The mind's negativity bias means to doubt your capacity to cope with the unexpected and*

exaggerate events to the detriment of your mental and emotional well-being.

- Surrender to the natural order of events by leaning into your fears and insecurities. Reason with your anxieties by perceiving them with a logical mind instead of becoming embroiled in them.
- You evolve by being exposed to uncertainty and confronting your fears; otherwise, they dominate your mental landscape and grow in intensity.
- Uncertainty allows you to re-evaluate the past and make new choices in light of what transpires. It presents opportunities to create a compelling future based on new information.

5

Conquer Your Fears

"Our deepest fear is not that we are inadequate. Our deepest fear is that we are powerful beyond measure....It is our light, not our darkness that most frightens us...."
—Marianne Williamson

Our Deepest Fear

To Awaken Your Authentic Self, you cannot be tied to your fears. An awakened mind is a mind liberated from fear. Marianne Williamson's header quote is a significant work from the world acclaimed spiritual activist, often misattributed to Nelson Mandela's inauguration speech. She suggests it is not our darkness which we are afraid of; rather, it is our magnificence. We are unwilling to reveal our brilliance in the event others are made to feel inferior. This is significant given the dynamics of peer pressure and culture nowadays. We feel safe playing small and blend in with the masses since it shifts the spotlight off us. The questions and self-doubts may arise: "What if I am

103

not good enough?" "What if I'm found out?" "There are others who are better than I am." This is evident in popular culture which epitomizes the tall poppy syndrome. Many people fear that revealing their uniqueness may be inappropriate to their friends, family, and colleagues. Playing small serves no one, especially yourself. You are unique in many ways and your gifts and talents are a unique expression of universal energy. To deny others your gifts and talents may be likened to a tree refusing to bear fruit in season since it doubts its source of intelligence.

I draw your attention to the famous inventor Thomas Edison. Had he withheld his invention of the electric light bulb, we would be living in darkness these days. Another steward of notable inventions was Benjamin Franklin, who was an accomplished printer and inventor. His famous Franklin stove may well have been patented had he chosen to do so. Instead, he donated his time and money to developing the invention by giving it away, believing it would benefit many people. We doubt our magnificence since it directly coincides with self-esteem. Self-doubt is toxic and debilitating, as it serves to convince you of your unworthiness. It is the silent voice within that we fear and judge our self-worth by. We are terrified of our personal power given the self-doubt which rears its ugly head from an early age. It is estimated that by the time you are seventeen years old you will have heard the phrase "NO, you can't" an average of 150,000 times. In contrast, you will have heard, "Yes, you can" approximately 5,000 times. It is no wonder we have been inured with disempowering beliefs and the inability to succeed.

You are entitled to goodness, abundance, and life's wondrous pleasures. They are there waiting for you to claim them.

Instead, we internalize a script that informs us otherwise. We follow this script and doubt our true potential, our future vision and goals. Paulo Coelho reminds us about honoring our personal legend in his acclaimed novel *The Alchemist.* You are not depriving others of greatness by playing small. Marianne Williamson's poem goes on to say, "Your playing small doesn't serve the world…as we let our own light shine we unconsciously give other people permission to do the same." As you claim and step into your glory, you allow others to see the possibility of attaining the same freedom. For this reason we applaud and salute the underdog. We identify with them since it is embedded into modern culture to thrive and succeed. There is an underdog within us all waiting to appear. We unconsciously hold ourselves down convinced of our unworthiness to remain in the darkness. To sit on the sidelines is safe since we cannot be judged, labeled, or criticized there. But safe never serves anyone, let alone yourself. Leadership expert and speaker Robin Sharma suggests, "If people aren't laughing at your dreams, they're not big enough."

I wish to remind you of the baby elephant principle which sums up the truth of our fears. Baby elephants in captivity are chained at the leg to a small wooden peg in the ground. As they mature to full size, they are capable of breaking free given their relative size. Yet as adults they remain tethered to the chain, conditioned to believe it has the power to hold them captive. In some ways our lives mimic the behavior of adult elephants. Many of us form limiting beliefs during childhood which keep us imprisoned as adults. To overcome your deepest fear, acknowledge your Authentic Self which is the recurring theme throughout the book. Allow it passage throughout your life. Connect with life at the soul level instead of intellectualizing it. Your soul is boundless and not defined by limitations.

As you identify with your soul nature, it becomes effortless to reveal your talents and genius to the world. Fear is an illusion which deprives you of your power. It stifles your growth and convinces you of your unworthiness—it limits your potential. Your soul nature is infinite by contrast, unbound by time or space. Learn to think in terms of limitless possibilities—acknowledge your inner richness. Once you make an inner declaration toward greatness, the universe acknowledges it by bringing forth opportunities which allow your magnificence to shine. You must take the lead. You must take the first step toward claiming your own power.

The Key To Overcoming Fear Of Change

Fear of change is normal, although how you respond to change is more relevant. The key question one needs to ask is, "Am I responding to the fear itself or the fear of not being in control?" There's an important distinction in that simple question since it makes sense to uphold a level of control. When you release control, the fear will advise you of an underlying belief or emotion which you've disregarded. Many years ago, fear of change was a common experience in my life. When I perceived change taking place, I delayed it by choosing to ignore it until it pushed back, intensifying until it overwhelmed me. Have you noticed when approaching a hill from a distance how steep it seems? It's disconcerting to note its scale because from afar it seems overwhelming until we approach and scale it. As you begin your ascent of a hill, it rarely appears steep. Yet as you engage the terrain your mind withdraws from fear to focus on the task at hand. Your perception will often cloud your judgment due to the mind's negativity bias. This is the phenomenon by which humans give more psychological weight to bad experiences than good ones.

Your mind searches its mental inventory of situations outside your comfort zone and labels them either *safe or threatening*. The problem with succumbing to fear is that it stifles personal growth and keeps us stuck. Fear serves a purpose from an evolutionary perspective, yet when we allow it to overcome us, we are at the mercy of the emotion. We cannot awaken our authenticity while dictated by our fears. The Authentic Self is not held captive by fear; it integrates them into life's experiences to evolve. If you fear change, make use of the metaphor of ascending hills to overcome them. The following principles will guide you toward implementing those changes.

1. Examine The Fear Of Change

When you examine your fear of change, you're inclined to perceive it from a conscious perspective. What is the basis for the fear? How does fear serve you? This is a powerful question to ask of oneself. How does a fear of change serve you? Fear of change does not serve us; it hinders our progress by revealing anxiety and inhibiting vital bodily processes. Fear and the fear of change is a hindrance. You may not know what is on the other side of change, though you trust that everything develops for your greatest good. Examine your life and take note of your resistance to changes in the past. Has life not always served you?

Fear is a façade orchestrated by the mind to protect you.

That's not bad, since nature's design is intended to protect us from danger. The fear becomes a threat to our survival when we become consumed by it. What is supposed to protect us, however, is turned against us if we perpetuate and feed the fear. The solution is to face our fears boldly to navigate your way out of it.

2. Reframe The Fear Of Change

You've heard the expression, *what would you do if you knew you couldn't fail?* The premise behind the passage is to face your fears if you wish to lead an authentic life. Without fear playing a role in your life, you wouldn't forge ahead, since the mind is notorious for thwarting your success. It thrives on the safe and the known. What is holding you back from embracing change that is ultimately for your greatest good? Perhaps life reveals an answer to overcome your fears by bringing you an experience that is the very thing you need to prevail. Fear of change can hold you back from accepting new and lasting change that accompanies it. Reframing fear to an empowering state allows you to navigate your way toward an authentic experience of yourself and reality.

3. Tame Fear Through Practice

To become proficient at a sport, performance, or otherwise, it makes sense to rehearse and practice. In his book *Outliers*, Malcolm Gladwell introduces us to the 10,000-hour rule. He suggests that to develop into a world-class performer in one's respective field, it requires approximately 10,000 hours of deliberate practice, equivalent to 10 years. While I'm not suggesting you attempt 10,000 hours at mastering your fears, through persistence it's possible to overcome the grip fear has on you. To overcome fear of change, embrace changes in your life as they occur. Gradually lean into the change as opposed to running away from it. Take small steps toward your fears, knowing you have the wherewithal to overcome life challenges.

Order a style of coffee you're unaccustomed to next time you're out. Remove your earphones when traveling on public transport and engage others in small talk. Smile at people in the street more often. Engage in friendly conversation with the cashier at the supermarket to learn something about them. The idea of these exercises is to accustom you to situations beyond your comfort zone since your mind will make new neural connections. To overcome fear of change, make a vow to confront the underlying fear. Don't allow it to overwhelm you and take small steps while accepting what shows up. The experience is there to teach you a valuable lesson, so stay open and receptive to it.

Gain Inner Strength Through Willpower

To overcome your fear of change, it is vital to harness willpower in your life. Likened as the distinguishable characteristic many strive to command, it slips from our hands like clutching at water. Every human endeavor requires willpower from the moment we wake until we retire to bed in the evening. Willpower demands our attention and tests our resolve when we least expect it. If we want to improve our health, willpower tries our commitment when we pass by the confectionery section at the supermarket. Some people claim they have little willpower when in fact they don't understand how to use it effectively. Popularized in the late '60s and early '70s, the marshmallow test was conducted by American psychologist Walter Mischel at Stanford University's Bing Nursery School using four-year-old children. Acknowledged as Emotional Intelligence (EI), or Emotional Quotient (EQ), the test sought to gauge children's capacity to delay gratification. Mischel claimed the results can accurately predict the children's success later in life. These include: higher SAT scores, lower levels of substance abuse, lower likelihood of obesity, better response to stress and enhanced social skills, as reported by their parents.

Despite people's perception, willpower can be gained. The mind can direct its focus on any task given the stimuli are held in the person's awareness long enough. "We act as though our supply of willpower were endless. As a result, we don't consider it a personal resource to be managed, like food or sleep. This repeatedly puts us in a tight spot, for when we need our willpower the most, it may not be there," affirm authors Gary Keller and Jay Papasan in *The One Thing: The Surprisingly Simple Truth Behind Extraordinary Results*. Willpower is called upon to make decisions in everyday life and sure enough, it gets used up well before we know it. We can react by being hard on ourselves for giving into the task we are trying so hard to control. Willpower is dependent on timing and bringing a full tank of it to the task at hand, because if we have already used it up on something, we can expect to have little of it in the next instance.

I consider the mind a chariot, tethered to wild horses ready to gallop at a moment's notice. As the commander, it's our mission to direct our mental energy on the task at hand. Inner strength results in developing this mental resiliency. In the study *The Physiology of Willpower: Linking Blood Glucose to Self-Control*, it is shown that a drop in blood sugar leads to a loss of willpower. This is because the brain needs high levels of glucose to exert self-control. When blood sugar runs low, the brain can't spend the energy to override impulses. Authors Gary Keller and Jay Papasan state, "Think of willpower like the power bar on your cell phone. Every morning you start out with a full charge. As the day goes on, every time you draw on it you're using it up. So as your green bar shrinks, so does your resolve, and when it eventually goes red, you're done." Consequently, delaying gratification calls us to exercise willpower which many of us do every day with food choices. It's no wonder when tired, we are most vulnerable because the brain's glucose resources are depleted.

Awareness is important for harnessing willpower. We must avoid slipping into subconscious states when pressed to make difficult decisions. A subconscious state is one devoid of conscious control or intent. It's as though we're on autopilot instead of directing our attention to the task at hand. Focus and attention are important when harnessing willpower. The ability to focus your attention on a task is vital. Yet you want to be mindful not to overindulge since you may be inclined to use it up. For this reason, don't keep yourself in a constant state of willpower depletion. The President of the United States wears the same suit every day because he doesn't want to deplete his willpower making choices on what to wear or what to eat. Vital decision-making is best left for more pressing matters. Charles Duhigg, author of *The Power Of Habit,* affirms, "Willpower isn't just a skill. It's a muscle, like the muscles in your arms or legs, and it gets tired as it works harder, so there's less power left over for other things." To overcome this restriction, develop strong habits to lean on when your willpower is low or exhausted. Sound habits are automatic resting points to fall back on. When you're most tired, hungry, anxious, thirsty, or uncomfortable, knowing you can shift to automatic behaviors helps you navigate a drop in willpower. Similarly, meditation or self-reflective activity is helpful in calming the mind during anxious periods when willpower is called upon. Meditation activates the parasympathetic nervous system which helps calm the body and mind during tense periods.

Author Charles Duhigg reminds us once more, "THE GOLDEN RULE OF HABIT CHANGE: You Can't Extinguish a Bad Habit, You Can Only Change It." This gives us a clue why many of our well-intended actions fail: We're trying to stop an old behavior, like snacking on junk food late at night instead of replacing the habit with a new behavior, like snacking on fruit instead. For willpower to be a source inner strength, we must expect it ahead of time. "This is how willpower becomes a habit: by choosing a certain behavior ahead of time, and then following that routine when an inflection point arrives," states Charles Duhigg. Despite people's beliefs, the more we use willpower in the right setting, the more of it we have to use when it matters most. Don't be hard on yourself when you slip up. Like any new habit, there's a period of learning and growth at the beginning until we master the skill. In no time, you will have gained inner strength and the willpower to overcome any obstacle life gives you.

Never Give Up Hope

Life can throw its twists and turns although you should never give up hope. There you are coasting along when an adversity shows up unannounced on your doorstep. I'm sure you agree life can change at the drop of a hat. One thing that can help you stay hopeful and optimistic is accepting that not everything in life will proceed the way you want it to…and that's all right. The acceptance that you will face obstacles, negative emotions, and people should ease your stress. If you are consumed by the fear of "what's next?" you will have to bear an unnecessary weight on your shoulders. If you adopt a hopeful and optimistic heart, you'll breathe easier and expect a more pleasant future. Hope is more valuable than we give it credit. It is like a soft burning flame that cannot be extinguished, withstanding the wind and rain to glow impervious to external elements. Hope has what it takes to get you through life's dramas.

Hope is like optimism. To believe circumstances will work out helps you to relax in the present when something less than desirable comes your way.

- Hope trusts you will get through it.
- Hope remembers the times you made it through.
- Hope teams up with faith to surmount the impossible.

I will admit when tough times arrive, emotions come alive in full vigor. When the boss tells you the company is downsizing and your position will be terminated, when your son gets expelled from school or your partner decides he/she doesn't know if they want to spend the rest of his life with you, emotions are ready for a rollercoaster ride. This is understandable, but if you have hope deep within you, your thoughts will gravitate toward the positive and your emotions will be more positive. For example, if Jack tells Amy that after three years of a serious relationship he does not know if she is the "forever" girl for him, Amy has several options. If she does not have an optimistic outlook, her thoughts will swing to the negative. She might consider, "What am I going to do? I gave him everything and he does this? My life is over! I will trust no one again!" Such thoughts could cause a nervous breakdown, depression, and perhaps to reach for something to anesthetize the pain. Alternatively, if Amy carries hope in her pocket and wearing optimism as her cloak, her thoughts may be more inclined to: "Wow! This is a painful thing to hear and my heart is sad, but I guess Jack is not the man I'm supposed to spend the rest of my life with. I'm sure things will work out regardless and when the time is right, I will meet my life partner." Though Amy may harbor emotions such as sadness, she may not go into a meltdown because she has learned to live with hope and optimism.

Sometimes when life appears bleak, you are called to master a lesson greater than you expect. This is when to rely on hope to get you through. For example, if you lose your job, you might want to learn valuable lessons during your transition of looking for another job. Perhaps you realize you dislike your job and will find a career path that makes you happy. Or maybe you want to start your own business. Consider your circumstances as a way to evolve from the experience. During tough times do your best to envision a positive future. Many times what you envision is what you will get. Call it a positive intention; what you reflect upon and visualize is what you will have served on your plate. What do you want your present and future to be comprised of? Close your eyes and visualize it and be optimistic you will receive what you see.

The world is full of those who have overcome incredible obstacles, failures to become successful and happy. Possibly they know to remain unattached to outcomes because they understand that not everything will go as planned. They understand when one door is closed, another door will lead them where they're meant to go. They understand enough about hope and optimism to have it work in their life. Allow life to weave her magic through you. Commit to a life of optimism no matter the circumstances. Optimistic people decide to raise the beacon of hope when times get tough, and so can you. The next time something does not go as planned, call on hope and declare "It will be all right. I believe the best in this situation," and chances are it will. To awaken your Authentic Self, you must muster your resources to envision and create the circumstances of your life.

Why It Pays To Be Relentless

In the film *The Pursuit of Happyness*, Chris Gardner (played by Will Smith) announces to his son during a moment of despair:

"Hey. Don't ever let somebody tell you…You can't do something. Not even me. All right?…You got a dream….You gotta protect it. People can't do somethin' themselves, they wanna tell you you can't do it. If you want somethin', go get it. Period."

Captured in that brief monologue is an inspiring though compelling reality of what it means to be relentless—persistence. To live an authentic life, we must be unwavering in our pursuit of it since life seldom rewards the undeserving. In the instance where achievement comes naturally, if one is not fully prepared, then *easy come, easy go*. It was Warren Buffett who said, "Until you can manage your emotions, don't expect to manage money." Regardless of assigning money to achievement, we need to manage our emotions to overcome obstacles on the road to victory.

An unwavering attitude arises from an indomitable will, characterized by a relentless pursuit of excellence. We can be determined in going after a dream, a goal, or a plan just as those who diligently toil away at their vocation. I'm reminded of Thomas Edison whose patience and uncompromising character contributed to numerous extraordinary inventions. A fierce desire is fueled by the determination to prosper. "There are a lot of great inventors and improvers in the world. But those who hack world-class success tend to be the ones who can focus relentlessly on a tiny number of things. In other words, to soar, we need to simplify," affirms author Shane Snow in *Smartcuts: How Hackers, Innovators, and Icons Accelerate Success.*

To develop persistence we soar above our difficulties instead of acquiesce to them. Because if our resolve is strong, nothing can stand in our way to realize victory. However well intentioned, an unyielding attitude cannot flourish in an impoverished mind. A great attitude blossoms when obstacles are observed as positive feedback that lead to victory. To be relentless demands tolerance, given events will seldom play out as we hope. The persistent person conspires with the forces of life and acts when the time is right. They commit to daily actions in pursuit of their objectives while savoring the journey—for the process is as significant as the goal. They foster a growth mindset that favors personal growth instead of a narrowed vision. Others may consider them with disdain and criticize their approach. Therefore, weigh up other people's opinions carefully without allowing them to hinder your plans. Author Robert Greene articulates it well in his book *Mastery*, "Be relentless in your pursuit of expansion. Whenever you feel like you are settling into some circle, force yourself to shake things up and look for new challenges..." A relentless outlook can make those around you uncomfortable and lead them to examine their own passion. They may impose their shortcomings on you to appease their indignity. To be exceptional we must pursue excellence and self-mastery. Those who achieve notable achievement polish their performance and enhance their skills daily.

It is no mystery that the bigger your dream, the harder it is to reach. This should not discourage you from going after it, despite chipping away at it deliberately and laboriously. I am drawn to the mantra of "consistent persistence." At times, victory may show up when we least expect it. There is no overnight success with the determined individual. Behind every rags-to-riches story lies a person who works assiduously to hone their craft and the ability to follow a well-laid plan. "Whatever you want out of life, you must go through a process to get it. The process will take time, energy, determination, sacrifice, and relentless focus. If you want it enough, you'll find a way to get it done," states author Larry Weidel in *Serial Winner: 5 Actions to Create Your Cycle of Success*. Determined individuals are meticulous with detail and research. They dot their i's and cross their t's, knowing the Devil lies in the details. They pursue their passion even when they're less inclined. The novelist who sits down to compose the written prose may not be motivated to work on this day. Yet their determination and unrelenting pursuit of mastery compels them to show up and transform their habits into accomplishments. A relentless approach demands pursuing objectives that work and discarding what is detrimental to the overall goal. This person is outcome oriented identifying when modifications need to be made. They take personal responsibility to overcome hurdles as they emerge, for they are not perfectionists, though they seek to be impeccable with the task at hand.

Being relentless builds character since we discover a hidden force influencing our every step. We forge the marble of our character to create an inner monument formed through determination, struggle, and resilience. These are the foundations of the relentless, unbounding in their quest for excellence. "The craftsman mindset, with its relentless focus on becoming 'so good they can't ignore you,' is a strategy well suited for acquiring career capital. This is why it trumps the passion mindset if your goal is to create work you love," affirms author Cal Newport in So Good They Can't Ignore You. Relentless characters are self-aware and play to their strengths instead of nourishing their weakness. They avoid succumbing to the voice of the ego since they know they are only as good as their last performance. They lead from the heart because pursuing their passion is an endeavor that emerges from their Authentic Self and not material gain. An uncompromising attitude requires perspective since it is natural to rest on one's laurels in the face of achievement. Yet when this happens we lose sight of the factors that contributed to our initial success. To be relentless we must think big and act big. As Chris Gardner reminds us, if we want something, we go get it.

Period!

Chapter Summary

- *Playing small serves no one, especially yourself. You are unique in many ways and your gifts and talents are a unique expression of universal energy.*
- *You doubt your magnificence since it directly coincides with self-esteem. Self-doubt is toxic and debilitating, as it serves to convince you of your unworthiness.*
- *The baby elephant principle: being held back by your self-imposed beliefs.*
- *Connect with life at the soul level, instead of intellectualizing it. Your soul is boundless and not defined by limitations.*
- *The problem with succumbing to fear is that it stifles your personal growth and keeps you stuck.*
- *Fear is a façade orchestrated by the mind to protect you.*
- *To overcome fear of change, confront the underlying fear behind it. Don't allow it to overwhelm you and take small steps while accepting what shows up.*
- *Willpower can be gained, since the mind can direct its focus on any task given the stimuli is held in the person's awareness long enough.*

- *A drop in blood sugar leads to a loss of willpower. This is because the brain needs high levels of glucose to exert self-control. When blood sugar runs low, the brain can't spend the energy to override impulses.*
- *Focus and attention are important when harnessing willpower. The ability to focus your attention on a task is vital.*
- *Don't keep yourself in a constant state of willpower depletion.*
- *Meditation or self-reflective activity is helpful in calming the mind during anxious periods when willpower is called upon.*
- *The more you use willpower in the right setting, the more of it you have to use when it matters most.*
- *During tough times do your best to envision a positive future. Many times what you envision is what you will get.*
- *The persistent person conspires with the forces of life and acts when the time is right.*
- *To be exceptional pursue excellence and self-mastery. Those who achieve notable achievement polish their performance and enhance their skills daily.*
- *Being relentless builds character since we discover a hidden force influencing our every step.*

- *Relentless characters are self-aware and play to their strengths instead of nourishing their weakness. They avoid succumbing to the voice of the ego since they know they are only as good as their last performance.*
- *To be relentless we must think big and act big.*

6

Overcoming Challenges and Setbacks

"Life is either a daring adventure or nothing at all."
—*Helen Keller*

Develop Power To Transcend Problems

I am astonished how rich an inner tapestry life gives us to handle the infinite ebb and flows. While I'm not suggesting I am bereft of problems, as I nourish and tend to my inner landscape the easier my life's passage becomes. How does one arrive at this point? How do you allow the beauty and majesty of life to show itself to you in a similar way? How can you access the rich woven force of life which nourishes you? The following points have served me well in my life's journey and so I wish to impart them to you with the hope they serve you the same. It was the Buddha who said, "Don't blindly believe what I say. Don't believe me because others convince you of my words. Don't believe anything you see, read, or hear from others, whether of authority, religious teachers, or texts. Don't rely on logic alone, nor speculation. Don't infer or be deceived by appearances. Do not give up your authority and follow blindly the will of others. This way will lead to only delusion. Find out for yourself what is truth, what is real."

Test these principles by incorporating them into your daily life. Start with one core principle until you have gained a grasp of it. Remember, don't rush the lesson. I remind you of the passage which states, *life is a great teacher—it presents us with the test before the lesson.* With that, personal growth and wisdom takes place at the level of the body and mind. It must be incorporated at the cellular level and should be breathed, lived, and known intimately. It is pointless quoting wisdom from a book if you've never embodied the lesson. So I offer the following wisdom in the hope you may incorporate the lessons by living their truth.

1. Undertake Personal Growth Daily

By personal growth, I mean an endeavor which will allow you to experience inner growth and expand your awareness and level of consciousness. You might face challenges from a loved one who brings out the worst in you. By growing, you see your loved one mirrors back your insecurities. Realize that when you are the outward expression of how others relate to you, inner growth is experienced.

2. Raise Your Consciousness And Awareness

When you raise your level of consciousness, you invite a high order of energy to course through you. You transcend problems since those problems are only clear at the level of awareness and consciousness which created them. Albert Einstein said: "Problems cannot be solved at the same level of thinking that created them." To transcend your problems, raise and transcend your consciousness. A useful analogy perceives life from a higher perspective; you're looking down on your problems instead of ensconced in them.

3. Respect Your Body And Mind By Living A Healthy Life

Honor your body as a miracle of nature. You are a living, breathing being with a soul and pure potential. When you live how nature intended, you allow the infinite expression of life to pulse through every cell. Eat healthy nutritious food which nourishes your mind, body, and soul. Avoid toxic foods and substances which lower your life force and vitality. When you eat according to your genetic constitution, you activate the DNA that brings forth radiant, abundant health and vitality.

4. Honor And Live YOUR Truth

Much of the New Age mumbo-jumbo is lined with metaphors and spiritual jargon that means little to help people incorporate into daily life. I find it impractical and wish they state how they want me to act. Honor yourself by living your truth states you live in congruence with your highest vision of yourself. It means honoring your heart by following those desires without being influenced, coerced, or swayed by others. This may be the hardest advice to follow since we're faced with challenges and obstacles which influence how we should act. The media advise us we need to gain material possessions to be happy. This is the furthest thing from the truth and intended to market products you don't need. It demands self-honesty and bravery to live your truth and become an example to others to do the same.

4. Know Yourself

By knowing yourself, I invite you to understand and appreciate the duality of your human nature. Nature can be ferocious and yet calm, silent, and serene. To know yourself invites you to connect with the essence of your spirit. Become attuned to the silent voice which lives within. Retreat into silence often to commune with this voice. Only in silence can you drown out the monkey mind (incessant chatter) to discover the essence of your essence.

5. Work With The Forces Of Life

As human beings we have needs. These needs range from material wants such as a nice home, car, and other luxuries. Our non-material needs include love, respect, acceptance (or validation), and understanding. Often our ego intervenes to advise us we need more than what we have. It convinces us we are lacking and that our neighbors have more than us. It tells us we should strive to seek more, that in doing so we will be happier. To collaborate with the forces of life you become grateful and mindful of what you have in your life. In doing so, you invite more of the same frequency and energy. When we place demands on what we should have instead of what IS, we oppose life. In opposing life, we create suffering.

To transcend suffering, stop resisting what shows up in your life. ALLOW what shows up as a call for inner growth and your life's lesson. The universe is perfect despite our ego mind which conceives otherwise. Transcend means to rise above and go beyond a limitation or obstacle. Next time you're faced with an insurmountable constraint, choose not only to rise above it, but to go beyond the problem and see multiple alternative scenarios. The enlightened among us talk of a non-linear consciousness, a consciousness which knows no limitations, no obstacles and is beyond time and space. It is my vision for you to call upon the same force when faced with similar challenges.

Obstacles Are Signposts For Inner Growth

The merits of pushing through fear and the unknown when evidence shows the contrary can be compelling. Allow me to cite a story involving a friend who left a full-time job with a well-known company as a senior sales manager to create his own company. He was unhappy with the company culture and the position offered him no personal and professional growth. My friend has a young family with three children under the ages of ten so it was important he considers his decision thoughtfully. He knew the risk to leave the comforts of a well-paid executive position to pursue a business venture which offered no financial security of success. Interestingly, at the same time I am reading *Delivering Happiness*, written by the founder of Zappos.com, Tony Hsieh. The book chronicles Hsieh's rise to create one of the leading online footwear retailers, which sold to Amazon for $1.2 billion, of which Hsieh took a large percentage.

I related to my friend how Tony Hsieh encountered many setbacks along his journey to build a successful online shoe business. A powerful idea is overcoming any hurdles life presents us with. I am fond of this principle and advised my friend his success is built on finding his own way to realize success. There is ALWAYS a path that leads us to overcome hurdles and obstacles. It is your job to find that path. Life will present you with insurmountable roadblocks, not because it intends for you to fail. Instead, that we are tested to decide how much we want the prize and if we're committed to staying the distance. There is little to stop me achieving my dream to impact humanity with my written and spoken message. I have great belief in myself, despite the many setbacks I've encountered. Over time, I resolved to change how I interpreted failure and reprogrammed my mind to an empowering dialogue. I affirmed that every time I experienced a setback, I was drawing closer to my goal. Every time it appeared I was moving further away from my goal, I am sent an even BETTER way to bring my dreams to reality. Gradually it began to work and I soon realized subtle changes taking shape in my reality to align with my purpose and vision. It was Dr. Wayne Dyer that stated, "Change the way you look at things and the things you look at will change."

Apply this principle to your current life by way of relationships, finance, career, business, health, etc. My advice to my friend was to overcome his obstacles because there is always a path that leads through. The universe is lined with roadblocks as you venture down life's path. Not because it wants to make it hard for you, because the greater your dream, the greater your load. To cite a similar analogy, the bigger the delivery truck, the more load you must carry. The more you push through to overcome challenges and setbacks, the greater your growth and reward.

What challenges are you facing in your personal or professional life? Is there a way through them?

What must you do or who must you become to overcome the challenge or obstacles?

These are empowering questions to ask oneself since they strike at the heart of what prevents you achieving your goal. I encounter many obstacles daily nowadays. My car stopped running yesterday during a torrential rainstorm. I was stranded on a hill and the ignition refused to start. I considered the possibilities to find a way out and drew on experience to navigate through. Sure I was mad; I was furious having to wait over an hour and a half for a tow truck to arrive while it's pouring rain. Yet I was stuck in a situation over which I had little control.

Harness the power of your mind which knows the best possible solution to overcome your challenges. Ask empowering questions when it matters and trust the power of your mind to find a way through. The mind is a powerful ally and comparable to working out: The more you train it and use it, the more it works on your behalf. There are no mistakes in this purposeful universe, only lessons we are yet to discover.

Staying Motivated When All Seems Lost

It's no surprise life is a game of ups and downs. It's not possible to experience the ups all the time. Sometimes life gives you lemons. But as they say—when life gives you lemons, make lemonade. While it's easier said than done, you must stay motivated. It is easy to stay down, sad and gloomy and to drown in insecurity or self-pity, but it will lead you into giving up and performing your worst. As I write this, I can relate to it because I've been there. We all have. But in those tough moments, you show your real strength. These are moments that tell you of your strength and determination for success. Such moments differentiate between winners and the rest of the world. If you are unmotivated, the following words of encouragement will help you find a path out of despair.

Mindset

You must harness a positive mindset. I'm certain I'm not the first person to tell you this. I experienced a transformation in myself and can avow that changing your mindset helps. Stop entertaining a fear-filled mindset. You might be insecure about your future, though if you have trust in yourself and the world, your outlook will change. You will be more balanced, stronger, more confident and happier. This will reflect in your work and personal life. By believing there will be a better tomorrow, you navigate your way out of misery. Keep in mind that change has to happen. If you are unhappy today, it will not stay the same and things will change because that is the cycle of life; nothing is permanent.

People

People around you play an important part. Are they motivating you or tearing you down? Are they affecting your mood in a positive or a negative way? No matter how strong you consider yourself to be, if you spend time with people who have a limited mindset, you cannot stay positive. Sooner or later you will develop a negative mindset because we are the sum of the people we associate with. Stay in the company of people who influence your life. People who achieve success have encountered failures. Such people can guide you in a better way. Successful people will be the ones to push you to new heights. The more successful and confident people you socialize with, the higher chances are for your success.

Inspiration

It is important to become inspired since there are many sources of inspiration. Attend self-help classes, read good books, listen to podcasts, or visit seminars. Inspiration dwells in many places. No matter how grave your situation, no matter how frustrated you are, you'll find someone who has encountered a similar condition and has managed. Draw inspiration from such sources. Read books that uplift your spirit more often, biographies of great leaders who have overcome challenges. Your thoughts will change and help you reinforce the positive person which dwells within. Successful people help you learn new things that may aid you. A positive outlook goes a long way.

Goals

When I experienced a rough spell in my life, it took months to recover. I was in that position for a year and lost my ability to navigate my way forward. I experienced anxiety and insecurity about my future, but I wanted to flourish. I realized deep inside there will be a better future and I strived for it. If people around you make things worse, find other company, but do not isolate yourself from the world. Make a few goals. Promise yourself you'll rekindle your friendship with an old friend. Watch a movie with friends. Form small goals that will let you experience the joys of life. When you know what you want, it's easier to achieve it. If you want to stay on-track, make sure you identify what the track is. Be persistent and keep pushing. Your situation will change; just stay positive.

Don't be disappointed. We all experience setbacks. Sometimes nothing works and life seems to go in the wrong direction. But having a positive mindset changes it all. Surround yourself with encouraging and successful people and stay inspired. Plan your goals and go after them with passion and enthusiasm. Authenticity is being real about your current state of life. It does not entail wearing rose-colored glasses hoping to experience a positive outlook when deep down you feel miserable. Authenticity involves connecting with your emotions no matter how intense or unfavorable they appear. Take solace knowing that when you experience intense emotions along the journey to reach your goals, you develop a deep understanding of who you are beneath the superfluous thoughts.

How To Overcome Challenges And Setbacks

Have you experienced challenges and setbacks? It can be difficult to face challenges. Many people avoid challenges and setbacks, yet we must face them rather than run away from them. No matter how much you avoid them, they will strike you back. You cannot avoid the challenges of life so instead face them with openness. You can overcome challenges and setbacks by applying the following rules that will help you build mental and emotional resilience as well as the wisdom to overcome setbacks.

Why Face Challenges?

Challenges are necessary for your growth. If you want to develop resilience, you need challenges in your life. Challenges polish your talents and improve your skills. They help us become successful individuals in the field we are involved in. Challenges help us discover who we are and how we behave under adversity. They reveal our authenticity to cope with the issues at hand rather than run away from them. When we're successful, we are confident, yet the difficult times allow us to know how we truly are.

Challenge Yourself

If you want to grow and become successful in reaching your full potential, you must challenge yourself. For that, you need to set goals that allow you to expand your creativity and imagination. These goals should motivate you. Though these should be achievable goals, don't make them too simple. A challenge should be difficult enough to develop your skills, otherwise known as deliberate practice which I mentioned in Chapter 5. Divide a big goal into smaller goals for simplicity.

How To Overcome Challenges

Follow these simple steps:

1. Clearly Understand The Problem

When you attempt to overcome a problem, make sure you understand what the problem is. If you don't clearly understand it, you can't solve it. Take time out to understand the problem from different perspectives. While it sounds like simple advice, many people assume they know what they're dealing with. They create a biased perspective of what they think is the issue, rather than the main problem to be tackled. If you face challenges, a sense of ill-fated doom comes over you, but do not panic. Stay calm to find a solution to your problems. Understanding your problem clearly will help you focus on the solution.

2. Identify Your Resources And Strengths

Identify the resources available to help you achieve your goals. Make a list of those resources.

- They may consist of: blogs, books, magazines, computer, and of course money. These materials can help you overcome your problems as an initial contact point. If you believe you are lacking in finances, start with what is available and raise the additional financial resources later. You don't need everything at hand to get started; start with what you have available to gather momentum.
- Personal strength and skills are important resources. If you are hardworking, there's no goal you cannot achieve. However, if you are inclined to being lazy after starting something and want to quit, you are at a

loss to succeed even with the right financial resources available.

- Motivation is a factor for success. If your friends and family motivate you, you can achieve success faster. If those devoted to welfare bring you down, it can be difficult to succeed in the face of additional burdens. Make sure you keep the right company and don't be afraid to demote people that interrupt or oppose your success. We need to be picky with whom we allow into our inner sphere of success, and that means being diligent with weeding out the grave diggers.

3. Create A Strategy

To face challenges, formulate a proper strategy. Consider carefully ways to find a suitable strategy to overcome your problems. Once you decide on the right strategy, execute it with precision and bring your whole self into it. That is, apply yourself to the task even though success may not be assured, don't lose heart. Most attempts rarely succeed the first time. Many successful people try and fail. Their failures become stepping stones for later success. So create a firm commitment to overcome your challenge until you succeed.

4. Implement Your Strategy

Once you devised a strategy, you need skill, intelligence, and creativity to carry it out. We must execute it with diligence, determination, and effort. Strive for excellence and try your best. However, if you don't overcome the challenge, don't be disheartened. Devise another strategy and try again. There can be only two reasons for failure: either the strategy wasn't good enough, or you didn't implement the strategy properly. Discover the cause, eliminate the problem, and try again.

Challenge yourself continuously. We all face challenges and none are immune to it. If you face setbacks, refuse to give up. Challenges are a way to improve your skills. They make you work under pressure and still survive. Setbacks should be taken as challenges you must accept. Make sure you don't give up on your goals. Once you cross the hurdles, you'll be welcomed with success.

The Power Of Consistency And Persistence

How many of you can claim with absolute certainty that you apply consistency and persistence in your daily life with a measure of success? [Cue silence] Consistency and persistence are two elusive virtues difficult to sustain if not regularly engaged. Let us take a moment to peer through the lens of what consistency and persistence have to offer. No doubt you are informed of the merits of consistency within a practical approach. Attend any weekend course and the instructor will validate the power of consistency as a key attribute toward accomplishment. Consistency may be defined as developing discipline in a chosen field with the goal of reaching a favorable outcome. Those who uphold discipline are rewarded with success since they have harnessed enduring focus through concerted effort. Let's be clear. Success in this context is not limited to particular areas of life. If losing weight and eating healthy are your primary goals, taking proper action on a consistent basis may be considered a success. Far too many people discount the power of consistent effort toward their goals. Consistency creates powerful neural networks in the brain known as grooving. These grooved neural networks help form strong connections within the brain's synaptic connections, thus enhancing your concentration on a task or goal.

When one applies intermittent effort to a goal, the brain does not receive enough stimuli to form powerful habits. It is the Hebbian theory, introduced by the Canadian psychologist Donald O. Hebb, who states that "nerves that fire together, wire together." With consistent effort, your brain gains the appropriate neural connections because of prolonged application. To focus your attention toward your goals allows the brain to *lock onto* the target. Consistency may be perceived as the ability to sustain continuous effort despite external forces. Ceaseless determination is paramount to draw a favorable outcome. Consistency builds character and sharpens the mind. Consistent people are triumphant, with an unyielding inner drive. They are firm in their resolve to invoke positive results and do not compromise by cutting corners or taking the road less traveled. This dedication pays off with the rewards that await. A thought worth mentioning. Consistency is essential in a task-oriented goal since it allows you to trace your results through to completion. For example, many people give up improving their nutritional and exercise goals as challenges arise. Following success without a measure of sustained performance is likely to produce ineffectual outcomes. In several instances, one's desired results may not be visible for any length of time, while changing nutritional and exercise goals. Often events are working in your favor, albeit behind the scenes while laying the foundations for future progress.

Let us turn our attention to the power of persistent effort.

It should be stated that persistence is a state of mind. It is the hallmark of accomplishment given that persistent people push through pain. Pain refers to the setbacks and roadblocks that are clear when plowing ahead. One's ability to recover from failure and setbacks forms the basis for future success. Persistence acknowledges the external forces which act on us. Such forces have the potential to derail or hinder one's progress. The persistent person acknowledges these forces are working against them, yet lingers on. In previous books, I drew the reader's attention toward establishing a compelling WHY? since I believe it to be a crucial measure of improvement. Persistent people have an indomitable will to succeed, having connected with a persuasive WHY? Behavioral psychologists have long believed that *showing up* is a good enough measure toward future success. I affirm that showing up is inadequate since people show up every day to dreary and mundane jobs which they loathe. While the body is present, their minds are on vacation somewhere on a tropical island. Showing up means being present and engaged with absolute intention and purpose.

Another key influence is the power of momentum, a formidable ally toward goal attainment. Without momentum, one applies partial effort while expecting victory. Think back to your last project in which you applied persistence and momentum. I daresay your efforts were met with ease and perfection as though you were in flow. Momentum is the accelerator driving persistence. As you maintain persistence, momentum takes the wheel to hasten progress. Artists will tell you that every creative pursuit takes a life of its own once a commitment is made, compelling it forward. A final principle which ties together the power of consistency and persistence is known as the compound effect. Author Darren Hardy wrote an insightful book titled *The Compound Effect* which outlines ways in which success is leveraged through building on consistency and persistence. According to the author, "The compound effect is the principle of reaping huge rewards from a series of small, smart choices. The most challenging aspect of the compound effect is that we have to keep working away for a while, **consistently** and **efficiently**, before we can begin to see the payoff." Thus the power of consistency and persistence are two fundamental forces that have the potential to generate powerful and lasting success in areas of your life.

Use them wisely.

Chapter Summary

- *You are the outward expression of how others relate to you.*
- *Raise your level of consciousness to invite high energy to course through you.*
- *Honor yourself by living your truth in congruence with your highest vision of yourself.*
- *Silence helps you drown out the monkey mind (incessant chatter) to discover the essence of your essence.*
- *When you place demands on what you should have instead of what IS, you oppose life. In opposing life, you create suffering.*
- *The greater your dream, the greater your load.*
- *There are no mistakes in this purposeful universe, only lessons we are yet to discover.*
- *If you are unhappy today, it will not stay the same. Your circumstances will change because that is the cycle of life; nothing is permanent.*
- *Stay in the company of people who influence your life.*
- *Authenticity involves connecting with your emotions no matter how intense or unfavorable they appear.*
- *Challenges help us discover who we are and how*

we behave in adversities. They reveal our authenticity to cope with the issues at hand, rather than run away from them.

- *To Overcome Challenges:*
  - *Clearly Understand The Problem*
  - *Identify Your Resources And Strengths*
  - *Create A Strategy*
  - *Implement Your Strategy*

- *Consistency creates powerful neural networks in the brain known as grooving. These grooved neural networks help form strong connections within the brain's synaptic connections, thus enhancing your concentration on a task or goal.*
- *Donald O. Hebb states that "nerves that fire together, wire together."*
- *Consistency builds character and sharpens the mind.*
- *Persistence is a state of mind and the hallmark of accomplishment, given persistent people push through pain.*
- *Consistency and persistence are two fundamental forces that have the potential to generate powerful and lasting success in areas of your life.*

7

Awaken Your Authentic Self

> *"Authenticity is a collection of choices that we have to make every day. It's about the choice to show up and be real. The choice to be honest. The choice to let our true selves be seen."*
> —Brené Brown

Will The Real You Please Stand Up?

Brilliance always seeks its own path to reveal itself. Ask anyone, "Who are you?" and they will reel off a list of attributes relating to their occupation, education, or familial status. "I am an architect, husband, father, mother, accountant, etc." What you do in your waking hours encompasses one facet of your life. It holds significance we identify with it, yet it doesn't tell us who we are at a deeper level.

Take a moment to consider who you truly are beneath the surface, irrespective of your title or status.

Who is the person you call the Self?

The person you identify with as "I?"

A facet of your being prevails beyond the individual you recognize in the mirror or see in photographs. This Self, although having transformed its external form over the years, remains the same. In his book *The Mind-Body Code,* clinical neuropsychologist Dr. Mario Martinez seeks to discover the key to longevity through interviews with centenarians. Having traversed the globe to uncover the secrets to long life, the common denominator among those who live beyond 100 years is that the person they call "the Self" remains much the same. Reflect on that for a moment. The person you know as "I" remains the same throughout your life because of your self-constructed image. While your external façade may change, the essence of the "Self" is unchanged. There is an underlying quality to your existence entrusted in goodness and recognized as the Authentic Self. Beneath your conditioning, the Authentic Self emerges to reveal the core self—the spiritual part of your nature. The Authentic Self is the embodiment of your soul nature—the immaterial Self which exists beyond the physical space-time continuum. This Self is not bound by the constraints of our culture to conform by way of rules and regulations. It is boundless, transcending the limitations of time, owing to its essence as simple awareness.

Equally, we recognize inauthenticity in others by labeling them as "fake." However, we are less likely to detect the same flaws in ourselves. This is because we associate with the dominant egoic self, which strives to achieve more and is never fulfilled until it gets what it wants. So we buy into its false demands of wanting more to ensure its survival. In contrast, the Authentic Self does not support the same needs as the ego. Through a quiet stillness, it communicates to us in silent whispers. The Authentic Self can be drowned out by the voice of the ego. Many people fail to merge with their deeper wisdom due to the overpowering ego which dominates their life. The American mythologist Joseph Campbell wrote, "The privilege of a lifetime is being who you are." The Authentic Self is concealed beneath the formed image of the Self while serving to obscure your spiritual nature. To realize the core self requires shedding the false image of who you think you are and allowing the real self to emerge. If we wish to venture beyond the pale as Dr. Martinez describes, we risk being excluded from belonging. Those who embark on a journey to realize success in the world are no longer considered part of the tribe. Our social need to identify with our tribe is an acknowledgment of our belonging.

This begs the question: How do we unite with our authentic nature, concealed under the weight of conditioning?

To reveal your authenticity means honoring the wisdom contained within the core self. At the deepest level, the soul's yearning to express itself through you remains vital to your personal evolution. The Authentic Self honors the wisdom that you are more than your thoughts. You created your image of self to exist and survive in the world, yet the eternal self does not associate with this likeness. An authentic life requires you live according to your highest truth. It means to embody your deepest values which serve as guideposts for genuine living. Those who live an inauthentic life are prone to life's struggle contained within the states of boredom, mid-life crisis, addictions, infidelity, etc. They stray from their Authentic Self by buying into the false belief they are lacking in this respect. Life succeeds through contrasts. It was Shakespeare who expressed through Hamlet that "there is nothing either good or bad, but thinking makes it so." While unsettling, life's conflicting nature highlights our struggle to make sense of the world. This becomes clear as we dip our toes in the water to experience the other side. Thus a mid-life crisis becomes a call to heal unpleasant emotional conflicts. To stay stuck in a mid-life crisis, however, becomes a healing crisis vying for our attention. As we merge with the Authentic Self, our problems, pain, and struggles give rise to inspired living. We harmonize with our essential self by integrating our highest values into the core of our being.

Self-examination is a means to reawaken the Authentic Self by making conscious what was unconscious. I use "reawaken" since your default state at conception is one of innocence and pure awareness. Byron Katie's program "The Work" is a valuable healing and transformation tool which offers powerful insights for enquiring into unconscious beliefs in order to awaken the Authentic Self. As you unite with the Authentic Self, a greater wholeness emerges to reveal the core self. To appreciate a bird in song requires one to recognize the same tune within their own being. Only then can we appreciate the wholeness of our being to emerge out of the fog of separation.

Recognizing The Voice Of The Ego

Being mindful of the ego's control could be the single factor that leads to our salvation. Alternative medicine advocate and author Deepak Chopra affirmed, "If you want to reach a state of bliss, then go beyond your ego. Make a decision to relinquish the need to control, the need to be approved, and the need to judge. Those are the three things the ego is doing all the time.

It's very important to be aware of them every time they come up." Many people are asleep to the vise-like grip the ego has and fall victim to it because they are unaware of its influence. The ego is the wounded and scorned child that poses a threat to a person's self-esteem. It manipulates you into the belief of separation, which is nothing more than an impulse intended to reinforce its position.

The ego thrives on dividing you from the wholeness of your Authentic Self and conspires to lure you into its ways. It is the splintered part of the soul serving to admonish you of your limitations. The ego takes its power from identifying with the "I" of your being. Every time you affirm, "I am lazy," "I am hopeless/incompetent," etc., it reinforces its influence. When this voice becomes overwhelming, it leads us further away from our soul nature. The ego undertakes to prove your unworthiness by bringing attention to the damaged aspects of your character. "All ego really is, is our opinions, which we take to be solid, real, and the absolute truth about how things are," states Buddhist nun Pema Chodron. We are complete beings, embodied in the duality of light and dark—yin and yang. The ego, however, prefers to bring attention to the darkness by reminding us of the concealed self, replete with faults and vulnerabilities. However, this is not who we are but merely a snapshot of our being.

It seeks to be heard to ensure its survival, since focusing attention on our soul nature diminishes the ego. To find harmony, we acknowledge our unconscious or suppressed thoughts while transforming them into empowering states. Mario Martinez states in *The MindBody Code*, "The solution to all your impasses and suffering is not to kill your ego or detach from your negative emotions. You need your ego to deal with

the practical aspects of life, and all emotions are essential biological information that tells you how your body is responding to the interpretations you make about your circumstances."
To draw attention to our Authentic Self, we must realize that
underneath our tangled story lies our core essence which is
love and light. For the ego is merely a façade masquerading as
a Venetian mask to conceal the real self. Consider this: Why do
we identify with the egoic voice instead of the expression of the
soul? Maybe it reminds us of the parent who criticizes us, in
contrast to the nurturing parent. Naturally, we are drawn to the
negative parent to appease them and justify our self-worth.

The ego is the worn-out script that plays out in our head to
convince us of our unworthiness. This is coupled with recalling negative thoughts that have us believe we are less than perfect. To transform the voice of the ego, we become conscious of
our limiting self-talk and examine our hurt and pain for what
it actually is—a smoke screen. We undertake this by going into
silence which allows us to connect with the stillness of the
inner self. Meditation practice is an effective means to connect with our soul, because it drowns out the mental chatter
in place of connecting with our Authentic Self. "The Authentic Self will never lead you to believe that you have anything to
defend, prove, or be puffed up about, because your true identity is not determined by what your ego or the world has to
say about you," affirms Dennis Merritt Jones. Regretfully, many
people distract themselves with extraneous noise that isolates
them from associating with their core self. If they retreat into
silence long enough, they discover beneath their thoughts is
someone they don't like. There is a vast undercurrent of longing to be noticed within. This pure awareness is known when

we shift our attention away from incessant thoughts and focus on the stillness within.

It was during meditation practice one day that I reached deep into my being and experienced this breathtaking stillness. I sensed returning home and yearned to associate with this pure silence. The clue to developing a relationship with this aspect of our being is to turn down the narrative of the egoic voice. We shouldn't try to destroy the ego, but to integrate it into the wholeness of our being so we are not a servant to it. Meditation teacher and psychotherapist Loch Kelly validates this position in his book *Shift into Freedom: The Science and Practice of Open-Hearted Awareness.* "What we let go of is our ego-identification. Our ego functions and ego personality become less stressed, defensive, and constricted; ego-identification is no longer experienced as the center of who we are." We must avoid supporting the ego's view of separateness, and instead highlight the principle of wholeness. Disempowering thoughts linked to fear is our soul calling us to reconnect with our authentic nature. Accordingly, fear is a signpost pointing us to the quietness within. So when a disempowering thought appears, simply notice it through pure awareness. I am reminded of the phrase my six-year-old nephew learned at kindergarten—"stop, look, and listen." We stop what we are doing, look within, and listen attentively to the voice calling our attention. As you practice this, the less the ego will reinforce its control, so in time it rescinds into the background. After all, if we seek to attain a state of bliss as Deepak Chopra affirms, we must reach beyond the ego while being attentive to its control.

Knowing The Language Of The Heart

I want you to close your eyes for a moment. Bring your attention to your chest and place your awareness on the feelings and sensations around your chest. While seated, continue to breathe easily and direct your focus on this region. You might encounter tingling feelings, images might flash across your mind—let them show up.

Now open your eyes.

Welcome to the resonance of the heart. You have embarked on the first step in experiencing your heart energy. The voice of the heart is quiet and assuring, though it can be drowned out by the relentless mental dialogue at play in our mind. The language of the heart is the call of the soul which echoes in a faint whisper. Upon closer examination, we see the ego is dominant, relentless, and ill-advised to help us navigate life. It is the cunning friend with honest intentions, spurring you toward insensitive acts of courage. In comparison, the heart speaks in a clear and reassuring way to reinforce our personal success and soul's transformation.

I am reminded of a delightful tale by the Jesuit priest and psychotherapist Anthony de Mello:

"What must I do to attain holiness?" said a traveler.

"Follow your heart," said the Master.

That seemed to please the traveler.

Before he left, however, the Master said to him in a whisper, "To follow your heart you are going to need a strong constitution." A strong constitution is required since the heart's wisdom will often conflict with the logic of the mind. It is experienced as an emotion, a sensation, or an inner experience, while the mind's narrative is firm and resolute. Soulful living is an invitation to live beyond the material world, rather than being led by our heart's wisdom. This is challenging because we are unfamiliar communicating with our heart, since our focus is fixed on left-brain logic. It is the analysis and over-analysis which leads to paralysis of the body. It is as simple and yet as involved as the message from author Gary Zukav who affirms in *The Seat Of The Soul,* "Feel your intentions in your heart. Feel not what your mind tells you, but what your heart tells you." Our addiction can lead us to react to external events while being insensitive to the call of our inner wisdom. To experience the way of the heart, we must develop the capacity to listen. This is challenging when our environment constantly summons our attention. We are exposed to fear-based news stories, products or services we don't need or, worse still, a celebrity scandal that carries limited importance in our lives. We don't have to be drawn into this endless drama and can choose to be pulled by life's circumstances or be led by the call of our spirit, which knows the way.

To know the language of the heart is the essence of love, the foundation of universal power. Love is the highest order conferred to us at the moment of conception. Millions of people spend their entire lives in search of their soul mate, while all along they seek to experience the essence of their soul. "The human heart is a keenly sensitive area of feeling and knowing that is a portal to our deepest self. Heart wisdom is a blend of deep feeling and understanding," states author John Prendergast, Ph.D. We must try to live from the heart instead of a self-centered existence imposed by what is missing in our life. This heart-based living I speak of is a return to wholeness. We never disconnect from this aspect of our being, aside from when we become distracted and lose our way. Similarly, language is not confined to that learned and communicated through words. It is conveyed through intuition, sensations, feelings, and an inner knowing. We must connect with this inner wisdom to know the entirety of our being. Meditation and regular silence are valuable to connect with the heart because we lower the volume on the endless chatter that occupies the spaces between our thoughts. For many, to retreat into silence means being alone with their thoughts, however disconcerting it may seem, rather than to realize their sacred nature. Spiritual teacher Adyashanti affirms, "Who would I be if I fell into the heart, not as some sort of ideal, not as something I imagine, but something that I actually allow to happen at the deepest level?"

The voice of the heart shows itself through feelings that connect you to your soul. When we honor these feelings and intentions they lead us back home where we yearn to be. It was Hans Christian Andersen who said, "Where words fail music speaks." This music lives in our heart and is discernible if we fall silent long enough to hear its message. To be guided by your heart while using the logic of the mind is to unify mind and body so that every thought and action emerges from intentional living. "When we are willing to set aside the contents of an 'overstuffed' mind and walk the trail unburdened, we'll discover that it's difficult not to hear what the heart wants to say," states author Dennis Merritt Jones. So as our attention deepens into our heart, we discover in that stillness our eternal soul calling us to be one again. For as the Master knew all along: To follow your heart demands a firm constitution. After all, the way of the heart will adopt everything the mind is unable to embrace.

Two Wolves Within And The One You Feed

Awakening the Authentic Self is illustrated in the following tale depicted as the supreme fight between good and evil. One evening, an elderly Cherokee brave told his grandson about a battle that goes on inside people.

"My dear one, the battle between two 'wolves' is inside us all. One is evil. It is anger, envy, jealousy, sorrow, regret, greed, arrogance, self-pity, guilt, resentment, inferiority, lies, false pride, superiority, and ego.

The other is good. It is joy, peace, love, hope, serenity, humility, kindness, benevolence, empathy, generosity, truth, compassion, and faith."

The grandson thought about it for a moment and then asked his grandfather: "Which wolf wins?"

The old Cherokee replied, "The one you feed."

The tale of the two wolves portrays the good and evil that lives within, represented by the conscious and the unconscious desire of man. If we are unconscious of our thoughts, we are at the mercy of feeding the evil wolf. Our unconscious thoughts are the unresolved or repressed parts of our psyche. The evil wolf asserts its power when we least expect it, because it is hidden from view. I'm aware of this darkness when a driver abruptly cuts me off in traffic and my ego is threatened. I react in a fit of simmering confrontation, believing I have been wronged. It is upon reflection that I recognize this as unconscious anger seeking to protect itself. The ego strives to assert its will to protect and strengthen itself and thus we fall prey to its needs. David Richo states, "Our ego was never meant to die, only to be tamed so that its wild energies could be put to better use." To mitigate acting out our unconscious desires, we become mindful of our thoughts instead of numb to them. We witness them with openness and tenderness instead of with binding judgment. Similarly, the shadow self comprises the unknown dark side of our personality. To disown the dark side means going to war with ourselves. Yet to accept ourselves as whole is to embody our strengths and limitations—our shadow self. This can be seen in the yin/yang symbol represented by the two halves that together complete wholeness.

Therefore, what we feed gives rise to goodness or the collapse of character. It was Frank Outlaw who said, "Watch your thoughts. They become words. Watch your words. They become deeds. Watch your deeds. They become habits. Watch your habits. They become character. Character is everything." We may not realize we are strengthening the ego until it grows in intensity, overshadowing our personality. Like a double-edged sword, what we feed is what we must coexist with.

So how can we stop feeding the fear and anger within?

Without being aware, we confer power to our dark side when we identify with disempowering states. Through a false persona we form an archetype where darkness prevails. If you walk into a pitch-black room without light, you assume darkness is all that exists. Yet when a light is switched on, you are motivated to identify with it instead of the darkness. The answer lies in knowing darkness is simply the absence of light. "Experience anger or fear or shock for what they are. But you don't have to think of them as evil—as intrinsically bad, as needing to be destroyed or driven from our midst. On the contrary, they need to be absorbed, healed, made whole," states author Steve Hagen in *Buddhism is Not What You Think: Finding Freedom Beyond Beliefs.*

How do we recognize our inner radiance?

It is the loving aspect of our being, imbued with an openness that infuses our hearts and minds. "When the Buddha found enlightenment, the demons felt consternation at the prospect of so much light coming into the world. This is the archetype of the combination of opposites: Light arouses shadow and shadow arouses light. Goodness is attacked by evil forces and forces of goodness battle forces of darkness," affirms David Richo. I recall on one occasion during meditation practice, drawing my awareness to this inner presence. I later explained to a friend, "I felt I was going deep into my being and I loved what was there." In contrast, if we feed the evil within, it grows in intensity since we give it life. Yet perpetuating evil cannot be maintained because the grim shadow leads to our self-destruction. Thus, by integrating our shadow into the wholeness of our being, we are called home to where we belong. I am drawn to Lama Surya Das's message, "To realize how karma works through insight into its actual mechanics is to become a master rather than a victim of our fate, and to realize freedom from and even autonomy within causes, circumstances, and conditions. That is why Buddha said, 'No one can make me angry unless I have it inside.'" In keeping with Lama Surya Das's declaration, we have the power to choose our path and not be victim to our inner demons.

Knowing whether our beliefs are beneficial allows us to let go of the negative karma of the past. How do we know if these beliefs serve us? We look to our external world to see life expressing our beliefs or opposing them. Do they create fulfillment and enrich our life, or do they keep us hostage? The narrative of the two wolves highlights the division inside us, vying for our attention. We can feed harmony and joy or light the flame of resentment and false pride. It was author of *The*

Celestine Prophecy, James Redfield, who said, "Where Attention goes, Energy flows; Where Intention goes, Energy flows." It is with this intention we direct our focus to nurture the goodness within. Like returning home, our soul calls us to find wholeness instead of remaining alienated by the fog of separation.

How To Cultivate Powerful Self-Esteem

Regrettably, many people experience low self-esteem which can arise in one's life for various reasons. A person with low self-esteem may have picked up verbal cues from those around them from a tender age. It is during these formative years where the child's mind is most impressionable. Those with low self-esteem are subjected to verbal abuse from loved ones or those close to them. Verbal abuse may be defined as any untoward or unwanted criticism from another person. Life is challenging in view of the demands of living in a modern world. To be subjected to criticism or emotional abuse can make life unbearable, mostly when one experiences suffering. You don't know what is beneath the surface of another person. Often we're only exposed to the façade of the people we meet. To draw on the *Iceberg Principle*, 90% of a person's constitution lies beneath the surface. Given that analogy, we have little knowledge of what is going on behind the scenes of others. The following are six principles to help you powerfully cultivate your self-esteem, thus awakening the authentic person within. I suggest you put them to practice at once. We cannot embrace a teaching until we've lived it and embodied it at a cellular level. As you carry out these principles, you'll notice a complete picture emerge. This is the essence of who you are. You are not defined by your thoughts, your beliefs, your values and principles. These are qualities you possess.

1. Self-Acceptance

Acceptance means embracing who you are. Part of this means acknowledging your imperfections and flaws. Remember, there are two sides to your nature—you cannot be imperfect. Focusing on your imperfections alone gives weight and energy to them. The principle may be akin to pain in the body. When you have a headache, your awareness is directed to the pain in your head. You are less aware of other body systems that are occurring. Similarly, to focus on your imperfections is like focusing only on your headache. Your awareness is drawn to the pain, thus amplifying its intensity.

2. Develop Self-Belief

Self-belief is a muscle that requires attention. Successful people attribute their success to *consistent persistence.* Their persistence arises from their self-belief and self-talk. Their inner dialogue is in the positive and affirmative sense. At their level of success, there's little negative self-talk. On the occasion self-talk emerges, successful people are mindful of their thoughts, thus not engaging nor accepting the thoughts as valid. It is vital you look for evidence in your own life where you've excelled. Develop an inner dialogue of kindness and empathy. You've heard the expression, *become your best friend.* Treat yourself as you would a family member or a loved one.

3. Be Present

Draw your mind out of the past by refusing to focus on prior failures and mistakes. When you draw on the past, you bring sad memories into the present moment. Come back to the moment by staying oriented in your present surroundings. Most people go about their life stuck recalling unfavorable memories, or in a stressed state expecting the future. The past is only a figment of your imagination and the future never arrives as you planned. Train your mind to stay grounded in the present moment when it looks to the past, by focusing on your immediate surroundings. Take regular walks in nature and observe your surroundings. Note the color of the trees, the grass, or something that grabs your attention. It might only be momentary, yet it orients your mind toward engaging in a current state of awareness.

4. Self-Improvement

Personal growth allows you to reframe failure by seeing opportunities in everything that has taken place in your life. You realize there are no mistakes in life. When combined with mindfulness and self-awareness, self-improvement is strong and powerful, helping you achieve your deepest wishes. It takes regular work and discipline to form a person of character.

5. Develop Mindfulness

Notice your predominant thought patterns—for example, are they self-sabotaging? Develop an inner dialogue to reframe such thought patterns. *Trip the circuit* of the mind by refusing to accept these thoughts as real. Thoughts are meaningless conversations that take place in your head. You needn't pay attention to the incessant chatter. As an exercise, learn to identify with the silent gaps in between your thoughts. As you become better acquainted with this practice, you'll be able to synchronize your thoughts with your breathing. This allows the mind and body to harmonize with one another, thus creating a peaceful physical state.

6. Create Empowering Beliefs

Examine and challenge outdated beliefs by writing a new script. Your current beliefs are formed long ago and are not relevant to your current life. Review them often, if they're related to your self-worth. Remember, you are more than the sum of your self-beliefs. Beliefs are stories you told yourself long ago and most times are redundant or obsolete. Successful people revise and review their predominant thoughts. They challenge the validity of these thoughts. They refuse to be drawn into the inner dialogue that takes place in their mind. To improve one's self-esteem can be a slow yet fulfilling journey. Don't be dissuaded by the time it takes to become the person you wish to be. An airplane can go no faster to arrive at its destination from one corner of the globe to the other. To hope for more self-esteem without doing the required work will not draw you closer to the person you wish to be. Be kind and gentle with yourself as you undertake your journey of improving your self-esteem. Become the observer when things don't go as planned. Instead of criticizing or judging yourself when you do wrong, see yourself as if your eyes are closed—don't label the thoughts. It is well worth every challenge that arises along your journey.

Chapter Summary

- *The person you know as "I" remains the same throughout your entire life because of the self-constructed image. While your external façade may change, the essence of the "Self" is unchanged.*

- *Beneath your conditioning, the Authentic Self emerges to reveal the core self—the spiritual part of your nature.*

- *The Authentic Self is concealed beneath the formed image of the Self while serving to obscure your spiritual nature. To realize the core self requires shedding the false image of who you think you are and allowing the real self to emerge.*

- *To reveal your authenticity means to honor the wisdom contained within the core self.*

- *An authentic life entails living according to your highest truth. It means to embody your deepest values which serve as guideposts for genuine living.*

- *As we merge with the Authentic Self, our problems, pain, and struggles give rise to inspired living.*

- *Self-examination is a means to reawaken the Authentic Self by making conscious what was unconscious, as your default state at conception is one of innocence and pure awareness.*

- *The ego is the wounded and scorned child that poses a threat to a person's self-esteem. It manipulates you into the belief of separation, which is nothing more than an impulse intended to reinforce its position.*
- *To align with our Authentic Self, we realize that underneath our tangled story lies our core essence which is love and light.*
- *To transform the voice of the ego, become conscious of your limiting self-talk and examine your hurt and pain for what it actually is—a smoke screen.*
- *Pure awareness is known when you shift your attention away from incessant thoughts and focus on the stillness within.*
- *Avoid supporting the ego's view of separateness, and instead highlight the principle of wholeness.*
- *The voice of the heart is quiet and assuring, though it can be drowned out by the relentless mental dialogue at play in your mind.*
- *To experience the way of the heart, develop the capacity to listen. This is challenging when your environment constantly summons your attention.*
- *Live from the heart, instead of a self-centered existence imposed by what is missing in your life.*

- *To be guided by your heart while using the logic of the mind is to unify mind and body so that every thought and action emerges from intentional living.*
- *To disown the dark side means going to war with yourself. To accept yourself as whole is to embody your strengths and limitations—your shadow self.*
- *Without being aware, you confer power to your dark side when you identify with disempowering states.*
- *By integrating your shadow into the wholeness of your being, you are called home to where you belong.*
- *The Iceberg Principle states that 90% of a person's constitution lies beneath the surface so you rarely know what a person is thinking.*
- *Train your mind to stay grounded in the present moment when it looks to the past by focusing on your immediate surroundings.*
- *Learn to identify with the silent gaps in between your thoughts. This allows the mind and body to harmonize with one another, thus creating a peaceful physical state.*
- *You are more than the sum of your self-beliefs. Beliefs are stories you told yourself long ago and most times are redundant or obsolete.*

Part 2

8

Discover Your Potential

"When you see what you're here for, the world begins to mirror your purpose in a magical way. It's almost as if you suddenly find yourself on a stage in a play that was written expressly for you."
—Betty Sue Flowers

Create A Future With Purpose

What is your purpose? That's an imposing question for an introduction in a self-help book. Let's get our hands dirty by uncovering those truths. You may have not entertained the idea that there may be a purpose to your life when life seems unbearable. Until disaster or tragedy strikes one questions their life's meaning. As outlined in my earlier book, *The Power to Navigate Life,* my life-threatening illness became the means to discover my life's purpose. My purpose is contained in the writing and speaking I perform and helping others awaken their potential. Your talents, skills, and the intangible gifts you are blessed with define your purpose. A notable book about discovering one's life purpose is by Richard J. Ledier called *The Power of Purpose.* Leider cites a quote in one of the book's chapters by renowned psychiatrist and Holocaust survivor Victor Frankl: "We can discover this meaning in life in three different ways: 1. by doing a deed; 2. by experiencing a value; and 3. by suffering." He suggests through loss and suffering, we experience the greatest personal growth. My experience of suffering through my illness and losing my father to type II diabetes had a huge impact on my outlook and life. I found my purpose in the midst of personal suffering and tragedy. I've had the privilege of working with remarkable people over the years who've shared similar experiences. They saw the beauty and miracle of life through their tragedy to triumph.

So let's return to the opening question related to your purpose. You might be surprised to learn you're living your purpose. It might be through your work, the people you impact, or your creative pursuits. I remember attending a seminar by behavioral expert Dr. John Demartini where he suggested you find your purpose through a self-examination exercise. When the words you write on paper bring tears to your eyes, you have connected with the truth of your purpose. That is a powerful message. For me, tears appear when I'm on stage inspiring people, talking about greatness or the human spirit. I discover my purpose by living it daily. It becomes a part of my being and I cannot hide from it or turn it off as it lives within me, having awakened it. Your purpose is your soul's call to life. When I'm in harmony and in alignment with my purpose, doors and opportunities open in the simplest way. My favorite affirmation testament to this is: "In an easy and relaxed manner. In a healthy and positive way, I allow life to flow through me." I suspend my ego to hear the silent whisper of my soul speaking.

How do you know you're in alignment and connected to your soul? There is an indescribable feeling washing over you when live with purpose. I am aware of it in my heart center and overwhelmed with emotion, euphoria, and rapture. Since I exercise, I'm attuned to the dopamine high during and after training. Nothing equates to being connected to your soul as you live and breathe your purpose. It becomes a part of your nature.

The following points relate to finding and connecting with your purpose. They are three points to guide you on your journey thus invoking an authentic life.

1. Discover Your Passion—What makes your heart sing with joy? Is it playing a musical instrument, singing, writing, dancing, or other? Perhaps you're still discovering your passion. That's great. Take your time. Your passion is a gift from the universe. Your gift back is to share it with others. Many people believe you cannot make a living pursuing your purpose. Yet take to the Internet and you will you see countless stories of people pursuing their passion. YouTube is awash these days with Internet sensations making videos of their favorite pastimes and sharing their passion with the world. Now is the best time in history to be pursuing your passion, given the interconnectedness modern technology has generated.

2. What's Been Your Life's Theme?—If I asked you to write a short narrative on your life as a play or motion picture, how would it look? What is the plot? Who are the main characters apart from you? What is the underlying theme, i.e., overcoming obstacles, learning to love, self-acceptance, discovering talents? These questions allow you to discover the mystery of your life. If you glance back over your life, you discover the uniqueness which shapes your purpose. Your past holds a reservoir of clues as inspiration to live your life's purpose. Delve deeper into your experiences to see what the main themes are and how you can draw from those. For example, for me it is about patience, trust, self-love, self-esteem, and overcoming fear to name a few. These are the threads which hold the canvas of life together to create my life's purpose.

3. What Experiences Shaped Your Life?—Is it graduating from college or high school? Your first romantic relationship? Being awarded a prize for achievement or service? It may be the loss of a loved one to a life-threatening illness or reconnecting with your paternal or maternal parent since they were absent when you were growing up. Write these major moments and reflect on what they mean to you. How can you use these to fuel your life's purpose? Referring to mine, I endured a health crisis and lost my father to illness. So it makes sense that my purpose relates to helping others overcome their life's challenges by inspiring them and awakening them to their potential. It is not an easy road and took many years to arrive at this point, but what's the rush? Better to have lived your purpose than to have died with a song waiting to be expressed.

If you are raised by a single parent or if a loved one died at a young age, relationships form an important part of your life. Perhaps your purpose is a meaningful relationship through deep and meaningful love. Deepak Chopra's quote sum it up well: "You find your path not by thinking, feeling, or doing but by surrendering. This reveals the impulses of spirit beneath the mask of ego." Connect with your spirit to find your purpose.

If you're living your purpose, may you continue to shine your talent and genius on the world. If you're discovering your purpose for the first time, fear not for every mistake or dead-end draws you closer to your pot of gold.

Guiding Principles For Success

In keeping with the theme of potential, it's said, following well laid out principles ensure success. The following key principles have served me well over the years. Inner growth requires patience and time to achieve inner mastery. When a lesson is skipped, the experience returns in another form until it's learned. With that in mind, don't rush the process. There is nowhere to get to—as soon as you attain the lesson, another experience will soon appear to challenge your understanding. I invite you to carry out the following principles in your daily life. Start with one at a time and live it until you embody it. You'll know when the time comes since everything will be effortless and there will be an inner peace and knowing which accompanies it.

1. You Are Not Your Thoughts

A Buddhist principle states: You are not your thoughts, rather the observer of the thoughts. Many people entertain limiting thoughts around what is lacking in their lives. *I am not good enough; I am overweight.* These thoughts lead to a feedback loop of self-deprecating thoughts which fuel our emotional body. The truth is: These thoughts do not represent the real you. Great leaders seldom entertain limiting thoughts like these. They don't allow them to enter their conscious mind. A great person does not think this way. You are a great person. Understand what that means for a moment. Leaders began their lives like others. They weren't always great and inspiring. Their minds did not allow them to buy into limiting thoughts. They envisioned being greater than they were. You can create the same life if you choose. When you are the observer of a thought, you might inquire: Who is having this thought? This allows you to be removed from the habitual pattern many of us fall into of identifying with our thoughts. Since we experience thoughts, we believe them to be true. We must become a silent witness standing at the shoreline, observing your thoughts as though they were waves coming in. Some waves arrive fast, yet others dissolve as soon they hit dry land. Other waves gently find their way in and fade away. By becoming the observer, you are allowing the witnessing of the thoughts to take shape. The observer does not become invested in the waves. They watch and appreciate the different waves coming in and identify less with their thoughts. This allows observing thoughts to become habitual.

2. Live In The Moment

In Eckhart Tolle's book *The Power of Now,* he states that being grounded and present allows the future to be created in each moment. Many people live in the past or the future. When living in the past, you dwell on thoughts, ideas, and beliefs that served you then. You might hold onto things that happened in the past, to any wrongs committed against you by others. To hold onto relationships or beliefs on how life should unfold. This prevents the moment developing as it should. For others, to live in the future means expecting how life will be when you [insert belief here]. You project yourself into your future self that may not arrive as you envision it. The future self escapes from the present moment believing this moment is less than perfect. To live in the moment requires mental commitment and discipline. Our minds are constantly agitated, fidgeting, and moving about. Our mind wanders from the present to the past to the future. It clings to thoughts to feel safe and protected. It might repeat the same thoughts because it becomes habitual. As mentioned earlier, this is not the real you. This is ego identifying with what is missing or lacking in your life. Through personal development and self-awareness, you form an awareness of your thoughts. The conscious awareness leads us from a person who is having runaway, fleeting moments to one aware of it. No fleeting thought is who you are. You are beyond that. A poignant quote by Jan Glidewell sums up how we respond to the moment: "You can clutch the past so tightly to your chest that it leaves your arms too full to embrace the present."

3. Feel The Fear And Do It Anyway

Fear can cripple you. Recall your fears of insects, heights, water, and public speaking. What happens to you when overcome with fear? Your heart beats faster, you experience shortness of breath, pupils dilate, palms sweat, muscles constrict, and blood pressure increases. These responses are hard-wired into us to warn of ensuing danger. Throughout your life, fear manifests in other ways not conducive to your personal growth. You might have a fear of being in social situations which require you to speak with complete strangers. Your mind assigns meaning to the encounters and drives your body into a spiral of strong emotions. Anxiety and panic sets in and you are powerless. Fear has taken hold. In these scenarios, the more you fuel the fear by running away from it, the stronger the intensity until it overpowers you. One of my early childhood fears was of drowning. I avoided swimming owing to my fear. I was overcome with anxiety and trepidation that my mother accompanied me to the swimming pool during swim training.

Though I overcame this fear one summer having taught myself to swim, the fear found its way into my life later in adult life. Fear became a theme most times. I dismissed it and avoided facing the situation that caused fear. The conditions are not the source of your problems. How you respond to it determines your quality of life. One day I had enough and confronted my fear with the help of others. I realized fear taught me to adopt faith and courage. It was my principal teaching moment and not my adversary as I once assumed. I experimented with my fears and approached conditions once out of my comfort zone. Little by little, fear lost its control over me. It is still present, yet I turn down the volume on it. I often ask myself when fear arises: "What if fear is disguised as love? How would I move forward? What would I do differently?" Fear teaches us the passage to courage and faith.

There is a notable lesson behind fear you must become attentive to. Whether your fear is body image issues, relationships, career, finances, health or other, connect with the frequency of love which waits on the other side of the mountain which blocks your view. I assure you it's there. You must break down fear's illusion. It is transparent and is penetrated the moment you move toward it. To run away from fear only intensifies the emotion so it follows you for the rest of your life. As you carry out these principles, you'll meet setbacks and failure. Go with it. It is part of the journey. These principles serve as a road map for navigating life, yet the reward is to chip away at your fears until you overcome them. You will discover the magnificence of life when you're in alignment with your Authentic Self and inner potential.

Find Your Greatness

"Some are born great, some achieve greatness, and some have greatness thrust upon them," declared William Shakespeare. Helen Keller contracted what is believed to have been meningitis or scarlet fever at the age of 19 months and was left permanently deaf and blind. Her parents knew their chances of finding a teacher to work with her were slim, given their remote location in Alabama. Yet this did not deter her mother Kate Keller from finding a teacher by the name of Anne Sullivan. Anne had overcome her own physical problems to include vision complications which required repeated surgery to correct. Over the coming years Sullivan taught the ten-year-old Keller to read braille to aid her learning capabilities. It later became evident that Keller was eager to gain knowledge. Soon after, she graduated magna cum laude from Radcliffe College. Keller became a lifelong advocate for the disabled and wrote twelve books, traveling to over 40 countries as a renowned speaker and author. Of the many honors received for her accomplishments, Keller obtained the Presidential Medal of Freedom, known as the highest civilian medal awarded by the President of the United States.

In light of Helen Keller's story, I'd like you to consider your definition of greatness.

In their book, *The Winner's Brain* by Dr. Jeff Brown and Mark Fenske the authors state, "In 1954, psychologist Julian Rotter coined the term locus of control to refer to people's belief about what causes good and bad things to happen in their lives. An internal locus of control reflects the belief you are master of your own destiny; an external locus of control reflects just the opposite." Helen Keller maintained a strong locus of control given her accomplishments and in view of her disabilities. It begs the question: Are we born into greatness, or does it develop it over time? I affirm that greatness is formed as a result of a nurturing environment. For some, hardship means to recoil in resignation. For others such as Keller, it presents the opportunity to overcome restrictions to win through. You are never presented with an experience to the sum of your conditioning. We must venture beyond our harbor of contentment if we wish to discover our genius.

Recognize your limitations but don't let them define you. Similarly, don't be deceived by a limited consciousness—expand your mind. In stating the obvious, being unaware of your potential means you're less inclined to unearth your greatness. Those who know of their potential have an unyielding self-belief to expose themselves to the unknown. Just as a tightrope walker knows death is imminent if he loses balance, he continues to push past the precipice of fear into the unknown. It is there he develops a deep respect for his pursuit, knowing his life can be taken away from him at any moment. Don't place limitations on what you perceive is possible. Far too many people discount what they're capable of, given self-imposed ceilings of limitations. Those same people set lofty goals yet wonder why life is not imbued with passion. Take charge by accepting responsibility for your actions, irrespective of whether circumstances play out in your favor or not. Greatness summons you to venture into the unknown, often without a clear vision.

There are no assurances when one yields to greatness. Talent, genius, and your impending gifts serve you when you step into your power. Greatness is attained when we follow our passions and build on our successes. As we pursue our dreams, our goals, and our desires, we invest in our greatness. "The greatest men and women are not competing against you; they are competing against themselves each and every day. You are your greatest competition," affirms Dr. Stan Beecham in his book *Elite Minds*. Greatness demands we overcome our inherent shortcomings as we are exposed to that which scares us. Author David Potter states, "We might gain perspective by considering how the Ancient Greeks determined greatness in athletes. Then and now, true greatness is as defined not by a single moment, but by the ability to **build a record of extraordinary achievement.**" Greatness is attained when we dare to play big. It is commensurate with humility. The great are humble, knowing their talents, gifts, and genius are expressed through them as infinite intelligence. Equally, others suggest greatness extends from the soul. When an individual cultivates their soul's gifts, greatness results to express this faculty. Those like Gandhi, Mother Teresa, Martin Luther King, Jr. and others understood that to have an emotional impact on people, they had to align with their soul's calling. It is written into their words and actions.

Pursue integrity by aligning with your deepest values. Honor these values to invest in your greatness. Just as connecting with your deepest nature reflects your soul's quality, integrity is the glue which binds actions to greatness. We are the sum of our actions and in the same way that actions express our thoughts, they also reflect our self-worth. You strengthen your self-esteem by elevating your internal locus of control every time you honor your integrity. Shakespeare proposed three conditions for greatness in the opening quote while the Roman philosopher Seneca suggested adversity commands the path to greatness. Either way, greatness is the journey to overcome our limitations. It was Michelangelo who affirmed, "In every block of marble I see a statue as plain as though it stood before me, shaped and perfect in attitude and action. I have only to hew away the rough walls that imprison the lovely apparition to reveal it to the other eyes as mine see it." I urge you to unearth your greatness, thus exposing the façade that obscures it. In time, your doubts and fears will break free revealing your true, strong self. It this self that shall be seen by all.

Live What You Love

What ignites your passion? What allows you to feel engaged in the moment? For many of you, being absorbed in your favorite hobby, sport, or pastime comes to mind. You might recite the countless hours spent in pursuit of that interest and the feelings associated with it. We find enormous pleasure in pursuing our passion. It must be stated that your 'work' is not the only area tied to your love. Many people find sanctuary in their pastimes or hobbies which bear no financial incentive other than to offer enjoyment and self-fulfillment. The state of flow one achieves when aligned with their passion has been well documented. Time stands still as we're overcome with pleasure, absorbed in our pursuit. Such activities give mental, emotional, and physical benefits to the individual. In recent times we've seen popular culture espouse turning your passion into profits as a practical success model. However, this may not appeal to all people. In his commencement speech at Stanford University in 2005, the late Steve Jobs imparted graduates with the wisdom, "…and the only way to do great work is to love what you do. If you haven't found it yet keep looking. Don't settle." While he was alluding to one's career, we can adapt this statement to reflect other aspects of our lives where our passions run deep. So how do you live what you love? The following points are ways to encapsulate your passion be becoming aligned with your highest potential.

1. Become What You Love: Embody what you love by being an extension of your passion. People who live their love can't wait to get up in the morning to spend another day immersed in their pursuit. As Steve Jobs reminds us in the earlier quote, "if you haven't found it yet—don't settle." There is nothing more meaningless and soul destroying than pursuing a life which does not resonate with your deepest self.

2. Find Purpose And Passion In Other Areas: I mentioned earlier that your love or passion does not have to be tied to your work. For example, many people have hobbies or interests which do not earn money, yet provide personal satisfaction. It takes persistence and focus to turn your passion into profits. Those who have achieved this crossover will remind you it often comes at a price—long hours, stress, health risks, family problems, etc. This should not dissuade you from pursuing this path; instead, you should realize what is involved.

3. Harmonize Mind And Body: When pursuing your passion, harmony and balance are preserved in the mind and body. The art of miniature bonsai tree pruning can bring a deep satisfaction and resonance to the individual as they watch their bonsai take shape. People who keep tropical fish report feeling the same connection. Cooking is said to have the same therapeutic effect to calm the mind and body.

4. Slow To The Speed Of Life: The Schumann resonances which have a frequency range of 7.83Hz (7-10 cycles per second), is common in the EEG readings of humans and many animals. It is known that the dominant brain wave frequency of shamans and healers comes close to 7.83 Hz and may beat in phase with the Earth's signal, causing harmonic resonance. This is scientific proof we are wired to synchronize with the speed and frequency of life.

5. Transcend Your Fears: Move through your fears. Fear is a debilitating emotion which discolors your perception of life. It shapes your inner landscape and reality. Let go of your fears by transforming them into peace, love, faith, and trust. As you let go of fear you will fall in love with life. You cannot appreciate life when your mind and body are gripped by fear, which is a lower state of consciousness. Love reflects a higher state of consciousness (logarithmic level—500) as represented in the map of consciousness whereas fear is depicted as (logarithmic level—100).

6. Look For Good In All Situations: Orient your senses to look for the positive in situations—not in a Pollyanna way. What may appear as an untoward situation contains the seed of something positive. As you widen your vista, you will look for the good in all situations. It won't come looking for you holding up a placard, screaming to get your attention. Look for evidence in the smallest details and you will find it. It was the German architect Ludwig Mies van der Rohe who said, "God is in the details."

7. Engage In Loving Relationships: Engage in loving relationships and let go of toxic ones. Remember, we coach others how to treat us. If you are not receiving the respect you deserve, on an unconscious level you may have attracted this relationship to experience personal growth. Learn from it by going inward to dissolve any conflicts. People's perception of life is discolored by their view of intimate relationships. They fail to acknowledge that life is a mirror reflecting back one's inner landscape—*as within, so without.* As you heal your wounds, life acknowledges your openness to live a life vested in love.

Never Give Up, Great Things Take Time

I am fascinated by billionaires. There, I said it.

Please don't hold me in contempt as I endeavor to explain myself. OK, it may be presumptuous of me, since you are not mistaken for assuming my fascination was owing to their wealth status—right? I should be forthcoming that my curiosity extends toward the **mindset** of self-made billionaires. Consider for a moment the conviction a self-made billionaire has to reach their level of success, in spite of the insurmountable hurdles along the way. While researching this topic in 2011, there were 946 billionaires in the world. At the time of writing in 2016, that number has swelled to 1,645 with an aggregate wealth of $6.5 trillion. That is a staggering figure. Despite people's beliefs toward the rich, the wealthy are not deceitful in their pursuit of wealth—they are astute and industrious. To become a billionaire requires one to overcome many mental and emotional hurdles. It requires a profound confidence to never give up, given the economic forces that oppose those reaching for success. To attain an astounding level of wealth, one must think and act in ways conducive to wealth attainment. There must be an inherent self-belief, an unyielding motivation and a desire to prevail. Represented in the quote, "The more you help people get what they want, the more you get what you want," this simple axiom forms the basis to a wealthy person's philosophy.

Self-made billionaires support an unwavering level of mental toughness and resiliency. According to authors who have written on talent and success, including Malcolm Gladwell, Cal Newport and Robert Greene, talent is not bestowed upon us at the time of our birth. Success is gained over time arising from firm persistence and dedication. While the nature vs. nurture discussion has eluded scientists and behavioral economists for years, many struggle to draw consensus on what it takes to be talented. In recent times, evolutionary psychologists now infer that nurture/nature is a more proper term which suggests that environment accounts for a large part of a person's success, while acknowledging DNA is just as important. In keeping with success as a motivator, the following points are valuable models for building on achievement—thus abolishing the need to *give up*:

1. A Relentless Desire To Succeed.
2. Extend Yourself Each Time.
3. Enjoy The Journey.

Let us examine them in detail:

A Relentless Desire To Succeed: Recall the last time you learned something new. You might have reached a point in the skill or task and proclaimed, "To hell with this, I give up?" I know I have. I wish to re-frame the notion of winning to include **NOT giving up** despite outward appearances. Leadership expert and author Robin Sharma offers the following sage advice: "If people aren't laughing at you at least once a week, your dreams are too small." That is, you're not reaching beyond your capabilities. Often you may expect to reap the rewards for the hard work you have put in. Signs of success may not be apparent for weeks, months, or years. You may even become disheartened and give up right when a breakthrough is imminent. This is a common scenario for most people. We strive for external confirmation, believing the fruits of our labor will yield a positive sign. At this point, we assume events are unfolding in our favor behind the scenes and beyond our limited senses. The aphorism which invites you to *believe it before you see it* underscores the message of deep optimism.

Extend Yourself Each Time: People succumb to the impression that they must put everything on the line to succeed, that they must sacrifice everything in the pursuit of their goal. This is a misleading assumption based on several reasons. Steady improvements over time often yield greater returns. While I am not advocating a new idea, it was author Darren Hardy who outlines this point in his prize-winning book, *Compound Effect*. Take the elastic rubber band as a metaphor: Your aim should be to extend yourself further each time, beyond your comfort zone. In doing so you discover more of yourself while taking calculated risks since you're able to identify mistakes with an enriched mind.

Enjoy The Journey: In refusing to give up, you reconnect with your underlying motivation for pursuing your goal. To maintain a purposeful vision while savoring the journey becomes the ultimate aphrodisiac. I work ten-hour days including weekends with adequate rest and exercise. As Sunday arrives, I often reflect on what I have achieved during the week and how I can build on my success in the following week. It's reassuring to note I haven't 'worked' in the true meaning of the word—I surrender to a flow experience called work, which I am passionate toward. I invite you to find your passion and pursue it with gusto—let the spirit of your quest come alive through you. If you contemplate giving up, I trust this has reignited your desire to move forward with enthusiasm. As a final thought, an unrelenting persistence and dedication are seen as defining attributes by successful people. With that in mind, create your ideal future by assuming a purposeful vision for success. Fill it with optimism and empowering beliefs owing to your overall success—never give up since you never know when the tides of fortune will come your way.

Chapter Summary

- *Your purpose is your soul's call to life.*
- *"What if fear is disguised as love, how would you move forward?" "What would you do differently?" Fear teaches you the passage to courage and faith.*
- *To run away from fear only intensifies the emotion so it follows you for the rest of your life.*
- *Recognize your limitations but don't let them define you. Similarly, don't be deceived by a limited consciousness—expand your mind.*
- *Don't place limitations on what you perceive is possible. Far too many people discount what they're capable of, given self-imposed ceilings of limitations.*
- *Take charge by accepting responsibility for your actions, irrespective of whether circumstances play out in your favor or not.*
- *Pursue integrity by aligning with your deepest values. Honor these values to invest in your greatness.*
- *Embody what you love by being an extension of your passion.*
- *Fear is a debilitating emotion which discolors*

your perception of life. It shapes your inner landscape and reality.

- *The three models for building on achievement:*
  - *A relentless desire to succeed.*
  - *Extend yourself each time.*
  - *Enjoy the journey.*

9

The Power To Transform Your Life

> *"I can affect change by transforming the only thing that I ever had control over in the first place and that is myself."*
> —*Deepak Chopra*

The Power To Transform Your Life

"When she transformed into a butterfly, the caterpillars spoke not of her beauty, but of her weirdness. They wanted her to change back into what she has always been."

"But she had wings," writes author Dean Jackson in *The Poetry of Oneness.*

Self-transformation remains fundamental to the human condition. The ability to impact our life through change remains our greatest virtue. Yet most people sail through life powerless to venture beyond their comfort zone. It is there they stay until circumstances compel them to take action. If we wish to transform, it must be framed within the proper context to make the change sustainable. Change is essential to living an authentic life because we discard that which no longer serves us to merge into our Authentic Self. One must become curious how they intend their life to be, while disregarding the negative aspects of the change. To focus on life's denials reinforces them, thus change emerges for the wrong reasons. Let's not sugar-coat it—change is difficult. One need only refer to the change cycle to note self-transformation is a tumultuous landslide interspersed with detours, highs, and lows. Yet if approached with the right intention, a change in circumstances yields life-lasting benefits. Many people resist change because it can be difficult and disruptive. Why disturb the status quo, they proclaim. Yet if we allow for change, an inner shift is made to usher in the new, fresh, and vital energy grounded in receptivity to the upcoming attractions. Transformation, like the overused caterpillar analogy, coincides with a shift in awareness to shape our reality.

Author Michael A. Singer states in his book *The Surrender Experiment,* "What I saw was that no matter who we are, life is going to put us through the changes we need to go through. The question is: Are we willing to use this force for our transformation? I saw that even very intense situations don't have to leave psychological scars, if we are willing to process our changes at a deeper level." To influence change and self-transformation, it must be approached intending to improve your life, while accepting your current circumstances.

Own Your Situation: If we seek change, no one will make the shift until we decide to. We are the sole investor in the corporation called Our Life. To own your situation means taking responsibility for the life you create. If you are unhappy with your current circumstances, acknowledge your unhappiness, yet do not believe reality is fixed. It is anything but fixed. As you shift from perpetuating a wounded mindset, power is realized to usher in the change. The wounded perpetuate a malicious cycle of self-torment, believing they are at the mercy of life. Owning your situation means empowering yourself to make changes congruent with an increase in personal power.

Accept Your Circumstances: Human suffering ensues when we resist what emerges. Your opposition to what is shows resistance and moves you into a disempowered state. Author Hale Dwoskin of the self-inquiry program *The Sedona Method* states, "That's because the most powerful place to create what we choose is from the position that it's 'okay' whether we get it or not. This model applies to all areas of our lives." Your life's circumstances are perfect to shape your personal development, irrespective of whether you see it that way. The moment you accept your circumstances, self-transformation sets into motion.

Let Go Of Resistance: Self-judgment and judgment of others keep us stuck recycling the past into the present moment. Judgment is a toxic emotion because we concede to it, believing we are not in control. Past conditioning governs our actions and limiting beliefs discourage positive change. We may be in a rut and unable to transform our life, owing to the distorted lens through which we perceive our current circumstances. From *The Power to Navigate* Life I avow, "Judging yourself and others is too easy, since it shifts the blame from looking within and dealing with those parts we dislike. Those who remain Parked in life feel the need to label and judge others, believing the world is wrong and they are right."

Honor Your Emotions: Are there circumstances which transpired long ago that you hold onto as pain or anger? Were you victimized, criticized, abused, or neglected? Investigate the negative feelings so you can take an honest look at them. Feel your feelings. Yes, that's right, connect with the emotions but do not attach meaning to them. To acknowledge your feelings requires courage, especially if they have been stowed away for years. Don't allow negative or untoward feelings come between you and the remarkable future which awaits. While it is daunting to deal with negative emotions, it pales into insignificance to the havoc wreaked if the emotions are neglected.

I am drawn once more to Hale Dwoskin's quote from *The Sedona Method*, "There are no problems in the present moment. I saved this piece for now, because I know this may be hard for you to accept, but—what if all the supposed problems you have right now are only memories? I challenge you to explore this question for yourself and at least entertain the possibility." The power of the human will is unbending—it can bring opportunities into being once your resolve is firm. It was the British politician Benjamin Disraeli who declared, "Nothing can withstand the power of the human will if it is willing to stake its very existence to the extent of its purpose." In transforming our lives we leave behind a part of us to gain something more powerful; the wings to experience a renewed existence for whom we aspire to become.

The Life You Deserve To Live

"The givens of life are gifts because they are the ingredients of character, depth and compassion," states David Richo in *The Five Things We Cannot Change.* There is celebrated wisdom in that simple message, which when overlooked results in life's ensuing dramas. Being irrational creatures, we fail to see past our tragedies to realize life gives us encouragement even though it may not appear in the form we expect. Your time here is not meant to be a cycle of pain and suffering. It is within your power to choose how you respond to life's unfolding events. Contained within that choice lies your greatest lessons if you withhold judgment on how life should develop. To concede defeat, you award power to those unpleasant events by perpetuating the victim role, which is an easy trap to fall into. It is with restrained patience we remain vigilant to how we respond to life's ups and downs.

Happiness is a choice, not an unattainable goal.

You move toward happiness the moment you declare your intention to do so. Equally, we may be content, yet happiness may elude us. When happiness entails our material and emotional needs being met, we allow it to permeate our lives with unbound richness. With our basic needs fulfilled, we want nothing more than the comfort of being present within our own body. Even unwanted thoughts fueled with fear or anxiety are powerless over us since they are transitory states. Your obligation is to abide by something deeper if you wish to live the life you deserve. Stand for something which commands power and a reason to attend to the day. We receive what we ask of life. What we claim equates to our self-worth. Our self-worth is in direct proportion to the sum of our life's experiences. You cannot demand more if you are undeserving on some level.

If you have issues with receiving, this is likely to show in how much life affords you. However, if your beliefs coincide with what you deserve, that becomes your reference point. Unresolved childhood wounds are often related to unworthiness issues that perpetuate through maturity. Perhaps your main caregiver convinced you of your unworthiness and you have held onto this all this time. In *The MindBody Code,* Dr. Mario Martinez affirms this point: "You were never robbed of your power or your worthiness; you inadvertently disowned them." For that reason, avoid responding to limiting thoughts to what is lacking in your life. Do not concede to disempowering thoughts based on an internal script. With enough energy, these learned beliefs sooner or later transform into negative states. Reality is formed by aligning with your deepest values, not by reciting worn-out childhood inner dialogues. This is not who you are, any more than choosing to associate with your childhood toys. Reality is reflected in your thoughts, desires, and beliefs on what you deserve and are willing to accept. "Because if the decisions you make about where you invest your blood, sweat, and tears are not consistent with the person you aspire to be, you'll never become that person," states Clayton M. Christensen in *How Will You Measure Your Life?*

Be bold in your willingness to commit to your dreams. Don't be pushed by life's failures since they often redirect you to a better-suited destination if you allow the journey to unfold. Be moved by your passion and your heart's desires. There is discussion these days on the merit of visualizing a purposeful future. While much of the advice comes from well-intentioned life coaches, the guidance invites you to call on your imagination to bring reality to life. You have to believe it before you see it, maintains the saying. To embrace the life we deserve, we step into our greatness, not cower from it. You have nothing to fear other than fear itself, which holds you captive by playing small. Marianne Williamson reminds us, "Our deepest fear is not that we are inadequate. Our deepest fear is that we are powerful beyond measure." Just like a double-edged sword, if we shy away from our magnificence, it has the potential to impair our growth if we fail to use those gifts. I enjoy Steven Pressfield's view, "A child has no trouble believing the unbelievable, nor does the genius or the madman. It's only you and I, with our big brains and our tiny hearts, who doubt and overthink and hesitate."

Be present and alive in each moment instead of floundering in the past or focusing on an imaginary future. Many people prevent a promising future from arriving due to negative thoughts and a belief they are undeserving of goodness. To create the life you deserve, take inspired action and move out of your comfort zone. "Life happens at the end of your comfort zone," declares Neale Donald Walsch. In honoring this intent, author David J. Schwartz acknowledges this belief in *The Magic of Thinking Big*, "Believe it can be done. When you believe something can be done, really believe, your mind will find the ways to do it. Believing a solution paves the way to a solution." David Richo Ph.D. asserts that life's gifts are the ingredients of character, depth, and compassion. To affirm these endowments we must face our challenges with binding conviction and a resolute heart. For in striving, we attain inner freedom and as the Buddhist nun Pema Chodron says, "No matter what the size, color, or shape is, the point is still to lean toward the discomfort of life and see it clearly rather than to protect ourselves from it."

The Art of Living Beautifully

In the 1996 movie *Jack*, the lead character played by Robin Williams announces at his graduation, "Please, don't worry so much. Because in the end none of us has very long on this earth. Life is fleeting. And if you're ever distressed, cast your eyes to the summer sky when the stars are strung across the velvety night. And when a shooting star streaks through the blackness, turning night into day, make a wish, and think of me. Make your life spectacular." There is something memorable about that passage that drives deep into our soul. True to his words, Robin Williams lived a remarkable life equaled with an illustrious career. This is not a surmise on the late actor, rather an invitation to "Make your life spectacular." The art of living beautifully is a call to know thyself without exception. Otherwise, we are at the mercy of external events which disrupt the foundations of our inner life. To know oneself means to align with our Authentic Self. Regretfully, many people seldom explore the complexity of their emotional constitution until it's too late. A life of beauty arises when we move beyond our fixed reality and dare to explore the life we dream possible. It means to live fearlessly, beyond the walls of a comfortable existence.

To live a beautiful life means to transform disempowering states into positive life experiences. Life's events can scar us, leaving us vulnerable. Seemingly we cease taking risks for fear of getting hurt. While universal, the drawback is to retreat without ever reaching for the treasures we long for. The greatest mind of our century, Albert Einstein, said, "The most beautiful thing we can experience is the mysterious. It is the source of all true art and science." I urge you to explore this sentiment by trusting in the mysterious where the seeds of opportunity lie. Life is hardly predictable. Like torrential rain on a sultry night, when change ushers through, it can leave a deluge of uncertainty in its wake. For that reason, consider your problems as an alluring adventure instead of a melting pot of frustration. While challenging, a change in perception allows you to appreciate difficult moments to cultivate personal growth. We must be mindful of these opportunities as they arise, rather than concede life is devoid of wonderful moments. Most people strive for happiness. Bookshelves are littered with advice proclaiming the secret to attain happiness in thirty days or less. Yet research shows we are less happy than in the past. Maybe technology is to blame for creating insincere connections devoid of social interactions.

To be in service of others is a way out of the unhappiness trap. It is not a transitory practice either, rather an opportunity to deepen our connection with ourselves. "Like the Dalai Lama and the Buddha himself, many modern era scientists and philosophers agree that serving others is the secret to happiness, fulfillment, and a good and beautiful life," asserts Lama Surya Das. Clearly, we know happiness is not tied to owning the latest smartphone or sports car. While the advice seems obvious, many people fill the emptiness within by amassing material objects. This creates more desires and if we have limited financial resources, it creates further pain and suffering. I assure you, no material object will complete you more than what lies deep within your soul. To live beautifully means to live according to our highest values. In doing so, we form meaningful connections with others that enrich our life. Likewise, we must avoid seeing life being a sequence of daily routines and events which pass by at the blink of an eye. If we subscribe to this erroneous thinking, we succumb to the monotony of living a *Groundhog Day* existence. Miracles take place right before our eyes. We miss them because we rush about our day scurrying to the next event or trying to meet deadlines. Dr. Wayne Dyer said, "Miracles come in moments. Be ready and willing." Miracles cannot be experienced by analyzing the past or future, for they will pass you by like a high-speed train if you are unaware.

So disconnect from processing thoughts for a moment and move into your heart, the source of all wisdom where your soul calls home. Similarly, a beautiful life calls us to recognize what is of value to us. One way to experience beauty is to stop, listen, and connect with our surroundings. This means to slow to the speed of life instead of running around like the mad hatter in *Alice in Wonderland,* hoping to get everything done yet achieving little. To be present in the moment is challenging because life leads us in different directions. Before long we succumb to external forces instead of abiding by our inner blueprint. We must relax and let go of unnecessary stressors that are not tied to our long-term happiness. Unwelcomed stress affects our capacity to enjoy life because we react to events, instead of allowing them to pass through our lives. Visualize a boxer backed into the ropes, battling punches from his opponent. He cannot move into an offensive stance because he is fixed in a parked state. Life can have that effect on us because we are pushed and pulled to our limits and retreat in resignation. Sure enough, the next blow arrives stronger than before and if our guard is down, we're knocked to the ground harder than before. I enjoy the quote from the epic motion picture *Braveheart* in which William Wallace declares to the Princess of Wales, "Every man dies, not every man really lives." To live a beautiful life is an invitation to live passionately while you can.

The Willingness To Change

Change is difficult.

If you hope to change a personal behavior, save money or otherwise, the gods of change are reluctant to smile upon you in those early stages. Yet within our willingness to change lies the yearning for something more. Personal transformation heralds our willingness to let go of the old to make room for the new in our lives. To merge into the Authentic Self, we must gradually shed our former self to step into the core self. Change heralds letting go of the tired, old, and outdated to usher in the new. It shows we have gone so far with an endeavor and must allow something new to fill its place. Change is the process of life, despite the unknown path ahead. The **willingness** to change is crucial in any transformation since it sets into motion what will soon become. Your willingness to change is a desire to embrace a new way of life. We must be prepared to commit to new actions and confront our fears if we wish to embody the changes at a deeper level. We must venture beyond the known, beyond our comfort zone if we seek to attain inner growth. The growth I am referring to is realized when we rouse our potential, our genius, gifts, and talents. Thus your willingness to change is measured by your ability to **adapt** to change. If we are discontented with life and seek more honest experiences, we must embrace change on all levels. Albert Einstein said: "We cannot solve our problems with the same level of thinking that created them." Thus a new mental landscape must be formed if you wish to perceive your circumstances in a new light. The commitment to change is an obligation to your personal growth and a promising future.

Change is the fabric of life—the seasons, the days, the landscape changes—yet we fear change. Thus we must abide by the cycles of life if we seek to reshape our circumstances. Fear of change is a natural response. You need not abolish your fears; integrate them into your experience. It was Susan Jeffers's acclaimed book *Feel The Fear and Do It Anyway* which reminds us of our commitment to embrace fear as we undergo change. Change is not indicative of losing control as many believe since we have limited control anyway. It implies surrender and detachment for the ultimate good of our personal evolution. An adjustment period is foundational to moments of growth and transformation. Allow time to acclimate to these changes, then allow it to sweep through. Life is not bound by our inner clock, so we must yield to what transpires with openness and receptivity. A change in circumstances disrupts the brain's thought process given its habituation to pattern recognition. Your mind considers historical evidence as memories to form assumptions about the future. Its habitual tendency is inclined toward established patterns. In his book *The Click Moment,* author Frans Johansson states, "Our brains have been designed to perceive order instead of randomness." We must acquaint ourselves with change if we wish to master change at any level. Justifiably we will slip up along the way as we integrate our new experiences into our life. This should not dissuade you from persisting, yet appreciate that the cycle of change diminishes suffering feelings of guilt along the way.

In Chapter Ten, I outlined five ways to create new habits while drawing your attention to the transformative cycle of change. I encourage you to embrace change by being open and receptive to it. Unite with your heart and mind to navigate through it. Reason and logic alone are insufficient measures to realize change since they obscure the voice of wisdom. Evidently, fear arises with any change due to uncertainty. Recall earlier that the mind is resistant to change. For that reason we must integrate new experiences into our life gradually so as not to disrupt the brain's homeostasis. Our response to this perceived fear may be expressed via the following question: "Am I responding to the fear itself or the fear of not being in control?" Our aim then is to delineate between a perceived threat to our well-being or an irrational fear. Fear is a façade orchestrated by the mind to protect you. While it should not be construed as deleterious, your mind protects you from imminent danger by arousing suspicion when change is imminent. Fear is considered a threat to your survival when you become consumed by it since it dominates your mental landscape. Resistance to change invites suffering by opposing what is. To avoid this, let go of your struggles and go along with the change ushered in—think *unlimited opportunities*. Recognize that change does not mean recoiling in hesitation, yet signifies an opportunity to move ahead into exciting times. Many people are dissatisfied with their circumstances nowadays owing to many reasons. We must develop a growth mindset as opposed to a fixed mindset according to Professor of Psychology at Stanford University, Carol Dweck.

Knowing change is difficult, we must stay grounded and

attentive if we wish to amend our circumstances. Do not wallow in the past nor expect a future to arrive as planned, given its impact to arouse fear. Trust that your willingness to change is enough to set into motion the power to transform oneself. It is this willingness which sets alight the flame to compel sweeping changes that linger well into the future.

The Art Of Contentment

Contentment is your trusted ambassador and revered statesman; your emotional safeguard. Contented people have a calm presence, neither striving nor resisting the currents of life. Contentment is tied to living a full life while seeing past the illusion that life is something more than it is. A popular expression in mainstream culture nowadays is cultivating gratitude. Taken out of context, people attempt to develop gratitude through logic and reason instead of heartfelt sincerity. Gratitude emanates from the heart and necessitates practice and commitment to be known. If you look for problems in untoward events, assuredly they will be there to greet you. However, if your attention is focused on opportunity, it too will be there. So, perception accounts for everything. It was the English essayist and poet Joseph Addison who states, "A contented mind is the greatest blessing a man can enjoy in this world." Contentment is an inner state of composure. I liken it to a majestic tree—a stone tower, solid and unmoveable; its branches shooting out to offer shelter like an umbrella. Its roots fixed, knowing what nature intended it to be. Contentment is sought in the smallest detail and fertilizes the seeds of happiness. It is a developed state of being—we drift into contentment just as slipping into our favorite pajamas. I find it interesting that people in Third World countries are the happiest, while in the West we struggle to find happiness outside us unless it shines, beeps, or blings.

Popular culture is built on the egoic belief we need more in order to be happy. The Zen Buddhist ideal leans toward the contrasting view—less is more. While you need not wander from one extreme to the other, consider adopting aspects of the Eastern view into your life. You need not live free of Western influences, yet find a suitable middle ground. In his book *Spontaneous Happiness,* Dr. Andrew Weil, medical doctor and author, asserts, "A better goal in life is to be content. Contentment is an inner sense of satisfaction that is not dependent on external factors." Contentment is to appreciate *what is* instead of *what could be.* We draw strength from the reserve of life for our current circumstances rather than focus on what is absent. For centuries, philosophers have debated what it takes to be happy versus content, believing the two are mutually exclusive. Contentment is the preceding level leading to happiness and is longer lasting. We can be content having our basic needs met: a job we enjoy, a fulfilling relationship, a home to go to, and a sense of security. It is shown that pursuing your passion is a good measure of contentment. Economic studies in the US suggest the earning level at which people no longer feel happier is $75,000 USD. Consequently, money is not a measure of happiness if something is missing from our lives. Added wealth only exaggerates what is already absent, i.e., loneliness, emptiness, fear, etc.

Knowing this, how can we find contentment in our everyday experience?

Cease comparing yourself to others since each individual

retains their own problems to contend with. We must embrace the richness of the present moment, standing steadfast in our commitment to the life we have. Dan Harris, ABC correspondent and *Nightline* anchor, states in his book *10% Happier*, "When you have one foot in the future and the other in the past, you piss on the present." Similarly, slow to the pace of life. There is nowhere to get to in a hurry. Trade the rat race for the gradual speed of life. As you know, the tortoise ultimately finds its way to the finish while soaking in the richness of life along the way. Let go of struggling by refusing to buy into the mental drama associated with it. There is a better way to control outcomes which rests in your hands. Life need not be one endless drama after another. "Outside events link up with our inner thoughts and feelings, giving us a sense of participation with the universe," state Charlene Belitz and Meg Lundstrom in their book *The Power of Flow*.

Similarly, connect with your inner wisdom. This has been a recurring theme throughout the book and worth reiterating. The source of your happiness is contained within, not in an external cause. Your search will be endless and only yield further craving and desire. Dr. Weil claims society has a skewed relationship of what it means to be happy, depicted in the pursuit of happiness. In this context happiness is viewed as an external pursuit to satisfy our emotional needs, instead of that contained within. He says, "The goal of working toward optimal emotional health is to enhance: contentment, comfort, serenity and resilience." In this way we roll with the ups and downs of life. I believe this to be worthwhile and practical advice. Stop chasing after the elixir of happiness to the detriment of your sanity. The promised chariot of hope is unattainable if we search outside ourselves for it. I encourage you to find contentment in the here and now rather than seek it in the unattainable. For you have no place to get to and nothing to attain if you have not embraced the life you have.

Chapter Summary

- *Change is essential to living an authentic life. Discard that which no longer serves you and merge into your Authentic Self.*
- *As you shift from perpetuating a wounded mindset, power is realized to usher in the change.*
- *While it is daunting to deal with negative emotions, it pales into insignificance to the havoc wreaked if the emotions are neglected.*
- *Happiness is a choice, not an unattainable goal.*
- *Unwanted thoughts fueled with fear or anxiety are powerless over you since they are transitory states.*
- *You receive what you ask of life. What you claim equates to your self-worth. Your self-worth is in direct proportion to the sum of your life's experiences.*
- *Unresolved childhood wounds are often related to unworthiness issues that perpetuate through maturity.*
- *Reality is reflected in your thoughts, desires, and beliefs on what you deserve and are willing to accept.*
- *Be bold in your willingness to commit to your*

dreams. Be moved by your passion and your heart's desires.

- To embrace the life you deserve, step into your greatness instead of cowering from it.
- A life of beauty arises when you move beyond your fixed reality and dare to explore the life you dream possible.
- Consider your problems as an alluring adventure instead of a melting pot of frustration.
- To be in service of others is a way out of the unhappiness trap. It is not a transitory practice either, rather an opportunity to deepen your connection with yourself.
- Slow to the speed of life instead of running around like the mad hatter in Alice in Wonderland, hoping to get everything done yet achieving little.
- Let go of unnecessary stressors that are not tied to your long-term happiness.
- The **willingness** to change is crucial in any transformation since it sets into motion what will become.
- Your willingness to change is measured by your ability to **adapt** to change.
- Life is not bound by your inner clock, so yield to what transpires with openness and receptivity.
- Change does not mean recoiling in hesitation, yet

it signifies an opportunity to move ahead into exciting times.

- *Contentment is sought in the smallest detail and fertilizes the seeds of happiness.*
- *Contentment is to appreciate what is instead of what could be. Draw strength from the reserve of life for your current circumstances rather than focus on what is absent.*
- *The source of your happiness is contained within, not in an external cause. Your search will be endless and only yield further craving and desire.*
- *Stop chasing after the elixir of happiness to the detriment of your sanity. The promised chariot of hope is unattainable if you search outside for it.*

10

Obstacles Illuminate The Path To Success

> *"Success is determined not by whether or not you face obstacles, but by your reaction to them. And if you look at these obstacles as a containing fence, they become your excuse for failure. If you look at them as a hurdle, each one strengthens you for the next."*
> —Ben Carson, *Gifted Hands*

How Do You Define Success?

What is your definition of success? Is it an elusive, unattainable dream? Are you the embodiment of success? There are people who attract success like a magnet and others who couldn't find success if it was sitting on their front door. To learn more about success, it's essential we define what success is, given one man's success may be another man's failure. People often compare their success to others. John lives in a lovely home with an expensive car, holidays four times a year, and has a beautiful wife and family. What they fail to see is the underlying attributes which make up John's life. It's easy to look at another man's riches being better than yours without appreciating the hidden factors. American entrepreneur, author, and speaker Jim Rohn suggests we strive for 'excellence,' not success. If one aims for success, it becomes elusive like trying to find happiness. If you focus on excellence, success is assured since it's the byproduct of great work and deeds. Reflect on your definition of success and draw a list of how success looks to you. What does it mean to be successful? To acquire material possessions? Perhaps sustain fulfilling relationships or be spiritually minded? Or any number of these points? How will you know when you're successful?

My definition of success has changed over the years. If I'm asked to define success during my twenties, it meant being rich and wealthy, working twenty days a year, and traveling the world. Success these days embodies more. The following is what I consider as worthy of success:

- Impact humanity through my work
- Help others turn their dreams into reality
- Be healthy in mind, body, and spirit
- Spiritually aligned to a higher source
- Enjoy fulfilling relationships with family, friends, and loved ones
- Be financially free
- Give back to others through charitable and/or volunteer work

I'm successful in these areas when I fulfill my purpose and destiny. Every day becomes a blessing, not a chore. Arising each morning becomes a joy, not a curse. I'm at peace with myself.

I realized success does not follow a straight line. There are many detours and roads which lead to success. The detours and dead ends are the lessons learned to become successful. They shape your character into the person you will become. Experience shapes your beliefs and thoughts. Experience and inner growth are two measurable qualities required for success. Success is a journey, not a destination. Read that again. "Success is a journey, not a destination." It's who you become that determines your success. Those who win the lottery are worse off a year after their win. Albeit, winning the lottery is not a terrible problem to have. People winning it have no experience managing that level of wealth. That's why it slips out of their hands. They do not create an inner shift related to money and finances. It is thrust upon them and so they must learn to manage large sums of money. The key to success lies not in the destination as much as the person you become. It's the endless failures, disappointments, highs, and lows that mold you into a person worthy of success.

I've experienced wanting to give up when it seems impossible. I wondered why I was striving on little income while my friends were making more. They enjoyed success, while I barely got by. Such moments are defining in one's life since they show how committed you are to turn your dreams into reality. I've grown during those times, having realized my desire to achieve my goals is far greater than I imagined. I'm willing to do whatever it takes to achieve it. If that means reading more books than the next person, working late at night to finish a project, or seeking resources that will speed up my success, I'm willing to make those sacrifices. What are you willing to do or be to achieve your goals? If life shows you otherwise, are you prepared to push through to make it happen? Your answer shows what you value and what you're willing to concede to turn your dreams into reality. What inner changes must take place to realize your vision of success?

Obstacles Illuminate The Path To Success

In his book *Meditations*, Roman Emperor Marcus Aurelius declared, "The impediment to action advances action. What stands in the way becomes the way." He was referring to the obstacles which stand in the way of success to reveal the path ahead. Consider the following fable to underline this ideal. Two identical acorns from the same oak tree are planted in distinct locations. One is grown in the middle of a dense forest while the other is planted on a steep hill by itself. The oak on the steep hillside is exposed to frequent storms and fierce gale winds. As a result, its roots plummet deep into the earth spreading in every direction, enfolding giant boulders to secure its position. While the tree isn't growing fast enough, the growth is occurring underground. It is as though the roots know they must protect the tree from the threatening elements by positioning themselves firmly beneath the soil. The acorn planted in the forest becomes a weak, frail sapling having to compete with other giant oaks for nutrients and space. Since protected by neighboring trees larger and stronger, the little oak does not see the need to spread its roots for support.

Obstacles compel you to turn your weaknesses into strengths, instead of cowering from them as many people do. They exist not to be surrendered to but to be overcome, for in overcoming do we gain the inner conviction and resilience to succeed. Obstacles illuminate the path to success by exposing challenges in which to overcome, thus ensuring victory is attainable. They are goalposts leading you toward goal achievement. Consider your most recent motivation to pursue a goal. What obstacles became clear to you along the way? How did you overcome the obstacle? What insights did you gain? For clients I work with, the single biggest impediment to success occurs months into their wellness campaign. Enthusiasm gives rise to unforeseen obstacles which impose upon their success to lose weight or improve their health. Yet contained within each obstacle, a renewed optimism to gain valuable lessons and key insights is made. Obstacles highlight limiting beliefs or neglected emotional conflicts, which need your attention if you seek to meet success. It is the opportunity to reconcile with facets of your character opposed to the obstacle. Take for example the fear of success, which cripples individuals well before they set out toward pursuing their goal. By attending to your fears before realizing your achievements, you are better suited to savor the victory when it arrives. A successful person inundated with fear is no more successful than the sum of his fears, looming over him like a dark cloud.

Obstacles reinforce a resilient mindset by allowing us to develop mental fortitude, mainly when victory is attainable. It underscores the person you have become in light of the obstacles faced. Comparable to the acorn tree roots plummeting deep into the earth, life exposes weeds from our psyche if we stay attentive to the lessons learned. Thus, obstacles serve as necessary mental and emotional growth. To highlight this, authors Jeff Brown and Mark Fenske state in their book, *The Winner's Brain*, "Resilience and Motivation are two of the critical abilities for which Winner's Brains are wired." Obstacles may be regarded as a transitory state, yet your thoughts relating to the obstacles may become permanent. In his book *Falling Into Grace*, author Adyashanti asserts, "when we believe what we think, when we take our thinking to be reality, we will suffer." In light of this, obstacles are not the cause of your problems. Your reaction to the obstacles which highlight an error in your thinking is what needs your attention.

It is vital to appreciate that nothing is fixed nor permanent. Life is subject to change and fluctuations which rise and fall in line with the seasons. Every so-called problem contains the seed of opportunity and the womb of creation. If we stay attentive to the underlying lessons, we transform the experience into personal triumph. Your obstacles give way to fundamental lessons and breakthroughs since they reinforce vital clues leading to success. Every attempt to overcome an obstacle strengthens a pathway to success. It is not in overcoming the obstacle we prevail. It is by being observant to the lessons conveyed on account of the obstacle that we gain valuable insights. As you reflect on your recent challenges, pause for a moment to consider the lessons gained to overcome them. Contemplate your answer to the following question: "What does the greater intelligence within me seek to learn from this experience?" There is always a greater lesson vested in the personal discovery of a gift you are yet to harness. As you awaken that potential, the path toward success is illuminated.

How To Form Successful Habits

The journey to awaken the Authentic Self is lined with detours, setbacks, and often derailments. However, this should not deter you from awakening the giant within. One of the ways to harness potential is through establishing powerful habits. It is author Stephen R. Covey who said in his book *Seven Habits of Highly Effective People,* "Start with the end in mind." So you've decided to create a new habit to curtail your recent indulgence for overeating. Those close to you have even made a passing remark, noticing your 'winter weight,' which has slowly crept up on you in recent times. The café lattes you sneak in throughout the day have become an unnecessary luxury. You concede defeat—it's time to trade in the coffee card for the gym membership. It must be said that forming new habits is challenging, since it disrupts both the mind and body's natural state of equilibrium. While the rational mind is quick to affirm an emphatic YES to the new habit, the emotional brain is not quite as enthusiastic to your newly laid plans. With any luck, you've given it considerable thought, along with your strong emotional desire to make the change. Oftentimes, we have very little idea on the journey ahead until we embark upon it. In my early adult life, I was at the mercy of my habits, given my susceptibility for my emotions to prevail. A number of well-intentioned habits were met with resistance midway due to unreasonable expectations. As I approach middle age, I've had the good fortune to establish sound habits in various areas of life that continue to serve me well. Moreover, in my work as a health and self-empowerment professional, my clients have benefited from my wise counsel and steep learning curve over the years.

To form and maintain new habits we must stick to key principles to help us cement the new learnings. Combined into your daily routine, they simultaneously shape the underlying desire to achieve lasting change.

1. Understand The Change Cycle: Having worked in collaboration with a sports psychologist in the past, I have come to understand the importance of the change cycle which we touched on in Chapter Nine in forming new habits. Undoubtedly as you adopt new habits, you will be met with inner resistance since you are disrupting the mind and body's stability. Knowing the six stages of change in advance affords you realistic expectations of the journey ahead. A relevant piece of trivia: 33% of people who undertake a fitness membership cancel or seldom attend after the third month. Knowing that people's motivational habits wane over time, gyms purposely lure you into signing twelve-month contracts paid in advance, with petty exit clauses.

2. Have A Compelling Reason: Avoid starting a new habit believing it is the right thing to do. Remember the conscious and emotional brain have different agendas. You will undoubtedly be met with resistance as the going gets tough since internal conflicts are bound to arise. It is advisable to adopt a purposeful intent why you wish to pursue the new habit. Motivational speaker Jim Rohn once quipped, "We must all suffer one of two things: the pain of discipline or the pain of regret or disappointment." We know the pain of discipline bears lighter on our conscience than the pain of regret. Reconnecting with your WHY? will help you connect with your conscious and emotional intentions. Connecting with your original intention to start a new habit is paramount for success. As the journey gathers momentum, setbacks and inner resistance are often enough to derail your progress.

3. Chunk It Down: Break down the goal into smaller goals. Pursue one habit or goal at a time until you have become proficient. For example, if your intention to 'get fit' means undertaking an exercise program, you might start with a series of gentle long walks early in the morning to test the waters. Don't have ambitious expectations of how your health journey might take shape. Starting slow with the intention of gaining momentum may be far more useful in the long run than quitting altogether. Allow the strength of the goal or habit to propel you toward action. As the saying goes, *slow and steady wins the race.*

4. Manage Your Environment: Remove temptations likely to derail your progress. If your new habit is to curb eating unhealthy foods, be sure to have your fridge and pantry stocked with healthy food options. While this may seem trivial, during times of emotional need, the conscious brain becomes irrational, leading to the probability of cheating. Therefore keep temptations out of sight where you can. Similarly, avoid falling into the lure of rewarding yourself with food. Your mind is incredibly astute at recognizing this, having undergone thousands of years of evolution—it will find ways to use the rewards against you. Opt for rewards that are non-food-related such as relaxing massages, buying a new item of clothing, music, etc. It is important to factor *resistance* into the equation since you will invariably become unstuck at times. Do not be hard on yourself when/if this occurs. Use the time wisely to regroup and continue pursuing your habit.

5. Commit To The Habit: Time to put the pedal to the metal. Smaller victories achieved early in the habit-forming period add crucial momentum to your habit. Undertaking daily activity for an entire month is a timely approach for forming sound disciplinary behavior. Daily action is paramount for maintaining impetus, rather than intermittent application. Aim for at least a 90%+ strike rate during the initial month. I find it useful to use a range of tools as motivational aids. I purposely place colored Post-it notes around the home in places I often frequent. If using technology to motivate yourself, avoid falling victim to the technology; instead, use it as support to help you stick to your newly laid plans.

Setbacks are unavoidable throughout the habit-forming period. Make a public declaration of your intended habit to a friend, work colleague, or loved one. Make yourself accountable to someone that is likely to offer much-needed support or who has walked in your shoes. Offer to return the favor. Being accountable to someone affords you a sound reason for keeping your word. This makes it all the more worthwhile for adhering to your habit. Resist overthinking or falling victim to your emotions as the going gets tough. Your mind will naturally find excuses to jeopardize your progress. Do not buy into the excuses. Remember why you set out to form the new habit in the first place.

Do You Suffer From Toxic Success Syndrome?

The earth spins fast even though we're unaware of it. In the same way, many people's lives spin out of control and they are oblivious to it. They believe their hectic lives are normal and necessary for success.

What is success?

Success is defined differently by most, although it has accomplishment attached to it. Some consider themselves successful undertaking a job they love. For others, it's a home and car. Another one believes being a stay-at-home mom makes her successful. Success is noble and worthwhile to pursue. Yet our culture has a "toxic success syndrome." There's a push to strive for success given the apparent lack in a person's life. This deficiency causes people to strive to outward tasks and accomplishments to fulfill them. To create goals and action plans toward completing those goals is wonderful. I consider it wise, yet the longing to be "successful" puts people on an insatiable path that frustrates them, instead of pursuing peace and joy. Observe the way children are busy these days with tasks, choirs, and events. Parents push their children to "be the best" and do while forsaking their childhood. Play soccer at age three, football at age four or five, karate, chorus, theater, dance, etc. I'm not saying children should not be active in their interests, yet I don't agree with the "push" toward being the best at a young age. Get first place. Make Mom and Dad proud, as if being mediocre isn't good enough. This can discourage children when they don't excel at something. We need accomplishments to satiate our self-worth and receive adequate attention. We want to accomplish our goals, but are we delaying peace and joy for some time down the road when we FINALLY arrive? Does this thinking run through your mind?

"I will be happy when…."

Toxic success syndrome implies you won't be happy until A, B, or C happens and is disheartening because you can be happy NOW. Regardless of how many goals you accomplish, how much money you have, whether you're in an intimate relationship, your book is published, the job you want, etc. You can be happy now when A, B, or C hasn't happened. The practice of yoga and meditation has exploded in recent years for good reason. We are tired of being deficient, coupled with a lack and emptiness. We make more money, find a different girlfriend or boyfriend, buy a new house, trade the mediocre car for a sports car, excel at work, etc. We numb our negative feelings with addictions such as food, pills, sex, and alcohol. It doesn't work because trying to fill a void, relieve the pain, or gain recognition does not come via external means. This is why yoga and meditation find their way into our lives. These techniques provide good results because even employers understand that healthy and happy employees mean less sick time and more productivity at work. Why don't we get quiet? Meditation is an easy practice, yet the majority will not take five minutes a day to sit quietly with themselves. Why not? We're accustomed to being on the go so that five minutes of stillness and solitude is difficult. Yet these techniques and practice can improve lives. Meditation is proven to reduce anxiety and stress. People report less sadness and fatigue. Yoga does the same. To get in touch with the mind and body is simple, yet we consider it is not worth it or don't have time. I assure you it's worth the time you put forth into it.

We sink time into striving for accomplishments. We sink thousands of dollars into schooling, therapy, and medicine. It's time to do less striving and more sitting with ourselves. Aren't you ready to stop trying to make yourself happy and relax so you can "be" happy no matter where you are in life? I might not know the specifics, but I know you can learn to let go of negative emotions and enjoy the present moment. Sure, you may feel sad or angry or frustrated (when something untoward happens), but you needn't be controlled by these states. You can learn to dance when the storms are raging, laugh when hell breaks loose, and rest when the wind blows. Struggles, pain, and dreams are part of the human condition. Yet we needn't strive and delay our happiness until the day A, B, or C occurs.

Be mindful of your present and enjoy life now. Celebrate the victories while you can. "But you don't know my situation, Tony!" Life is a journey and we can be peaceful and happy throughout the journey.

Intuition Is The Key To Success

Have you been in a situation where you did something with little thought to the action? As though someone is whispering to you or to talk to a certain person? If so, this could be intuition prompting you as intuition is the key to success. Your intuition speaks in a gentle and subtle way. It nudges you rather than imposes itself in a loud voice. Given the subtlety, it's important to learn how to listen to its guidance. If you are busy with a million thoughts and hustle about your day, you will miss intuition communicating to you. Intuition is spontaneous and reassuring. You could stand in line waiting for coffee and be inclined to pay for the person's drink behind you for no reason. You might wonder if the thought is coming from you or if it's intuition beckoning. They key is to act on our intuition despite lack of evidence to the contrary. Intuition is not limited to thoughts and yet is a real spiritual force. You can tune into this force and allow it to guide you by being attentive to it as it arises. Intuition is not limited to emotions or feelings. If you're aware of intense emotions, it may not be attributed to intuition, but your thoughts. Researchers assert that intuition is associated with right brain activity because it impresses images upon the right hemisphere of the brain. The left brain is associated with thoughts and is the logical processor. Due to the correlation with the right side of the brain, meditation is helpful for becoming in tune with your intuition. Meditation requires sitting silently, focusing on your breath, and observing your thoughts in silence. It is easy to get caught up in external noise; we drown out the silent whisper of intuition. To be guided by intuition, turn the radio and television off and get in tune with silence—the Authentic Self. A wonderful place to practice is in nature. Take a walk or sit in a serene place where you can connect with the environment to be at peace. Those who meditate report being calmer and happier. If you incorporate 10 minutes a day of meditation, you are likely to experience less stress, more joy, and perceive your intuition.

Intuition can help you to become more successful. As you attend to your day, become focused within. If you receive a prompt or gentle nudge, go with it. The key is to hear your intuition and take action. Initially you may not be engaged with it, but the more you tune in, the easier you distinguish intuition from other influences. When you wake up in the morning, take a few minutes to lie in bed, take a few deep breaths, and turn your focus inward. Ask for guidance for the day. Offer gratitude for the good in your life. Listen to the whisper of intuition while paying attention to images or thoughts that emerge. You might see a quick image flash by of a friend you haven't spoken to in a while. If you do, your intuition is telling you to get in touch with them. You might be compelled to visit the library that day and meet an individual in your line of work who offers you a job proposition. You never know what eventuates when you tune into intuition daily. As you pursue success in every area of your life, don't leave intuition out. Listen for its lead and offer gratitude for this powerful force and the power within.

Leave No Stone Unturned In Your Desire For Success

In an ancient Greek fable, the playwright Euripides conveys a story of an army general who buries a large treasure in his tent following his defeat in battle. When the conquering general and his troops could not locate the treasure, they consult the Oracle of Delphi, who advised them to look under every stone. The conquering general returned to the site where the tent was situated, ordering his troops to search under every stone until the treasure was uncovered. The tale by Euripides depicts man's unbending desire to pursue every course of action to achieve his outcome. Consider the relevance of this story in your own life. Is there a goal or dream you're determined to achieve with a vehement desire? Giving up is an easy way out since it abandons the need to concede failure and the ensuing emotions which arise from defeat. Yet character is formed in defeat, similar to carbon dioxide applied with intense heat and pressure, gives rise to form a diamond. I'd like you to consider leaving no stone unturned in your pursuit to realize a particular goal or outcome. That is, adopt an unrelenting desire to pursue that which burns deep in your heart. Have you noticed that those who strike upon success have an unyielding tenacity not to lose sight of their vision? Similar to a dog who refuses to let go of his bone until he has gnawed at it, thus reducing it to nothing more than bone fragments, you must strive to exhaust all avenues before retreating into defeat. Often we believe every course of action is being undertaken, yet something is always lurking around the corner, waiting to command our attention.

People who seek a cure for disease or illness may spend years searching for a solution to no avail. Yet as they abandon hope, a likely solution is brought to light when they least expect it. Therefore, I urge you to stay vigilant, yet in a state of expectation without a projected outcome of how your goal will come to bear. Consider your answer to this question—what is it you desire? We spend a great deal of time protesting what we don't want, to the detriment of our true desires. Your subconscious mind is constantly scanning your innermost thoughts and daydreams. It does so by filtering pertinent information to reveal patterns of thought particular to your character. Therefore, given your commitment, giving up should be the last resort until all avenues have been exhausted. Similarly, what you set out to achieve may not be realized in the form you intended. Many of the world's greatest inventions came to life because of an accident or mishap. Consider the inventions we take for granted such as: Post-it notes, penicillin, the microwave oven, Velcro, and X-rays. Such inventions arose out of mere accident and countless errors. It is no surprise that vigilance, tenacity, and an unrelenting desire are paramount in your quest to succeed. This principle applies to most areas of life: improving personal finances, career, entrepreneurship, and seeking a committed relationship. I invite you to think in terms of infinite possibilities. In their book, *The Winner's Brain: 8 Strategies Great Minds Use to Achieve Success,* authors Jeff Brown and Mark Fenske state, "A Winner's Brain is very good at tuning out distractions and choosing the best way to focus on a task (there are different types of focus the brain is capable of) in order to get the best outcome." The ability to tune out distractions becomes a focal point to realize your intended outcome. The winner's mind is goal-oriented, given its laser focus to stay committed to the project until it has come to life.

Regrettably, most people adopt the suck-it-and-see

approach to goal attainment, alluding to the English expression of "giving it a go" while attentive to what eventuates in the process. While merit is gained in adopting this approach, it is better suited toward smaller goals rather than risk gambling with the game of life. A more likely strategy calls for developing a compelling inner resolve to pursue the goal 'til the end. Far too many people give up just when the tide turns. While you may not appreciate how close you are, in hindsight you might lament your missed opportunity. To leave no stone unturned in your quest for success requires restrained patience and biding your time. In support, a steadfast vigilance to realize a successful outcome is similarly paramount. I suggest you alternate between these two states, given patience and vigilance oppose one another. Do not abandon hope when all seems lost; that is the time when the tide turns in your favor. Life is bound by unexpected change when you least expect it.

In concluding this chapter, pursue everything in your power to realize your goal, then turn it over to the universe to usher in the ideal outcome. Dan Millman's book *Way of the Peaceful Warrior* reminds us of the following affirmation: "I no longer presume to know how life should come or go; letting go in this way brings a sense of freedom. This doesn't mean I don't care or have no preferences. My actions naturally follow the call of my heart, my interests and values. I make efforts in my personal and professional life in alignment with my goals. But once I've taken aim and loosed the arrows from the bow, I can only wait with interest to see where it will land." Assume the same inner conviction toward your vision of success. Sure enough, when you least expect it, success will greet you in the timeliest hour.

Chapter Summary

- *Experience and inner growth are two measurable qualities required for success.*
- *Obstacles compel you to turn your weaknesses into strengths instead of cowering from them.*
- *Obstacles illuminate the path to success by exposing challenges to overcome, thus ensuring victory is attainable.*
- *Obstacles reinforce a resilient mindset by allowing you to develop mental fortitude, mainly when victory is attainable.*
- *Obstacles may be regarded as a transitory state, yet your thoughts relating to the obstacles may become permanent.*
- *There is always a greater lesson vested in the personal discovery of a gift you are yet to harness.*
- *Jim Rohn quipped, "We must all suffer one of two things: the pain of discipline or the pain of regret or disappointment."*
- *Intuition is not limited to thoughts and is a real spiritual force.*
- *Character is formed in defeat, similar to how carbon dioxide applied with intense heat and pressure gives rise to form a diamond.*

- *Your subconscious mind is constantly scanning your innermost thoughts and daydreams. It filters pertinent information to reveal patterns of thought particular to your character.*
- *The winner's mind is goal-oriented, given its laser focus to stay committed to the project until it has come to life.*
- *Developing a compelling inner resolve to pursue the goal 'til the end. Far too many people give up just when the tide turns.*
- *A steadfast vigilance to realize a successful outcome is similarly paramount.*
- *Life is bound by unexpected change when you least expect it.*

11

The Art Of Effortless Living

> "*By letting it go it all gets done. The world is won by those who let it go. But when you try and try, the world is beyond winning.*"
> —*Lao Tzu*

The Art Of Effortless Living

There is an inherent rhythm to life—everything follows an intricate order as observed in a flock of birds flying and ducking in unison. You needn't clutch to things since life takes care of matters in due course. It was the Chinese philosopher Lao Tzu who said, "Nature does not hurry, yet everything is accomplished." Every condition maintains its own self-organizing system to yield a perfect outcome. Everything flows in harmony without needless worry. As we abide by this awareness, our willingness to trust life exceeds our reasoning. Authors Charlene Belitz and Meg Lundstrom reinforce this message stating, "Flow is the natural, effortless unfolding of our life in a way that moves us toward wholeness and harmony." Effortless living is the willingness to embrace the flow experience while setting aside our need for intended outcomes. We let go of circumstances which no longer serve us instead of anxiously clutching at life. To let go signifies mental and emotional withdrawal from situations outside our control. Energy is spent opposing life rather than going with the flow. It is the egoic mind which affirms it knows better than the infinite intelligence which guides the stars and planets. We recognize the folly in that assumption since we are a small cog in a well-orchestrated process. In her book *The Art of Effortless Living*, author Ingrid Bacci, Ph.D. reminds us, "…if we let go of doing and move toward being, every part of our lives will change for the better." Ingrid's passage reminds us to yield to the natural order instead of resist it. Accept what transpires by allowing it to work for you even when the details are obscure. The seeds of fortune are contained within adversity. We must look for hidden opportunities in every condition.

We must avoid hastily casting judgment given the capacity to convey a biased opinion. Have you tried to rush through something and have it fall apart on you? Thomas Edison's invention of the lightbulb required 10,000 trials and errors before it came to life. You can't rush what needs to evolve on its own timeline. Effortless living acknowledges cooperation with the forces of life. Explore patience as a virtue if you are inclined to rush through life. What are you missing out by rushing? A hamster scurrying on a wheel recognizes the harder it runs, the less it gets to where it needs to. Trade the hamster wheel for the slow path—everything that must come to pass will do so naturally. If you are in a hurry, examine the root cause.

What are you avoiding?

What are you afraid to see if life slows?

That you are not in control?

Remain open to new experiences, new vistas, and new doors which usher in welcomed change. Those who claim life is dull resist this facet of life. It might be unclear to you, yet your presence in this space-time continuum is a testimony to your magnificence. Allow this knowing to sink into your being. Change forms the process of life and is essential to harness our personal power. "You just have to let things be and not do anything about them. That is probably the greatest discipline in the world because our whole thing is about making it happen. The point is to be present and trust the process," state Charlene Belitz and Meg Lundstrom. Similarly, focus on what is important and let everything else fall away. You needn't do more than is required at the time. In fact, doing less often yields greater results. Avoid your attachment to people, places, or events since everything is impermanent. Clinging is rooted in fear, which per- petuates more fear. Transform your thoughts into empowering ones to allow what needs to flow into your experience with ease. Let go of possessions for which you no longer have any use. If you haven't used it in the last three months, consider repurposing it. Having fewer material goods liberates us from the need to manage more. I'm not suggesting you live an austere life; instead, you should not seek solace in material possessions to reinforce your sense of self. "Want what life wants," affirms philosopher and spiri- tual teacher Guy Finley.

Avoid following the masses given their tendency to perpetuate mindless thinking. Popular culture expresses a recycled thought consciousness. If you seek to blend in, a place awaits you and you need not fight your way for it. Yet if you wish to be a thinker, a rad- ical, an inventor, an optimist, or creator, go out on a limb where the fruit is more satisfying. Life invites you to take risks. Those risks may or may not pay off, while other ways inspire you to experience yourself with renewed enthusiasm. In his book *The Luck Factor*, renowned author and psychologist Dr. Richard Wiseman affirms, "Being in the right place at the right time is actually all about being in the right state of mind." The state of mind Dr. Wiseman is referring to is possible when we honor our true nature instead of waging an inner battle that we are bound to lose. Effortless living follows from our resolve to quiet the muddy waters of our mind to allow the stillness to echo through us. Lao Tzu reminds us that **everything** is accomplishing when we harmonize with the flow of life—not some things, yet all things to include the life we seek to live. The Authentic Self abides by the flow of life and does not seek to hurry what should unfold naturally and effortlessly.

Happiness Is A Journey Not A Destination

The American author and poet Henry David Thoreau once expressed: "Happiness is like a butterfly; the more you chase it, the more it will elude you, but if you turn your attention to other things, it will come and sit softly on your shoulder…." To resolve happiness being an elusive quality, we assume it to be so by framing it in the negative. In light of the suffering in the world nowadays, many of us are inclined to consider happiness as intangible. "How can happiness prevail when there is suffering in the world?" one might assume. It would be remiss of me to answer this question in a book, when religion and philosophy have tried unsuccessfully to settle this dilemma for centuries. I can only reason that despite the suffering in the world, happiness is still an attainable goal. How might this be possible, you may ask? In underdeveloped countries, in spite of poverty, happiness prevails when people's basic needs are met. Contrast to the developed countries where daily life is chaotic with high rates of stress and mental illness because of demanding lifestyles.

In drawing awareness to our suffering and those of others, we lose sight of happiness as an attainable goal. Happiness cannot be a fleeting experience when we our focused attention is directed toward it. Many people believe when happiness is attained, it will transform their life. Hence the seeker travels far and wide, merely to discover it is contained within him. Our hectic lifestyle makes happiness harder to reach since our minds are always preoccupied with something. Technology and communication devices vie for our attention. Many find it challenging to be alone in silence without a communication device attached to them. The pursuit of happiness rests in letting go of unnecessary distractions. These include toxic thoughts, habits, disempowering emotions, destructive relationships, events, commitments, etc. By simplifying life, we create the idyllic conditions for happiness to thrive. As we direct our attention toward the negative aspects of life, i.e., daily news, gossip and tabloid magazines, etc., our minds are drawn to the stimuli on an ongoing basis. You cannot read the gossip magazines without being fixated on the next ensuing drama. Our awareness should be channeled into worthwhile experiences which offer us joy and happiness instead. The notion that happiness is elusive stems from our inability to hold our concentration on it long enough. If we believe happiness is an unattainable goal, we firmly reject it as a possibility, thus becoming elusive. You might have heard it said that your beliefs shape your perception, which creates your experience of life. Regrettably many people unknowingly drive happiness away via their thoughts. Their constant attention on their external reality shapes their inner world so that suffering becomes the focal point in their life. Popular culture has left an indelible mark on us so we look to our external conditions as a measure of success.

Many travel the world in search of happiness, seeking new and exciting experiences to discover it has vanished when they return home. At this point they direct their interest toward gaining more 'things' or associating with certain people in the hope it will bring them the happiness they strive for. Assuredly the novelty wears off and soon enough they are back where they started—struggling to fill an empty void within. It begs the question: Does happiness happen to us? Is it an externally generated experience or a user generated experience? If we subscribe to the belief that happiness occurs without our control, we remain at the mercy of it being a fleeting experience. Conversely, if we believe we are the wellspring of our own happiness, it will present itself in everyday life. This is empowering for several reasons, least of which being that we become the source of our joy instead of presuming it is not within our own volition.

In his book *Hardwiring Happiness*, neuropsychologist and author Rick Hanson states that happiness can be attained in everyday life by applying a four-step protocol, he calls H.E.A.L.:

- Have a positive experience
- Enrich it
- Absorb it
- Link a positive experience to it (optional)

Striving toward a goal while pursuing one's dream or passion, although contains its own challenges, may still be a positive experience. Some of the world's greatest inventors and creative people before our time struggled with success in their respective fields amid the backdrop of pursuing happiness. To attain happiness, we must connect with our deepest nature. Look for happiness in your everyday life experiences and undoubtedly it will surprise you how inviting the world can be. Allow the joy and rapture to emanate from within, not without. If you rush about daily life plugged into electronic devices with little or no quiet time, happiness will pass you by like a high-speed rail train. Make a vow to honor the happiness within you. Reconnect with your childlike nature. Be curious toward the simple things in life and I can assure you happiness will not be so elusive.

How To Live A More Conscious Life

To live a conscious life means knowing yourself beyond the superficial façade. If you are conscious, you are aware of the present moment and your inner self is awakened. To be conscious means to be mindful of your thoughts and emotions. Most people don't live conscious lives in the sense I speak of. They live in their heads with thoughts swirling around and miss their NOW experience of life. Have you been on holiday and your perception of life expanded? You smell the fresh air, smile at the lush green trees and gorgeous flowers while aware of the birds humming. You are alive and happier because you forget the hundreds of thoughts running around in your mind. You are conscious of your present surroundings. Those same surroundings are present in your neighborhood, but you focus on other things to notice them. Our spirit longs to be experienced. However, it may be covered up by layers of negativity and limiting beliefs we consider to be normal. Childhood wounds, negative feelings, limiting beliefs, etc. pile on year after year and it gets harder to connect with our spirit. To become conscious requires peeling away these layers. To live a more conscious life requires you to slow down, become quiet, and allow the painful wounds to surface so you can process them and let them go. By doing so, you plow through layers of buried emotions to be in tune with your spirit. As you do this, wounds heal and wholeness arises, leading to a wonderful transformation.

You might think, "Who wants to go back to childhood and face old wounds?" I understand, yet it's an important process if you want to live a conscious life.

Ponder these questions:

Are you happy with your life?

Do you love who you are?

Do you know your primary purpose in life?

Are your relationships up to par?

If your answers to these questions are not what you want them to be, take time to move into silence, whatever that means to you. Be present with your thoughts and feelings. Learn to sit in silence and let your mind rest. Even 10 minutes a day is helpful. Sit in a comfortable position, take a few deep breaths, and focus on your breath. As you inhale, notice the air moving into your lungs and leaving your body as you exhale. As you focus on your breathing, other thoughts melt away and you are at peace. Random thoughts and feelings such as old wounds will surface and when they do, acknowledge them and let them go. Some call becoming more conscious "enlightenment." The more enlightened you become, the more peace, joy, and contentment you enjoy. You won't lie in bed at night with your thoughts keeping you awake obsessing over things. Along with silence and meditation, you can live a conscious life by being mindful and present throughout the day. Be mindful of your thoughts and if they must be there, be sure they are positive. Be mindful of your surroundings. Play with your pets. Sit outside and breathe the aroma of nature. Smile often. Notice yourself inhaling and exhaling. Notice the core of your being alive and well. Get to the core of who you are. You are much more than your flesh and bones. Intend to live a more conscious life and as you do, you will discover more and more what a magnificent spirit you are.

The Art Of Simplicity: It's Time To Simplify Your Life

In a busy and hectic world, people long for the simple life. With work, kids, chores, and never-ending errands, it's easy to become overstressed and exhausted. Stress levels are at an all-time high with health problems on the increase. Parents scurry from place to place to raise their all-star soccer and dance-competing children and lie in bed at night thinking, "What am I doing? Will life ever settle down? I'm exhausted!" Don't get me wrong; productivity requires action. Nothing would be achieved if we contemplated our to-do list without action. Learning the art of simplicity and balance is where we find happiness and peace. Those who simplify their life live with less stress. They find a spiritual path that leads them to more authentic joy which is the underlying premise of the book. To awaken the Authentic Self, we must let go of defeating habits and lifestyle choices that impede the process. Living a simple life is not a new idea. It has been popular from the turn of civilization. Early Christians advised followers to let go of what they didn't need and live a simple life, devoted to others. Buddhists encouraged followers to let go of desire and seek nothing more than was necessary to live. Native Americans lived simple lives, utilizing natural resources as often as possible for sustenance and shelter. Over time, the pursuit of material possessions and money led people to drown out simplicity. To keep up with the Joneses is the new norm. The pursuit of happiness through status and wealth leads people to push against the tide so they can be better, have more, and strive to be the best. The concern with this is a drain on our energy leaving people tired, empty, and discontented.

What does simplicity look like? Why do some people lead simpler lives than others? Oftentimes, a person gets stretched to their limit before realizing their busy lifestyle is not self-serving. They seek happiness and status via outside means while starving on the inside. Finally, an epiphany occurs and they realize they must simplify life to find peace and joy. Simplicity means different things to different people but has common characteristics. It means to live day-to-day with the necessary essentials whether they be material or immaterial. Here are ways others have chosen to simplify:

- Get rid of things (clutter) you don't need. Have a garage sale, donate items or give them to friends and family members.
- Let go of negative emotions.
- Downsize. Get rid of expensive payments that weigh you down.
- Stop perusing time-consuming activities.

- Commit to doing more of what you love.
- Take up a hobby.
- Let go of miserable relationships.
- Go on a spiritual retreat.

As you take time to gauge your life, you'll discover how to simplify along the way. Make a list of things you can do and commit to attempting them on a trial basis. Everyone has 24 hours in a day and many pack it full of tasks that prevent them growing in happiness. It's the hamster on the exercise wheel running 'round but never getting anywhere. It's time to get off the hamster wheel and carve out a life that is balanced and satisfying. Pursue that which resonates with your deepest self and remove what does not serve you. Make a "Not to Do" list and eliminate what impedes upon your time. Read stories of people who have simplified their life and know you can, too. Ask friends to join you in the endeavor. Join the simplicity movement so that you can enjoy life to the fullest. The Authentic Self thrives on being expressed through actions that align with your soul nature. Creativity and expressions are ways in which we harness authenticity so it is wise to make room in your life for these pursuits. Suddenly, life appears joyous and invigorating because you have taken the time to cultivate the essence of your authentic nature.

Perception Creates Reality

Perception is a remarkable phenomenon. Author Gregory Berns states in *Iconoclast*, "Perception is the brain's way of interpreting ambiguous visual signals in the most likely explanation possible. These explanations are a direct result of past experience." In short, perception equates to the sum of your past conditioning. In keeping with this idea, I invite you to participate in the following thought experiment to test this model. Suppose you are raised in a poor family with little material possessions to account for. Your constant concern for money leads you to adopt a scarcity mentality. Over time, you develop negative beliefs related to money, since your past was replete with evidence of money being in short supply.

Now, let's consider an alternative outlook.

You are raised in a wealthy family living in an affluent neighborhood: equipped with maids, butlers, and a chauffeur. You are provided with the finest luxuries you could ever need. Your family holds media interests in a thriving global empire in which you are involved. Regular travel on the company's private plane and holidays in exotic resorts are the norm for you. What do you think your perception of money is likely to be given the above scenario? I'm certain prosperity, abundance, and wealth would be common to your experience, given your relationship to wealth. You expect money to be readily available since reality dictates its abundant supply. The nature of living in a material world means our reality becomes the canvas upon which we make sense of our environment. Perception is based on our mind-constructed model of the world, such that life reflects our held beliefs and opinions. Stephen R. Covey reminds us, "To change ourselves effectively, we first had to change our perceptions." In a similar example, some people believe in the institution of marriage while others consider relationships to end in disillusionment or divorce. Yet neither party is right nor wrong. Their perception is colored by their experience of reality. Your life's experiences give rise to a *distorted* view of the world, observed through your self-made filters. I mean that in the best possible sense. The filters we use to create reality are biased for several reasons, least of which affirms they are the product of our past. At the beginning of seminars, I often remind audiences of the Thomas Dewar quote which states, "Minds are like parachutes; they work best when open." Thus to appreciate reality and connect with the truth, it serves us well to consider opposing views and find agreement somewhere in the middle. It is my opinion most people are quick to pass judgment before giving others the benefit of the doubt. They reference formed memories to construct inaccurate assessments of a situation.

Reflect on a recent setting in which you were quick to jump to conclusions. You may have assumed you were right and the other party was wrong. I have an instance that springs to mind. A friend of mine relates a story which involves a young man on a bus who neglected to offer his seat to an elderly passenger standing nearby. My friend was quick to conclude he lacked manners for failing to offer his seat to the senior passenger. Little did my friend realize at the time that the young man had been fitted with a prosthetic leg that afternoon related to a motorcycle accident. The prosthetist had advised him to occupy a seat on the bus since standing on the artificial leg would cause further swelling in the amputated limb. Since the bus was packed with commuters, the young man was glad to find a seat to rest his limbs. After arriving at the same stop, my friend struck up a conversation with the man which revealed the complete story. Suffice it to say she felt remorseful, given the elderly woman did not appear to be impaired and was capable of standing unassisted. The above scenario is an extreme example illustrating how our judgments impair our perception. Seldom do we have a detailed picture of a situation until we dig deeper. In his highly praised book *Influence: The Psychology of Persuasion,* Robert B. Cialdini states, "Often we don't realize that our attitude toward something has been influenced by the number of times we have been exposed to it in the past." In her presuming her judgment, my friend called on her biased memory to interpret the case at hand. Based on past reference, she wrongly concluded the young man to be rude, which was clearly not the case.

This simple story reinforces the need to suspend judgment because we often bring our own bias to the moment. To be tolerant of others reinforces our self-compassion and self-tolerance. We shape our reality by assuming a different filter in which to perceive life. When a situation arises with which you are unfamiliar, rather than add a narrative to it, consider the following viewpoint: "What else could be going on underneath the surface which I'm unaware of?" Assuredly, something is always festering behind the scenes which we are unaware of. If you are quick to cast aspersions, you limit your experience of reality. Relationships allow us to explore new ideas within a unique setting. In exploring and integrating those ideas we form new vistas upon which our reality expands. Your perception of reality is subject to past experiences and beliefs. To be aware and awake, you become a conscious creator of your destiny, while appreciating there will always be more than meets the eye in our existence.

No Matter What, Live The Life You Desire

I want you to realize, no matter what, that you'll strive to live the life you desire with passion and enthusiasm. What do

Michael Jordan, Colonel Sanders, J. K. Rowling, and Oprah Winfrey have in common? They beat the odds to achieve their career goals despite adverse circumstances, lack of resources, other people's lack of support, and financial obstacles. They didn't quit. How will you know when to cut your losses or stay the course? What is the difference between dwelling on something and persevering? You've set your sights on a goal and determinedly pursued it. But you're not seeing the results you expect. You're at the point where you decide if this is a temporary defeat, to continue on in faith, yet doubt creeps in that you're barking up the wrong tree. Whether you decide to fish a particular spot on the lake or stay in an unhappy marriage hoping things change, the decision to persevere is one of the hardest ones to make. When do we call it quits? Only you can decide when to change direction or tactics. Only you decide what is right to invest in time and energy in a career or relationship that is not working. The key is doing something different, not quitting. Success is imminent as long as you don't concede defeat. For those who want to find a wonderful partner, there's someone out there except for the person who gives up. In those moments of frustration and doubt, when you've worked hard for success but only see evidence to the contrary, consider the following to persevere.

1. Step Away And Regroup: Taking a break can lead to a breakthrough. A change in your perspective unleashes creative thinking. Sometimes we can be overly invested in a situation to see a solution. Yet the moment we step back we consult our creative intelligence which has the answers we seek. That is why great ideas emerge in the shower.

2. Call In Reinforcements: Seek counsel. Consult a professional. Seek guidance from a mentor. Get advice from an expert. Ask someone you hold in high regard for their opinion. To consult someone you trust is a wise decision since they traversed the path and recognize the easiest way through. Often they're in a position to make suitable recommendations to fine-tune your course, which may require minor adjustments instead of giant transitions.

3. Redefine Your Goal: Do you want to be happy in your current job, or do you want to have a rewarding career? Don't give up on your goal; make adjustments to your goal. If you wish to enjoy your current job without pursuing a stable career, your decision will influence your choices. Do you pursue job promotions in your existing job, or do you enroll in further education to become suitably qualified for a career that offers you greater job satisfaction?

4. Pace Yourself: You are more prone to quitting when exhausted and overwhelmed. Maintain a healthy balance and realize there's nowhere to get to in a hurry. Remember, the goalpost is an ever-changing landscape so that when you reach your goal, you'll undoubtedly want to establish a new one. Be happy and content with progress and adopt a growth mindset as outlined in Chapter 9. A fixed mindset is limited since it does not reason in terms of opportunities but is preoccupied with a fixed line of thought.

5. Take Baby Steps: When you are overwhelmed and frustrated, take one baby step toward your goal to keep momentum. People assume they mistake giant steps daily to reach their goal, yet this limited perspective is misleading. In the book *One Small Step Can Change Your Life: The Kaizen Way* author Robert Maurer states, "When life gets scary and difficult, we tend to look for solutions in places where it is easy or at least familiar to do so, and not in the dark, uncomfortable places where real solutions might lie." We must adapt and get comfortable being uncomfortable and to do this we can stretch beyond our comfort zone each time.

6. Surrender To Life: Live life on her terms. Don't spend energy swimming against the tide. This means being flexible in your thinking. Life is efficient. As you move two steps forward and one step back, there are no mistakes. That one step back is a blessing because it provides you with knowledge and experience to attain your goal. Pursue your passion but don't be rigid how you achieve success. Rather than resist what looks to be a dead end, embrace it as a blessed detour. Allow life to open doors and show you ways to achieve your dreams that never occurred to you. Surrender is not giving up. It is part of the process and a state of allowing. Your ability to persist is not possible without your ability to allow.

Continue to follow your heart. Believe in yourself and your dreams. Anything is possible and miracles happen every day. Goals are not meant to be reached in a straightforward fashion. Consider the above illustration as a testament to this and re-evaluate your plans. The greatest discoveries and inventions resulted from divine "mistakes." Progress is often made via a zig-zag toward your goal. The universe is aligned for the attainment of our purpose and passion.

We should enjoy the journey.

Chapter Summary

- *Effortless living is the willingness to embrace the flow experience while setting aside your need for intended outcomes.*
- *The seeds of fortune are contained within adversity. Look for hidden opportunities in every condition.*
- *You can't rush what needs to evolve on its own timeline. Effortless living acknowledges cooperation with the forces of life.*
- *Remain open to new experiences, new vistas, and new doors which usher in welcomed change.*
- *Avoid your attachment to people, places, or events since everything is impermanent. Clinging is rooted in fear which perpetuates more fear.*
- *Despite the suffering in the world, happiness is still an attainable goal.*
- *The pursuit of happiness rests in letting go of unnecessary distractions.*
- *If you believe you are the wellspring of your own happiness, it will present itself in everyday life.*
- *Look for happiness in your everyday life experiences and undoubtedly it will surprise you how inviting the world can be. Allow the joy and rapture to emanate from within, not without.*

- *Your spirit longs to be experienced. However, it may be covered up by layers of negativity and limiting beliefs you consider to be normal.*
- *To live a more conscious life requires you to slow down, become quiet, and allow the painful wounds to surface so you can process them and let them go.*
- *Perception is based on your mind-constructed model of the world, such that life reflects your held beliefs and opinions.*
- *To appreciate reality and connect with the truth, it serves you to consider opposing views and find agreement somewhere in the middle.*
- *When a situation arises which you are unfamiliar with, rather than add a narrative to it, consider the following viewpoint instead: "What else could be going on underneath the surface which I'm unaware of?"*
- *Allow life to open doors and show you ways to achieve your dreams that never occurred to you. Surrender is not giving up. It is part of the process and a state of allowing.*

How To Live While You're Alive

Find Your Inspiration

Are you an artist? Or someone with creative skills? You cannot complete your work if you're not inspired. You need to find inspiration to allow your creative juices to find expression. It is not limited to artists alone but anyone who wants to harness the power of inspiration in their life. If you want direction in your life, you need to be inspired. The problem is, most people don't know what inspires them. Let's see how you can find your true inspiration. While artists are inspired by nature, others are inspired by humans and their way of living. We all have different inspiration sources. Some of us look within while others outwards. There are multiple sources for inspiration and the key is to be on the lookout for it. I find inspiration in many things and in everyday life. Nobody can tell you what should or shouldn't inspire you, as you must find inspiration for yourself. When I reflect back at my life, I am inspired by different things at different times. As a teenager, my inspiration was my father who was a tailor and becoming a successful designer appealed to me then. As times change, our inspirations and role models change. While I still enjoy fashion, I don't want to become a designer anymore. Today I have different goals and I'm inspired by writing, speaking, entrepreneurs, and leadership. I find people amazing in their abilities and accomplishments. But I find becoming inspired by people alone isn't enough. This is why I draw my inspiration from other mediums such as art, music, nature, and from within.

Since inspiration sources keep changing, you need not look to the past for inspiration. What inspires you and sets your soul free right now? What do you want now, or where do you wish you were? That will lead you to your source of inspiration. Nature can be a source of inspiration. If you are feeling uninspired, go wandering. Clear your mind of worries and go out in cool weather to enjoy the scenic beauties of nature. This will take your mind off worries. From different plants to water bodies, to exciting animals—nature is full of surprises. Just relax and enjoy it, and you'll be inspired.

If you still cannot find your source of inspiration, try these:

- Read biographies of successful people
- Travel and visit other cultures.
- Go to photography exhibitions and see the beauty captured in images

- Visit the beach and enjoy a quiet walk. This will give you time to reflect on your inner self
- Visit new restaurants and try different foods. Many chefs get their inspiration this way
- Go out with friends and have a chat over a long coffee break
- Read interesting blogs related to your field of interest
- Listen to new kinds of music. Select a new genre and enjoy it
- Teach other people. Impart your knowledge.

If you want to gain spiritual knowledge and inspiration, you need to be open-minded. If you hold hatred toward someone because they belong to a particular country or religion, you cannot gain spiritual freedom. Remember, free your heart of hatred. Be free and you'll be inspired. Avoid being biased or intolerant. Treat everyone with love and compassion and you'll find love around you in the smallest details. If you're wandering in nature, be sure you leave your iPhone at home. I've seen people who go on early morning jogs and plug in their earphones so they can cut themselves from the 'noise' of nature. Enjoy nature and be one with it. Pay attention to what it's trying to tell you. Listen to relaxing nature sounds which can be a source of peaceful joy. Your favorite music might be great, but there's nothing better than the music of nature. Enjoy it for a change. Another thing to help you get inspired is to socialize. The more you socialize with others, the more you learn. Without socializing, you are prone to sit in one place foster a particular mindset. Leave that place. Stop stagnating. Meet different people and learn new things from them.

Why You Should Follow Your Bliss

What fuels your spirit? What are you most passionate about? To follow your passion, you not only serve others, you serve yourself. By aligning with your authentic nature you explore your gifts, talents, and wisdom. This is the foundation to awakening the Authentic Self: being in alignment with universal intention. A useful metaphor to illustrate this point is seen in nature's design through a snowflake viewed under a microscope. The intricate fractal design comprised of symmetrical structures reveals the shimmering wonder that lies beneath. I invite you to model your thinking on nature's inherent wisdom since you are expressed through her inspired brilliance. Sadly, most people never experience the joy of becoming their best since they fail to acknowledge their genius. They believe they are undeserving of such gifts. To highlight the misleading basis of this belief, consider snowflakes refusing to fall in winter because they are inferior to other snowflakes that are much more brilliant in design. The analogy, though simple, illustrates that your bliss is symbolic of your personal story. It is the reason you are alive at this point in the Earth's history. I am not inviting you to believe in reincarnation or otherwise, simply that you recognize your presence serves a purpose in the grand scheme of things. "Each exists for but a short time, and in that time explore but a small part of the whole universe," states Stephen Hawking in his epic book *The Grand Design*.

Have you been to the ballet and observed dancers gracefully move onstage as though floating on thin air? Audiences are captivated by their poise and the ethereal state in which they effortlessly glide through a performance. From the dancer's viewpoint, they are in reverie: a state of flow as psychology professor Mihaly Csíkszentmihályi noted. They are present, grounded, and in sync with their repertoire. If you were to ask a dancer why they perform, they tell you that dancing is a way of life, emanating from their inner being. Dance is the performance art in which they express their soul. It is their passion and purpose that gives meaning to their life. It's not something they do, it's who they are. A dancer does not refer to their performance as something they enjoy, for such a description is much too passive. They inform you I am a dancer, choosing to embody it at a deeper level. Consider a similar standpoint in your life. How do you respond when asked, "Who are you?" Do you identify with your work, your marital status or ethnicity? Do not associate with your skills or passion alone since these are fleeting states. Many people have multiple careers throughout their lifetime, so to equate with them all is misleading.

So what is your bliss?

Your bliss is what you are willing to chase irrespective of financial gain. You cannot wait to engage in your passion after waking up each morning since you are entirely consumed by it. Your friends and loved ones notice how much time you devote being absorbed in this pursuit. You are oblivious to time, a quality particular to being in flow. It feels as though you are caught in a black hole as time passes. Your bliss may represent your calling. If you find joy conveying happiness and fulfillment to others, your bliss is a blessing. Artists and creative people experience this enthusiasm when undertaking their vocation. The hours are long, with sacrifices along the way to gain mastery. However, the rewards are clear when one retires at the end of a working week to realize they haven't actually worked; they have engaged in purposeful play. It is an uncontained ambition that no undertaking is too big, given that time is always available to pursue your passion.

When you follow your bliss, the path reveals itself. Obstacles which impede your success gradually fall away. The right people show up to help you advance ahead. It's not that life lacks challenges, they appear nevertheless to serve you and not obstruct you. The ideal circumstances transpire when you're in alignment with universal intelligence and the creative force of the universe. Take a moment to consider friends or loved ones in jobs, relationships, or circumstances they dislike. Reflect on the energy they spend caught up in circumstances that do not serve them. They are consumed by their life-force; forlorn and exhausted. It is echoed in their words and reflected in their body language. Don't become that person. Yes, many have obligations to their families or business, yet they chose the path. Some opted not to pursue their bliss for various reasons and yet those same people criticize others who set out to follow theirs. They support the erroneous belief it is impossible to follow your bliss.

In contrast, consider those people joyfully pursuing their bliss. I venture to say despite the obvious challenges, they carve out a unique place in the world. Challenges and obstacles are part of the journey; they illuminate the path to success and none are immune to it. Make a steadfast declaration on what you seek to attain in this life. If you're following your bliss, I wish you continued success and joy. If you're not there yet I hope these words ignite a deep desire to take inspired action. You are never too old, unqualified, set in your ways, lacking talent, or whatever justification your ego uses to convince you otherwise. I enjoy the quote from Stephen Pressfield's acclaimed book *The War of Art,* "Our job in this life is not to shape ourselves into some ideal we imagine we ought to be, but to find out who we already are and become it."

Overcome Self-Doubt To Live Passionately

You've been in this scenario before, the silent self-talk seeks to remind you of your destructive thoughts. The voice grows louder, repeating your known weaknesses. It continues to annoy you until you surrender. You give up, knowing it has taken hold. Welcome to 'self-doubt,' the intimidating inner critic which lives in your mind. The modest detractor determined to undermine your success. You're unable to release its hold on you. You know it's there, so why won't it leave you alone? You cannot vanish doubts despite your best intentions. Doubts are a part of our nature. It is a learned quality formed during your growth into adulthood. It begins with loved ones calling out not to climb that tree as a child for fear you might fall. The advice is echoed by imminent doom if you perform that action that leads us to self-doubt. I was a mischievous child as reminded by my mother. I pushed the boundaries of what was safe for children. The words 'no' and 'don't' were often recited at home to save me from my peril. If parents restricted their use of 'no' to children I'm certain they would not entertain self-doubt to the degree they do. It's no surprise that children need boundaries. I'm aware of it with my nephew at an impressionable age exploring the world: grabbing, touching, pulling apart, and destroying things in his line of vision. It's pleasing to see him learn and discover life around him. I am mindful as a caring adult that he plays safe and careful with my communication to avoid commands such as 'no,' 'can't,' or 'don't.' Instead, I distract him when he's destructive, offering something of better value which he responds to.

Your behavior results from childhood programming, and adults are notorious for creating incorrect stories about themselves. Doubt is a story often repeated through adulthood. It is healthy to have a level of doubt to make decisions. It allows you to be selective in considering other options. You examine ideas thoughtfully before engaging in your pursuit. There is another form of doubt more sinister and self-deprecating. One tells themselves stories and lies related to qualities they lack. I've witnessed self-doubt in my work assisting clients regain their health. They lie to themselves that they're not worthy of being healthy, loved, or respected. Perhaps this is thrust upon them as children and they adopt these beliefs into adult life.

Self-doubt requires examination if it prevents you living an authentic, rich, and abundant life. It requires investigation if you live in doubt of your abilities. Most people are content not to live for something greater than themselves. They store their emotions under the rug hoping it will go away. Years later, the emotions resurface as illness, destructive relationships or addiction to substances or behavior etc. Author Bruce Lipton in his book Spontaneous Evolution states that 95% of your behavior is controlled by your subconscious mind. Most of your learned behavior from birth to six years is subconscious. Most of what you learn is acquired during those formative years. Articles, books, and resources are written on self-doubt and most use 'conquering' dismissively like overcoming an illness. I'm suggesting doubt is part of your nature—your shadow self. You mustn't deny any aspect of yourself, for in doing so means that part of you will continue to seek representation.

Self-doubt means while being aware of the inner critic you

still take action in spite of it. In a documentary on accelerated free-falling, the interviewer asked the adventurer if he felt fear during jumps. His stated fear was present during every jump, yet he turned down the volume that prevented him from achieving his goal. My advice: Examine the root cause of self-doubt and what it may be inviting you to become. Is it concealing something you denied long ago? If your dream is to sing in front of thousands of people yet you entertain self-doubt, perhaps it teaches you to have faith in yourself. Often an internal shift is needed to fulfill your goal and self-doubt may be the way to attain it. Take inventory regarding your goals and vision. It's essential you examine the tools and resources required to get you there. Doubt is a speed hump in your journey. Speed humps slow you down but don't stop you. If you face self-doubt, examine the reason behind it. Don't allow it to get the better of you. Your vision should be greater than the obstacles in your path. Be kind and gentle with yourself. Beating yourself up over past failures and mistakes leads to more of the same thinking. Take action toward your goals by removing the doubts that hold you back. Seek guidance from loved ones or close friends if you're unable to navigate your way around. Remember, your journey toward awakening the Authentic Self is fraught with many detours, obstacles, and learnings. Don't recoil from the challenge; embrace and face it with open arms. Draw valuable lessons and insights along the way.

Play Big In The Game Of Life

Consider the following story of a man reading the morning newspaper who noticed his name in the obituary column.

Much to his surprise, the newspapers had reported the death of the wrong person. His first response was shock. When he regained his composure, he sought to find out what people said of him. The obituary read, "Dynamite King Dies" and "He was the merchant of death." Given the man was the inventor of dynamite, being christened the "merchant of death" was not how he wanted to be remembered. After a moment of reflection, he decided to renew his life purpose. From that day on, he vowed to work toward peace. His name was Alfred Nobel and he is widely known today by the great Nobel Prize.

How do you want to be remembered?

What lasting impression do you wish to leave behind?

While we seldom contemplate our own mortality, reflecting on the value of our life allows us to consider what is important. Life can be lived at an incredible pace that we sometimes fail to recognize its significance, no sooner than it vanishes. I urge you to play big in the game of life irrespective of fame, fortune, or success. It is vital we honor our talents, resources, and gifts to the best of our ability. It is your duty to bring to life the best version of yourself regardless of your limitations. To be your best is an evolving process, yet the one true constant is that you improve without settling. "What you believe about yourself and your world is the primary determinant to what you do and, ultimately, how well you do it," affirms sports psychologist Stan Beecham. What we receive in life is proportional to what we believe we deserve. History has shown less talented people having achieved outstanding success owing to their commanding self-belief.

I invite you to overcome your fears and push past your resistance as you make the leap forward. These two aspects alone keep you stranded because your life's objectives become diluted through the fog of separation. Sacrifice is essential in any field where the prize is big. Nothing is gained standing on the sidelines. Even time is a sacrifice when pursuing your passion. Those who play small receive smaller rewards. Those who take risks with little assurances are compensated owing to their enduring commitment. Life honors those willing to risk it all and play big. Author Robert Greene states, "In the end, the money and success that truly last come not to those who focus on such things as goals, but rather to those who focus on mastery and fulfilling their Life's Task." The life task he speaks of is your one true purpose that flames your inner desires and awakens your potential. Life mirrors your commitment to excellence. For this reason, be vigilant about how you spend your time and energy.

Similarly reframe failure as an investment in future success. Why have we become so scared of failure nowadays? I believe it's because we equate failure to self-worth. You are not a failure if an outcome does not result as planned. The outcome has failed, directing you to try a different approach next time. It was Albert Einstein who said if you want to live a happy life, tie it to a goal, not to people or things. You cannot lose in the game of life where lessons are learned and wisdom is gained. Success arrives when you least expect it, due to the hard work and tireless commitment to greatness. Self-doubt is a killer of many dreams; one should conquer it before it flourishes. Avoid cowering in defeat to rising doubts, yet rise above your challenges with renewed strength. Doubts are lingering thoughts that disappear when you take inspired action. In light of this, develop an insatiable self-belief and nurture it daily. Become the CEO of your own enterprise and command it with steadfast leadership. Don't wait for others to acknowledge your talents, genius, and gifts. Greet the world with passion and enthusiasm. Stan Beecham writes, "Beliefs control biology, biology controls behavior, and behavior determines success." Moreover, create your own definition of success. Don't be lulled into other people's definition of success since you'll forever chase your tail trying to live up to others' expectations. Focus on what matters and allow everything else not conducive to your potential to fall away. If it does not resonate with you, let it go so something better will fill its place.

Overcome your fears and focus on what you can achieve. If you are pulled by your fears, you perceive life from a constrained mindset. Reaching for the skies while lying on your back is not conducive to your potential. Get on your feet and make daily advances toward that which you seek. "Courage is your compass. It illuminates your path," avows Sean Patrick in *Awakening Your Inner Genius.* We all know success is attained through hard work and commitment. The mental and emotional resilience gained over time forms a successful mindset to attract the right opportunities. If we wish to be remembered after we're gone, we must live for something deeper while still alive. Alfred Nobel knew being an explosives expert was not how he intended to live out his days, so he created a new destiny. I urge you to think with the end in mind to live a significant life. From that space you create an exceptional life using your talents, gifts, and genius to serve others.

Go With The Flow

You are no doubt familiar with the expression, "Go with the flow." Those with honorable intentions like to advise us to sail with the speed of life. But what does it mean to go with the flow? What is flow and how do we benefit from being in flow? To go with the flow means offering less resistance to the currents of life. It means practicing the art of allowing than disallowing. For example, you might be resistant to the changes taking place in your life right now. Things may appear to be falling apart on the surface. This might be expressed as a distorted view of reality, an inaccurate view based on one's biased perception of what is taking place. What may be falling apart is may be making way for the new to enter. Some say that nature abhors a vacuum. The old and new cannot coexist, so parts of your life must recede to allow something better to fill its place.

Better said than done you might acknowledge. I appreciate chaos is an essential part of change. Tension often occurs right before a big breakthrough. It might be helpful to think of chaos as *ordered chaos* instead. Ordered chaos may be defined as disorganization leading to a significant breakthrough. According to the book *Flow: The Psychology of Optimal Experience*, Mihaly Csíkszentmihályi suggests that flow is a state of being measured by one's level of consciousness. He proposes that we have control how we interpret external events. He highlights examples of those inflicted with misfortune, showing how they created meaning amidst adversity. The distinction between Flow and the flow of life must be noted here. Yet the two can coexist at the same time. When we achieve a state of Flow as Mihaly Csíkszentmihályi suggests, we experience a state referred to as **optimal experience.** The longer we are in flow, the higher the state of consciousness is experienced. Those who experience flow include musicians, athletes, dancers or anyone tied to their passion.

Returning to the flow of life. As we become accustomed to

stepping back from the mental drama, we allow life to permeate through us. This requires courage as we are not privileged to knowing the outcome, which may be terrifying. Although, what may appear terrifying at first may become a blessing in disguise and your greatest learning experience. Surrendering control of how life should unfold amid the backdrop of drama and uncertainty, is valuable to maintain perspective. I relinquish the need to control life's outcomes as I have little control how life develops. You cannot influence the forces of life. Often one cannot even control their external environment let alone their thoughts. Life is subject to change so the universe thrives and expands. Have you noticed the natural rhythms and momentum of life? It may be too slow for some who prefer to ride in the fast lane. Frustration ensues when we wish events unfold faster than they do. Yet purpose is maintained for the speed at which life evolves. Instead of opposing these forces, you may find it worthwhile to cooperate with them. If we slowed to the speed of life, we offset our inner suffering and emotional turmoil. Our needs are met when we acknowledge universal energy to course through us. This often means getting out of our mind and into our hearts. To turn within means tuning in to your heart's desires. When mental chatter is prevalent, the language of the heart is drowned out by the drama playing out in the mind.

The egoic mind needs to be heard, since the heart expresses itself in silent whispers. The egoic mind clings to events and circumstances in order for it to survive. Break for a moment to become acquainted with the language of the ego. If you listen closely there is a constant need for "more," "not enough" or "missing out." These are ways it uses to communicate to you. It advises us if our needs are not met, we will be unhappy.

Although, we are likely to be unhappy regardless since that which we attract may not meet our expectations. It becomes a futile battle waged against your deeper self and reality—how can you win? By minding your inner sanctuary with gentleness and compassion. As you do so, your external reality harmonizes with your inner domain. Your outer world reflects your inner world. I am not suggesting we abandon our goals, dreams or ambitions. What if we *rolled with punches* by allowing what needs to happen do so with minimal interference? Life knows and sees all beyond our limited senses. A good starting point to go with the flow is learning to transform your worries, fears and anxieties. These lower emotional states feed off one another. The more energy you give them, the greater the emotional intensity. Transforming these energies into higher emotional states allows you to make peace with them, by attending to the messages the emotions convey. There is a hidden message contained within every experience. Delve deeper to discover that message and I can assure you a profound learning experience awaits you.

Chapter Summary

- *Free your heart of hatred and you'll be inspired. Avoid being biased or intolerant.*
- *Treat everyone with love and compassion and you'll find love around you in the smallest details.*
- *Sadly, most people never experience the joy of becoming their best since they fail to acknowledge their genius.*
- *Do not associate with your skills or passion alone since these are fleeting states.*
- *Your bliss may represent your calling. If you find joy conveying happiness and fulfillment to others, your bliss is a blessing.*
- *You are never too old, unqualified, set in your ways, lacking talent or whatever justification your ego uses to convince you otherwise.*
- *95% of behavior is controlled by your subconscious mind. Most of your learned behavior from birth to six years is subconscious.*
- *Self-doubt means while being aware of the inner critic you take action in spite of it.*
- *Doubt is a speed hump in your journey. Speed humps slow you down, not stop you.*
- *To be your best is an evolving process, yet the one*

true constant is that you improve without settling.

- *What you receive in life is proportional to what you believe you deserve.*
- *Life honors those willing to risk it all and play big.*
- *Reframe failure as an investment in future success.*
- *Develop an insatiable self-belief and nurture it daily. Become the CEO of your own enterprise and command it with steadfast leadership.*
- *Create your own definition of success. Don't be lulled into other people's definition of success since you'll forever chase your tail trying to live up to other's expectations.*
- *Think with the end in mind to live a significant life*
- *To go with the flow means offering less resistance to the currents of life. It means practicing the art of allowing rather than disallowing.*
- *When you achieve a state of flow as Mihaly Csíkszentmihályi suggests, you experience a state referred to as* **optimal experience.**
- *Frustration ensues when you wish events unfold faster than they do. Yet purpose is maintained for the speed at which life evolves.*
- *A good starting point to go with the flow is to*

transform your worries, fears, and anxieties. These lower emotional states feed off one another.

13

How To Create Meaningful Moments

> *"Do the difficult things while they are easy and do the great things while they are small. A journey of a thousand miles must begin with a single step."*
> —Lao Tzu

What Goes Around Comes Around

Fleming was a poor Scottish farmer. One day while out working in the fields, he heard a cry for help come from a nearby swamp. He dropped his tools and rushed to the swamp. There, stuck to his waist in black muck, was a terrified boy, screaming and struggling to free himself. Farmer Fleming saved the lad from what could have been a slow and terrifying death. The next day, a fancy carriage pulled up to the Scotsman's meager surroundings. A well-dressed nobleman stepped out and introduced himself as the father of the boy Farmer Fleming had saved.

"I want to repay you," said the nobleman. "You saved my son's life."

"No, I can't accept payment for what I did," the Scottish farmer replied, waving off the offer.

At that moment, the farmer's own son came to the door of the family cottage.

"Is that your son?" the nobleman asked.

"Yes," the farmer replied proudly.

"I'll make you a deal. Let me take him and give him a good education. If the lad is anything like his father, he'll grow to a man you can be proud of." And that he did. In time, Farmer Fleming's son graduated from St. Mary's Hospital Medical School in London and became known throughout the world as the noted Sir Alexander Fleming, the discoverer of penicillin. Years afterward, the nobleman's son was stricken with pneumonia. What saved him? Penicillin. The name of the nobleman? Lord Randolph Churchill. His son's name? Sir Winston Churchill.

What goes around comes around.

For many the notion of karma is a common theme which permeates throughout their life. The adage *what goes around comes around* is identified by those unfairly treated. The understanding that dishonest acts against others catch up to the offender is acknowledged. Karma is far more complicated and yet simpler than that. Karma functions within the backdrop of our lives. Newton's Third Law states that every action has an equal and opposite reaction. There is a cause and effect, so that every action creates another reaction, which produces a new counteraction. Thus an endless chain of actions and reactions is created. In a similar vein to Newton's Law, the butterfly effect by the American mathematician and meteorologist Edward Lorenz affirms, "When a butterfly flutters its wings in one part of the world, it can eventually cause a hurricane in another." Lorenz unified the theory that events within the cosmos have a ripple effect, which extends beyond the space and time realm. Closer to home, karma's actions have a ripple and boomerang effect in your life and the lives of others. Karma is the exchange of energy from one form to another. It should be viewed as neither good nor bad since it allows us to assume purposeful action if we are to balance out karma in our lives. In the same way, karmic clutter represents unresolved matters of the past. If karma is not balanced out, it invites negative consequences of past actions into the present moment. To heal the emotional baggage associated with anger, frustration, and disappointment, balance is upheld. From this viewpoint, karma preserves balance—no debt goes unpaid, no act of good service is turned a blind eye to. Our actions are supported within the moral landscape of, "Do unto others what you would have done unto yourself."

However well-meaning your intentions, upholding your moral duties does not assume others will return your goodwill. We are endowed with free will and how others treat you becomes their karma. For we repeatedly write the script of our karmic destiny through our actions. In the scheme of things, bad things happen to good people every day. Our obligation is to abide by our highest moral code since it allows us to become a righteous culture. We can become victims of our choices or write an empowering moral script for the future. It begs the question, "Is the universe vested in goodness?" I affirm the underlying structure governing universal laws is aligned within the framework of love—the highest functioning order. Good deeds are returned when your intentions are honorable and entrusted with love. The universe eavesdrops on your actions, intending to balance out the exchange of energy. It was the Greek physicist-philosopher Parmenides who stated that *nature abhors a vacuum*. Which means, as you let go of the old (thoughts, beliefs, energy, ideas, and toxic emotions), the universe rushes in to fill the void. As energy is repaid through favorable action, you abide by universal forces when you act in accordance with nature. Think of universal forces as observing road and traffic laws; everything flows seamlessly in the presence of order instead of chaos. Have you noticed how some people attract their desires in a relaxed manner while others struggle? It might be said those same people are working with the laws of karma in a conducive manner.

On a personal level as I honor my path in life, I harness the law of karma to act in a meaningful way. Wisdom has shown me that when I am wronged, rather than seek revenge, I trust karma to balance any improper actions against me or others. It is not my place to enact retribution or revenge—my karma is to play my role within the function of universal order. It is Dr. Wayne Dyer who reminds us to uphold this virtue: "How people treat you is their karma; how you react is yours." Life is neither fair nor unfair. To evaluate life according to this way of thinking fails to acknowledge the harmony present when we play by her rules. You have the wherewithal to change your future karma through awareness gained within the present moment. Do not be directed by subconscious actions alone. Be mindful, present, and aware of your choices. I am drawn to the aphorism by the Chinese philosopher Lao Tzu: "Watch your thoughts; they become words. Watch your words;

they become actions. Watch your actions; they become habit. Watch your habits; they become character. Watch your character; it becomes your destiny."

You Can't Always Get What You Want

To create meaningful moments, we must be mindful of not getting what we want. This becomes the root cause of suffering for many, yet this is the process of life and we take refuge knowing our needs are met at the right time. In the famous Rolling Stones song it was singer Mick Jagger who reminds us of life's greatest paradox. Over the years, the song line has evoked mixed feelings with me, given aspects I do not side with. Life has a mysterious force unbeknown to us. Often events transpire from an experience in which a lesson ensues. For example, if life seeks to teach you trust, it gives you an experience opposed to what you expect. You may be involved in a business relationship with someone who undermines your well-meaning intentions. In doing so, life tests your resolve to trust others so you learn self-empowerment. Mainstream culture affirms we can have whatever we want as long as we pursue it with honorable intentions. I am of the opinion we do not have free will; rather, we have **free choice**, operating within the container of a universe co-creating your life's experience. Therefore, when we don't get what we want, free will takes a backseat in the orchestration of life's events. When I exercise free choice and collaborate with universal forces, everything I **want** and **need** shows up at the right time.

Allow me to illustrate with a personal example. Having graduated from high school I had mixed feelings about the course of study to pursue at university. Like most high school students, I had strengths and weaknesses in certain subjects, although I did not excel in one stream. Upon my final year of school, I applied to study commerce at university and an opposing course, a bachelor of arts in fashion design. Since I grew up in a household of skilled artisans—my father was a tailor and my mother was a dressmaker—I showed an inclination toward the fine arts late in childhood. I recall sitting beside my father's antique sewing machine as a child. I observed for hours as he crafted fine luxurious fabrics into high-quality suits. Later, a university lecturer inferred I learned a visual language in tailoring after these years. I'm selected among thousands of applicants for the fashion design course. Equally, I miss out on selection for the commerce course which leads me to believe there are no accidents in life. The fashion design selection committee was fascinated by my technical knowledge of menswear, and thus began my time studying to become a designer.

Fast-forward several years to my final year of study. I collaborate with an Italian fashion company to produce a tailored menswear collection, inspired by my late father's work. The collection catches the eye of those abroad and I'm offered design positions in Italy and New York respectively. But life had other plans. While in Italy, I'm struck down with chicken pox within days of my arrival and bedridden for two weeks. I packed my portfolio intending to visit various design houses to present my work. Several years later my father passes away from complications from type II diabetes. This heralds yet another turning point in my life, in which my time as a successful menswear designer is eroded. As I write, I recollect how unpredictable my journey has been. I could not have expected nor scripted the outcome of my life in such detail. Nowadays I remain in awe of the incredible gift and wisdom to communicate the message of health and self-empowerment to people. Some step into their purpose while others are called to theirs. Thankfully I'm glad things worked out the way they did. I affirm we get what we need because what we need serves our highest potential. What we want is what the ego wants and is not aligned with our highest self.

In his writings, author Neale Donald Walsch talks of the soul's agenda opposing the ego's. He suggests your soul's agenda is not vested in the material world; rather it is rooted in the personal evolution of your soul. What the soul desires and what the ego needs are distinct. When ego conflicts with your soul's agenda we experience suffering and inner turmoil. For those blessed to discover their passion and purpose, there's great fulfillment knowing you are in alignment with your soul's plan. I believe when our soul's needs are met, we achieve harmony and inner bliss. Remember the words of the mystic Joseph Campbell: "following your bliss and the universe will open doors for you where there were only walls." The benevolent cosmos knows our needs and keeps us moving toward a greater plan. When you veer off track, the universe guides you back as a reminder of your purpose and dharma is greater than your ego's agenda.

How To Live Fully In The Present Moment

Meaningful moments appear when we are focused on the present moment. You cannot be recalling the past hurt and live fully in the now because your mind is not engaged with your present moment experience. The mind and body must learn to occupy this space in time together to live an authentic life. Your mind can fluctuate between a stressful thought about a future event while simultaneously recalling a thought from the past. You become caught in a vise-like grip buried between two thoughts which hold you captive. You abandon hope of remaining grounded in the present moment, despite your best intentions to let go of the incessant thoughts. This scenario is an all-too-familiar scene in our lives. Our minds are consumed with thinking and analyzing, not to mention the accompanying emotions which drive our thought patterns.

In his book *A Whole New Mind,* author Daniel Pink believes the future will belong to the "right brain" thinkers who think in whole terms. The right brain is considered to be complete, integrated, and holistic while the left is logical, analytical, and objective. To live in the present moment invites you to draw on your right brain, which is the seat of intuition. The importance of leaning toward right-brain thinking allows the integration of our sixth sense, intuition. This faculty or subtle knowledge weaves itself throughout our life, allowing us to reconnect back to the importance of being in the present moment. You have heard it said that the past and the future are merely illusions, since they don't exist in the NOW. Where are they? The past is a memory and the future has not yet arrived. We replay aspects of our past, whether consciously or unconsciously and bring it into the present moment. Our interactions with others are referenced by past conditioning. If a friend does not return a phone call, you feel hurt, angry, and betrayed even though there may be a logical reason for not calling. We are quick to jump to conclusions that we have been unfairly treated. Our subconscious thoughts recall our past hurts by creating the accompanying emotions to support them. This happens in a split second and we fall victim to ourselves. *In Way of The Peaceful Warrior,* self-help author and speaker Dan Millman reminds us of the importance of this moment: "The time is now, the place is here. Stay in the present. You can do nothing to change the past, and the future will never come exactly as you plan or hope for."

To experience timeless health and well-being it is important to be centered in the moment. Those who live in the past invite mental stress disguised as regret, fear, and anxiety. Similarly, those who are future oriented live with fear, worry, and anger since they anticipate a future which never arrives as planned. A well-known aphorism states that since your body is in the present moment, so should your thoughts be. This is what is meant when one talks about the mind-body connection—integrating the mind and body so they are in harmony and union with one another. Mind and body cannot be united if your thoughts are anywhere but in the present moment. It is widely accepted that those who live in the past or future surrender their personal power, reducing the capacity to create their ideal life circumstances. Opportunities are lost since they wish things to be as they were or hope life unfolds in a certain way. Their minds are caught up in a battle yearning for something more. As evident via Dan Millman's quote, the future never arrives as we plan or hope for. It stands to reason that we attend to the present moment with deep attentiveness. While it is good for me to espouse the virtues of living in the present moment, it is a challenge to keep our attention focused in the present, since we are at the mercy of our thoughts. These thoughts would have you know of your opposition to this moment. The ego will convince you the present moment does not live up to what you imagined, so suffering ensues.

So what can you do about it? How can you live fully in the present? Firstly, learn to witness your thoughts with an open heart and through the eyes of compassion. Many people who notice their thoughts are out of control respond unkindly. Do not attempt to silence your mind, since that only agitates it. To witness means to observe without creating a dialogue to support the thoughts. An effective way for reconnecting with one's Authentic Self and the present moment is to draw your attention to your breath. Earlier I spoke about the mind-body connection. To integrate your thoughts with your body allows you to be present and aware. You shift your attention away from the incessant thoughts and into your body. Close your eyes and focus your awareness on your nostrils. Don't allow other distractions to enter your mind. Focus on breathing in and out for five breaths. Do this as often as you need to throughout the day, when you find yourself stressed for no reason. The practice of mindfulness allows you to reconnect to the present moment because we shift our attention to what is taking place within us. Mindfulness tames the mind through focused attention. So a simple act of doing the dishes can be a rewarding experience. Of course, it takes practice and patience to become mindful, yet the rewards are certainly worth it.

Connect With Mind Body & Spirit

I wish to present you with an uncommon view of reality. For the next five minutes, the time it takes you to read and integrate this information, I intend to put forward an alternative view of life which you may not have previously considered. Indulge me as I outline a case for the benefits of merging mind, body, and spirit. I have written considerably about the mind, body, and spirit association in recent times, going so far as to devote a book on this topic which outlines how to integrate these aspects. I uphold to reconcile with these elements is vital for living an authentic life. When I talk about authentic, I am referring to living in harmony with your true nature. When you are aligned with your essential being, you transcend imposed limitations. Life resides through moments of inspiration rather than perspiration. Life has meaning and purpose at this level of being. As you connect with mind, body, and spirit, you experience success, happiness, joy, and the fullness of life. You cease to identify with fear and lower emotional states, which place immense resources on your mental, physical, and emotional well-being—in essence, you rise above these limitations. Your thoughts and emotions become an extension of your deepest self. You develop a deep-rooted connection to your spiritual self which is aligned with your life's purpose.

To awaken to your Authentic Self is to allow universal intelligence to direct your personal evolution. Throughout your childhood and adult life you may have created a fictitious mind-made tale based on who you thought you were. You painted a distorted image upon the canvas of your life by reinforcing the beliefs: "I am not good enough," "I am not talented enough," and "I am not worthy of receiving love." It is essential that you cease to identify with these beliefs, since this is not who you really are. To live in harmony with nature's plan requires you to unite with mind, body, and spirit. If you identify with your body for example, as many people do, your happiness is subject to your material form. What happens to your self-image as your body ages or you become ill? It is for this reason many people mistakenly identify with their illness or their aging body at this point in their life—but that is not who they are. Similarly, ego seeks to reinforce its image through your material form, while spirit does not define itself through labels—it is eternal and formless. As you come to appreciate that you are comprised of the material and non-material self, your body moves toward higher states of health, radiant energy, beauty, and the vitality of life flowing through it. Allow me to render a caveat—it takes time and commitment to evolve into the person I am describing. What is the hurry? The urgency to lose weight NOW is merely a marketing tactic to deprive you of your hard-earned dollars. Nature does not subscribe to this ideal, nor should you. She is patient and enduring. Humans are the only mammals where the young have the longest developmental period—there is a reason and purpose to nature's timing. Slow and steady are nature's trademark; there is no haste or urgency to life.

In keeping with this line of thought, health is not an event, rather it is a PROCESS which evolves over time. There is no need to rush the process of life. A person in alignment with their authentic nature knows any disturbance to their well-being is only transient. They have a universal view that life is an enduring process. They are not invested in their mental or emotional state, knowing thoughts and emotions come and go like ocean tides. They witness their thoughts like waves crashing into the shoreline. They know that in time, these thoughts too shall pass, much like the changing seasons. I trust you will value your health and well-being in a different light. I assure you that as you connect with mind, body, and spirit, your life will transform in numerous ways. You will look back with uncertainty and not understand why it took so long to achieve a blissful state of being. Remember, patience and persistence will undoubtedly prosper in the long term. You should make it a priority from this moment forward to evolve into somebody worthy of living an authentic and captivating life.

How To Create Meaningful Moments In Life

Life can pass by and we neglect to appreciate the pockets of time interwoven into meaningful moments. Throughout this book you are called to experience reality, rather than make sense of it at the level of the mind. Life's captivating mysteries can flash by in an instant if we dwell on the past too long or expect the future to arrive as we hope. To create meaningful moments is to stay present and grounded while letting go of mental distractions. For that is the capricious monkey mind seeking to assert its will because it strives to be heard. Meaningful moments exist in everyday life, yet when reality does not conform to our mental image, suffering ensues. "This is one way we can practice cultivating, on a daily basis, the radiant moment-to-moment awareness of interbeing, of meaningful connection and profound belonging of undefended openness and warm-hearted oneness with one and all," states Lama Surya Das. The answer lies in letting go of diversions and disempowering thoughts which disallow us to connect to the present moment. To be mindful of our thoughts instead of stuck in a subconscious state is a good reason to avoid reacting to life's events. Mindfulness engages us to be present and inhabit our body with intention and receptivity. We let go of expecting life to unfold in a particular way and accept what shows up to embrace it with curiosity. If we are irritated by life's events and react to it, we reinforce our suffering. Consider this, do you want to be right or do you want to be happy?

In the film *Anna and The King*, Prince Chulalongkorn played by actor Keith Chin declares to Anna Leonowens, played by Jodie Foster, "It is always surprising how small a part of life is taken up by meaningful moments. Most often they're over before they start even though they cast a light on the future and make the person who originated them unforgettable." To recognize meaningful moments, stop rushing to the next event and consider what is taking place before you. Our thoughts convince us there's something wrong with the present moment and we need to fix it to feel better. There are no problems in this moment, except our perception of it. It was Victor Frankl, the Austrian psychiatrist and Holocaust survivor who said, "When we are no longer able to change a situation—we are challenged to change ourselves." To create meaningful moments, we connect with others on a deeper level. In today's technologically advanced society, people hide behind screens to connect with others. While it has allowed us to stay connected, many of these connections are insincere relationships devoid of human contact. Do you want to go through life collecting human thumbnails to display on your computer screen "wall," or do you want to form deeper meaningful connections? Relationships create an opportunity for meaningful moments because they enrich our life. Regretfully, many people perceive them with disillusionment, because they orient their attention on the negative aspects. There is balance in every relationship, which means there's equal harmony and disharmony. To focus on disharmony alone distorts our view of the intricate connection between people.

Life can be notorious for pulling us in different directions. We become distracted and lose our way. Yet if we stay focused on what's essential, we place esteemed value on those areas. Dennis Merritt Jones reminds us to live an authentic life from which meaningful moments arise: "Living an authentic life is probably the most challenging thing a human being can endeavor to undertake because it is not the way of the world, but it is the way of the heart that connects you to what is real, what is meaningful, and what is eternal." The courage to live life on our terms can be profoundly meaningful when we follow our inner compass instead of abiding by other people's terms. It must be said, we alone ascribe meaning to the events of our life. Some attach deeper meaning while others see no causal relationship to that which transpires. I've often felt profound meaningful moments immersed in nature. In that instance I feel a deep connection to life. I get out of my head and allow life to flow through me.

Meaningful moments are interspersed throughout life, not in the acquisition of material possessions. So make it a priority to lean toward events which enrich your life, such as traveling to new places. Embark on these journeys with loved ones to reinforce your connection to life and those around you. Likewise, being of service to others fosters meaningful moments. In donating our time and self, we enhance our life through altruistic deeds. Similarly, we must adopt the right mindset to become attuned to such moments, instead of dismissing them as unimportant. Or else, we fail to miss out on wonderful experiences obscured as otherwise ordinary moments. Rather than speculate on reality we must embody it. Meaningful moments are a fabric of everyday life masquerading as familiar events. Don't let them pass you by.

Chapter Summary

- *Karma functions within the backdrop of your life. Newton's Third Law states that every action has an equal and opposite reaction.*
- *Karma is the exchange of energy from one form to another. It should be viewed as neither good nor bad, since it allows for purposeful action to balance out karma in your life.*
- *Karma preserves balance—no debt goes unpaid, no act of good service is turned a blind eye to.*
- *You are endowed with free will and how others treat you becomes their karma.*
- *Good deeds are returned when your intentions are honorable and entrusted with love. The universe eavesdrops on your actions, intending to balance out the exchange of energy.*
- *Do not be directed by subconscious actions alone. Be mindful, present, and aware of your choices.*
- *We do not have free will, rather, you have **free choice**, operating within the container of a universe co-creating your life's experience.*
- *When your soul's needs are met, you achieve harmony and inner bliss.*

- *Meaningful moments appear when you are focused on the present moment.*
- *The right brain is considered to be complete, integrated, and holistic, while the left is logical, analytical, and objective.*
- *To live in the present moment invites you to draw on your right brain, which is the seat of intuition.*
- *To experience timeless health and well-being, it is important to be centered in the moment.*
- *A well-known aphorism states that since your body is in the present moment, so should your thoughts be.*
- *To witness means to observe without creating a dialogue to support the thoughts.*
- *Mindfulness tames the mind through focused attention. So a simple act of doing the dishes can be a rewarding experience.*
- *Life resides through moments of inspiration rather than perspiration. Life has meaning and purpose at this level of being.*
- *Ego seeks to reinforce its image through your material form, while spirit does not define itself through labels—it is eternal and formless.*
- *To create meaningful moments is to stay present and grounded while letting go of mental distractions.*
- *Meaningful moments exist in everyday life, yet*

when reality does not conform to your mental image, suffering ensues.

- *Let go of diversions and disempowering thoughts which disallow you from connecting to the present moment.*
- *To recognize meaningful moments, stop rushing to the next event and consider what is taking place before you.*
- *To create meaningful moments, connect with others on a deeper level.*
- *The courage to live life on your terms can be profoundly meaningful when you follow your inner compass instead of abiding by other people's terms.*
- *You alone ascribe meaning to the events of your life. Some attach deeper meaning while others see no causal relationship to that which transpires.*

14

Live The Life You Desire

> *"The will to win, the desire to succeed, the urge to reach your full potential...these are the keys that will unlock the door to personal excellence."*
> —*Confucius*

The Road To Excellence

I wish to impress upon you that excellence arises when we develop the mental discipline to obey and collaborate with nature's laws. Richo writes, "The Zen poet Basho says: 'All who have achieved real excellence in any art possess one thing in common, a mind to obey nature, to be one with nature throughout the four seasons of the year.' Individual plans are therefore secondary to the larger purposes of a flowing universe." To attain excellence, we must be acquainted with its qualities. For example, success is measured against others' achievements while excellence is an individual pursuit. Leadership expert Robin Sharma says we should strive to be our best to attain excellence: "Be so ridiculously great at what you do that the world cannot help but give you an audience." In a similar vein the comedic genius Steve Martin said, "Be so good they can't ignore you." Excellence is the hallmark of an Authentic Self because we harness our wisdom, genius, and talents to enrich the lives of others. Excellence is attained by providing more than expected. Not only do we exceed others' expectations, we enrich their lives by being of service and adding value. There is much discussion these days regarding achieving success. Thought leaders offer wavering advice on strategies to climb your way to the top. Yet as we pursue excellence, success is there to greet us if our actions are firm. Consider the following formula for excellence:

Excellence→Personal Growth→Results→Success = Prosperity

In discussing excellence I'm reminded of those who surpass our wildest expectations. They are: Olympic athletes, music performers, artists, and dancers to name a few, having accumulated 10,000 hours of deliberate practice. "It is a lifetime accumulation of deliberate practice that again and again ends up explaining excellence," states Cal Newport in *So Good They Can't Ignore You*. Excellence invites us to become the center of our universe. We live life defined by smaller acts of distinction once we have mastered our inner domain. "Achieving excellence is one part human participation, but the other part is some kind of divine intervention that I am yet to fully understand. It is these types of questions that make me believe that life really is worth living, despite all the pain and gnashing of teeth we must go through," states Sport Psychologist Stan

Beecham. The ancient Greek philosopher Epicurus considered excellence to be natural in that we inherently seek pleasure and avoid pain. In the Ancient Greek language, the word Areté means excellence of any kind and signifies moral virtue. Human excellence is the psychological basis for carrying out the activities of a human life in a positive manner; to that extent human excellence is also happiness.1 Similarly, we can see excellence is characterized by moral virtues. The moral virtue relevant to fear, for instance, is courage.1 Likewise, it was Aristotle who said, "We are what we repeatedly do. Excellence, then, is not an act, but a habit." To live a life of excellence we must identify with our core values and live them as best we can. To live according to our highest virtues while aware of the complexity of our human nature. To know oneself at a deeper level, we overcome the restraints of our unconscious past to realize inner freedom. In a similar vein, honoring our emotional well-being is paramount for living an authentic life. This is recognized by our commitment to honor our self-worth rather than be dictated to by disempowering states. We refuse to be defined by our limiting beliefs and challenge them when they no longer serve us.

Many people navigate life unaware of their limiting beliefs and accept them as the fabric of their being. Yet through our understanding of brain neuroplasticity and epigenetics, we know nothing is fixed or permanent including our thoughts. It would be remiss of me to get this far and not mention the work of Carol Dweck who states, "This growth mindset is based on the belief that your basic qualities are things you can cultivate through your efforts. Although people may differ in every which way—in their initial talents and aptitudes, interests, or temperaments—everyone can change and grow through application and experience." So by adopting a growth mindset we surge toward excellence and the springboard to success. Excellence is attained when we let go of thoughts and beliefs which no longer harmonize with our deepest being. If they don't allow us to live to our highest moral code, we must dispose of them in place of those that uphold our best conduct. To live a life of excellence is a call toward wholehearted living, irrespective of our comparisons to others. It is our authentic power that permits mutual cooperation with ourselves and others. We answer the call of our inner spirit when we pursue integrity and nurture our commitment to support our highest position. It is well known that success can lead to complacency, because we are lulled into settling once our goals and objectives are met. In contrast, excellence is marked by continued improvement instead of being outcome-focused. This is what Carol Dweck refers to when she favors developing a Growth Mindset instead of a Fixed Mindset.

The path to excellence is lined with many detours, failures, and setbacks. The greatest inventors of our century experienced countless failures and disasters, yet these blunders did not discourage them from eventual success. Therefore, an unwavering passion and commitment is paramount for attaining excellence. Let us not be blinded by the promise of success; rather, we pursue excellence for what it brings to our life. After all, success is a destination while excellence is an enduring journey of self-discovery and blinding detours. May those detours lead you to the highest excellence throughout your life.

The Value Of Following Through

There's a story of a well-known motivational speaker who showed up onstage to an auditorium packed full of paid members. They come to hear him talk about wealth creation and the auditorium is filled with twenty thousand people. Following an introduction, he asked the audience to raise their hands if they want to know how to create wealth. Naturally, everyone's hand went up. The next bit was interesting. He states less than 90% of the people present will not follow through with their intention and those people should go home because they are wasting their time. Each person paid close to $1,000 to learn about wealth creation and was told to go home because they don't have the wherewithal to follow through. If you are one of those 90%, I'm certain you would find that confrontational. Yet he's right. John Assaraf, who featured in the film *The Secret* and is an international best-selling author, speaker, and entrepreneur, states that out of 100 people who state they wish to make $1,000,000 dollars a year, only three people will follow through to succeed. Here's his breakdown:

- 20% of the 100 have an excuse why they fail
- Of the remaining 80 people, 16% will drop off
- Of the 64 who remain, 32 will give up within 6 months
- Of the 32 remaining, 90% of them will give up since they did it their way

Therefore, of the 100 people who start, only three have what it takes to follow through with their commitment. The same statistic can be seen during Navy Seal training, known as BUD/

S (Basic Underwater Demolition/SEAL) which boasts an attrition rate of 75% to 80%. According to John, only 3% of the total population have what it takes to listen, learn, apply, and make things happen. I find it interesting as a statistic, yet compelling given the few people who succeed in their respective field. In my work as a health and self-empowerment speaker and coach, I've observed the same incidence with people looking to improve their health. At first glance, physical changes manifest once a health regime is implemented. You're eating and sleeping right, coupled with regular movement and reduced stress levels. Suddenly, a major challenge arises and you find yourself derailed from your goal. You make excuses about how busy you are, how little time you have, or other pressing matters that impede your health goals. Soon enough, your hard work is thrown out the window and you're right where you started. At this stage, you confirm how difficult it is to achieve the goals after all. Sadly, this represents 90% of the world population's thinking regarding goal attainment.

Self-improvement and health are a perfect union based on this scenario. When you work on yourself at the mental and physical level, wonderful things happen. What appear as obstacles now turn into opportunities. Challenges give rise to inner growth and transformation instead of setbacks. You edge closer to the imagined self you entertained when first setting out on your journey. The person who succeeds in their goals, their vision, and mastery of self is the one who follows through and sticks with it, **no matter what life throws at them.** Read that sentence aloud and commit it to memory. To achieve a goal, your WHY must be greater than any challenge or obstacle life presents you; otherwise, you will crumble at the first sign of resistance. Your WHY must be great enough, you leap out of bed before the alarm goes off each morning. Your setbacks point you toward your personal growth, so embrace the experience and lessons that show up. Your mind sees the seeds of opportunity in each failure instead of retreat in defeat. This is the hallmark of the successful mind. It is oriented to look for opportunities, even in the direst situations. It is world-acclaimed motivational speaker Tony Robbins who states: "There is no such thing as failure, only undesired outcomes."

Are you prepared to live the life you desire? Do you look for excuses when the going gets tough? Do you sabotage your success when things go well? Personal development entails personal growth. We experience inner growth when stretched to our limit and step out of our comfort zone. You recognize inner impediments are the reason you are limited in your success. You nurture those impediments while being attentive to transform them from obstacles to victories. A gardener acts the same way when weeding a garden. He knows crops cannot thrive in a garden bed ridden with weeds. Your mind is the garden, while the weeds and limiting beliefs must be attended to if you wish to harvest healthy crops. No matter the challenge, be it health, relationships, career, money, or otherwise, turn inward to examine the resistance. Pull out the weeds and replace them with empowering thoughts of success and excellence. You deserve to be the best you can be and what holds you back is perpetuated by inner resistance alone. Release the shackles to lead you closer to the greatness that awaits.

How To Successfully Navigate Life

To demonstrate how resistance infiltrates our life, a friend was considering his options for the following years of his academic life. Upon completion of studies, he will take a year off to work serving as a gap year; a pivotal period in a student's academic life. In his early twenties, my friend is concerned he will not be interested in working in his respective field of study. I suggested that life is a journey with many bridges to cross. When you approach a decision to your future path, you must first cross the bridge. The bridge may be likened to a major life decision. To navigate your way forward, you must know the direction you're headed, for the path will reveal itself. You never know what surprises await you along this journey and that is the exciting and anxiety driven part of life. The past serves as a guide to the future, given life unfolds in perpetual moments.

Your thoughts and emotions creates the future from the present moment. To navigate life, be aware and conscious of the present moment—that is, the thoughts and decisions you make now will influence your future. The future is created from the seed of opportunity within the present moment. Future events are only present moment possibilities. While this may sound abstract, you have little knowledge of future events from your present-day awareness, given it's yet to arrive. However, you have control of your thoughts, emotions and actions in each present moment. The future is created in the NOW. It is worth re-addressing this idea again. If you fail to embrace this principle, you will experience mental suffering which arises when we don't get what we want or it doesn't manifest in the form we wish. The future arrives quicker than you realize. It reveals itself in ways you cannot expect. Be prepared, be awake and receptive to what shows up. Follow your intuition, for the heart communicates in wisdom the mind cannot grasp. With that reflect on the following three steps toward creating the future you desire.

1. Honor Your Path

To honor your path invites you stay true to yourself no matter the obstacles that show up during the journey. Many give up too soon when they meet the slightest challenges. They believe life is better lived having fun and not making sacrifices. How much do you want to fulfill your goal, ambitions, or dreams? Is it a burning desire that emanates from within? If so, there's a good chance you'll be committed to it when the going gets tough. If your goal is that of another person's, you're not living life supported by your desires. Ask yourself WHY am I doing this? What do I wish to achieve? How will life look when I achieve this goal? Who can I help along the way while using my talents and genius? When you have the answers that resonate with you, you're committed to honoring your path despite the roadblocks or obstacles.

2. Be Well Prepared

Preparation not only means being physically prepared but mentally and emotionally. Learning about universal laws has been instrumental to navigate my way through life. Knowing life presents us with ebbs and flows allows me to understand things will not always go according to MY plan. I remain receptive to the cycle of life and work with those forces. I trust I am being supported in my endeavors when I honor my path. If I venture outside my jurisdiction, the universe advises me in no uncertain terms to regain my focus. To be prepared means no matter the obstacles you encounter, they are placed in your path for your greatest growth. You may fall upon circumstances which you believe unfair. The breakup of a romantic relationship may appear devastating at first. While there's a period of grief, these are transitional leading toward a greater lesson—an inner resolve that everything will turn out for the best. Look at your next challenge as a blessing, an opportunity to learn and gain a new insight. It may not be the lesson you want or hope for, yet its arrival is orchestrated to awaken your Authentic Self. If life seeks to teach you love, be willing to experience heartbreak. Life gives you the opposite experience so you may have wings to fly.

3. Remain Vigilant

The toughest terrain in the world lay waiting in the recesses of your mind. When you overcome these obstacles, your journey takes on new meaning. Remain vigilant and committed when honoring your path, despite the difficult times ahead. Vigilance is a state of being. It's a way of asserting one's mental state, despite outward conditions. You stay receptive that your journey is fulfilled. These principles work together in harmony when put into practice. You cannot have one without the other. To achieve your goals far exceeds the turmoils of life. Use these principles as foundations to navigate your way toward the life of your dreams. Decide that you'll stay on the path no matter the challenges. Trust you'll be shown the path ahead as you approach a bridge or crossing. The bridge serves as a connection between the past and the future. Be daring to cross each bridge to pave the way ahead to a remarkable life.

The Power Of Persistence

To live an authentic life, it's vital to harness the power of persistence which yields positive outcomes. Observe a child nag his mother to buy him something from a store, yet the child persists and receives what he wants. He may even resort to whining or crying to get his way. Chances are persistence paid off, because children recognize persistence pays off most times, as mum and dad will give in if enough whining or crying occurs. There is a power in persistence that can be used in negative ways (like the child) or positive ways. If you ask successful businessmen how they got to where they are today, they will say persistence is a key characteristic that helped them become successful.

Persistence means to keep going despite obstacles or setbacks, to continue moving forward despite the terrain. Persistence is a powerful force that can be harnessed toward success. Success doesn't fall into your lap; you must take action and like climbing a ladder; it takes action one step at a time. Abraham Lincoln is a prime example of persistence in action. Known as one of the greatest presidents in history, he lost eight elections before he became president. He lost his business twice and could've written himself off from being a failure, but he didn't. He was persistent and believed he could achieve his dreams. Another great example is the wonderful children's writer, Dr. Seuss. His book *And to Think I Saw It on Mulberry Street* was rejected by twenty-seven publishers before being published. Many people give up after a handful of rejections, but he persisted. Dr. Seuss became one of the greatest children's book writers around, selling more than 200 million copies of his books. If you're passionate, chances are you're persistent in moving toward it. Is it your goal to become a published author? Then you must be persistent in your writing and even after you receive 10 or 100 rejection letters for your book proposal. I've read about many professional athletes, artists, business owners, etc. that faced setbacks yet determined to persist their way to success. What's your passion? Were you once passionate toward something, yet shelved your plans because things weren't going as fast as you'd liked? I admonish you to dig deep and rediscover the passions and make a plan to go forward with persistence toward fulfilling them. It's easier to give up on your dreams than to persist through disappointments and setbacks, but easy won't fulfill you. A sense of plowing through obstacles, fears, and setbacks will fulfill you day in and day out. To know you're set on persisting through obstacles to get what you want is a liberating.

Now you appreciate that persistence is powerful and necessary, you might wonder how to incorporate it into your life. It's not as difficult as you think. To be persistent means not giving up on your goals no matter what happens. It's looking at whatever comes along and being determined to overcome it as best as you can, so you can continue on your journey toward success. Sometimes hurdles emerge and you're not sure what course of action to take. It's all right not to have all the answers. When you're unsure of your next step, research to learn how you can handle the situation. There are tools and resources to handle life's situations and people who faced what you're dealing with. Are you experiencing a halt in your progress? Talk to someone who's been there and seek advice. Are you frustrated or considering giving up? Look at your problems from a different perspective, go to a seminar, or hire a Life Coach to breathe new life into your dreams. Sometimes it takes sharing your frustration with others to gain fresh insights and revelations. You can learn to harness the power of persistence to achieve your goals and dreams. Adopt an "I can do it no matter what!" attitude and see how your forward motion picks up speed. It might not always go as planned but you will move forward. Give yourself permission to move forward, soaring on the power of persistence toward fulfilling your passions.

Don't Give Up On Your Dreams

Life happens to us. Sometimes situations arise which we must meet head on, other times it feels like we're putting out spot fire. To highlight this, I've been in a precarious position recently. Sure I experience bad days and weeks like many others, yet on this occasion, I was in despair. In reviewing my finances, I was alarmed how much it cost to pursue my dream. I realized if I continue under these circumstances, I'll be looking for employment instead. It was a daunting period of personal growth since I was unaware of the financial burden imposed on me. It's said raising that a child is a communal responsibility, I suggest the same is true of success. Reflect on these questions for a moment. Who are influential people in your life? How are they shaping your success? People come into our lives at the right time whether for a reason or a season and often your greatest breakthroughs occur within a short time. You may be faced with an insurmountable challenge or obstacle. The weight of the world is on your shoulders with little way to navigate ahead. Fear not, every time you face obstacles, you're invited to grow. While this advice may not be understood at the level of awareness to aid you at the time, trust you are taken care of.

Pursuing one's dream is filled with obstacles, dead ends, stop signs, and speed humps. The right path will be made known to you when the going gets tough. Sometimes, it's revealed when you least expect it, in a way you unbeknownst to the rational mind. Stay alert, remain aware and open to receiving information vital to your continued journey. If this message finds you at a time when in need of this wisdom, take comfort you have found your way home. The following words of encouragement will help you with your journey and navigate your way through.

1. Don't Despair. You Are Not Alone

You are never alone pursuing your dreams. Contrary to the circumstances at the time, lean on people for assistance. The help you need may be as simple as emotional support or guidance. When I'm in despair, I need a sounding board, someone to listen without judgment. I don't need an answer or a fix to my problems. When faced with such a scenario, we rely on support from loved ones that we are not alone on this journey. Reach out to those you trust. If your loved ones are unable to support you, refrain from seeking their support in the future. Instead, consult people who comfort you in times of need. Find a niche of supporters, friends, colleagues, and allies to trust in times of need.

2. You Are Closer Than You Realize

In an online blog article, I wrote about finding an unquenchable thirst and hunger toward your goals. During your lowest times, you may call on that inner resource to pull you through. You may be closer to realizing your goals than you expect. Most people who give up are within reach of their goals. It may not be clear at the time, yet you are closer than you realize. The moments you want to abandon are signs that test your resolve. The lesson asked you're called to learn is how much do you want to achieve your goals? A YouTube video called *Inspiration: How Bad Do You Want It?* is by a well-known motivational speaker. The speaker draws the analogy of wanting success like being submerged in water, needing that last gasp of air to survive. Your lowest point toward releasing your goals may be a test and you are invited to persist or give up. Either way you choose, you will live with the consequences of your choices, so choose wisely.

I embody pursuing my dream as my life's purpose. There's nothing to stop me fulfilling my dreams. I implore you to adopt a similar mindset. Take comfort that it's not meant to be easy. Tough times build character and resolve. They build strength of mind for when you reach your goal or dream. To recognize that you came close to giving up makes the victory sweeter when you reach your goals. Keep going. Stay poised. Stay vigilant. Yes, it will be hard and it will get harder, but that pales into insignificance when you reflect on your life that you did not give up on your dreams.

The Journey Matters More Than The Destination

It comes as no surprise that the journey to reach your goals far exceeds the goal itself. Moreover, the final outcome may not be as significant as you've been led to believe. Two bold statements, yes I know. Indulge me for a moment as we explore further. Reflect on a substantial goal you accomplished in the past year. Would you have reached the goal were it not for the steps taken to get there? Goal attainment is a byproduct of one's journey. In the same way, losing weight is inevitable when you implement healthy nutritional habits and lifestyle changes. The journey to achieve a goal is governed by the person you become along the way, the skills acquired, the connections made and the inner growth. Goal setting is a term burned into our psyche from an early age. We learn that goals represent the cornerstone of every victory, notwithstanding the foundations which are crucial to support those goals. While there is some merit in that advice, you'll be surprised to know many successful people set out with little or no goals, yet still managed to achieve notable success. Their underlying motivation was grounded in continuous improvement and acquiring valuable skills. Nowadays, countless self-help books, blogs, and master classes are devoted to coaching people on goal setting. We're counseled against setting unrealistic goals since they're less likely to be realized. Rather, it is advised to outline clear and manageable goals which affords you the opportunity to chart your progress more effectively.

Depicted in the following quote by Woody Allen is the understanding there is a greater force operating in the backdrop of our lives managing the finer details: "If you want to make God laugh, tell him your plans." The underlying message is that life never goes according to plan. Life becomes replete with the meaning you assign it. It is upheld by your passion toward your purpose. In keeping with the message of shifting focus off your goal, author Michael Neil reaffirms this point in his book *Supercoach*, "Obsessing about goals is like playing a game of fetch with yourself, using your happiness and self-worth as the bone." I offer the following thoughts echoed in the advice to savor the journey rather than having a fixed outcome for your goals.

Arriving Rather Than Striving: Life is a series of minor destinations. The goal is not to acquire things or people to complete you. Such goals are bound to cause suffering once they vanish from your life—easy come, easy go. When your focus is on the goal alone, you forfeit the lessons and wonderful experiences that lie in between. Your subconscious mind and accompanying biology are formed in such a way as to support your success. Appreciate the journey and trust you have the wherewithal to accomplish any task you set your mind upon, once your will and intention are firmly grounded. The journey is the essence of where life exists in all her glory.

Take Your Eyes Off The Prize: Have you ever undertaken a goal to lose weight, with a number in mind? Do you recall what method you employed to arrive at such a figure? I'm confident it was about as random as selecting numbers for the weekly lottery. Goals are meaningless without the intermediary process to get you there. The journey is where your goals are formed and realized. You may find that in losing weight, you acquire certain skills or undertake several lifestyle changes which you previously would not have considered. If you rush the process and achieve your goal in the shortest amount of time, you forego the experiences along the way which cement your new habits. As you take your eyes off the prize and enjoy the journey, you develop the ability to sharpen the saw as Stephen

Covey lays out in *The 7 Habits of Highly Effective People*. That is, you learn to preserve and enhance your personal self.

The Journey Builds Character: Character is shaped on the path to your goals. Strength of character is developed throughout the journey via the trials and lessons experienced. You will call upon these lessons when you attain your goal, much like an athlete who spends countless hours in training, honing their performance. Those skills will be harnessed at the appropriate time. Helen Keller reminds us of the virtue of character in the following quote, "Character cannot be developed in ease and quiet. Only through experience of trial and suffering can the soul be strengthened, ambition inspired, and success achieved." You see, the journey becomes the focal point since you gain innumerable resources along the way which renders the goal far more rewarding in the end. You've heard it said successful people are adaptable. They know what they want and pursue it with intense determination. They are receptive to the process of life and do not have fixed outcomes on how their goals will be achieved.

Now is a good time as any to take your foot off the accelerator and slip into cruise control. Rest assured you'll continue to arrive at smaller destinations, which pave the way for a rewarding and fulfilling journey, replete with fulfilling life experiences. More importantly, the journey becomes a continual process of refinement, leading you toward your ultimate victory—the accomplishment of your goal and the strength of character to match.

Chapter Summary

- *Excellence arises when you develop the mental discipline to obey and collaborate with nature's laws.*
- *Excellence is the hallmark of an Authentic Self because you harness your wisdom, genius, and talents to enrich the lives of others.*
- *Excellence invites you to become the center of your universe. You live life defined by smaller acts of distinction once you have mastered your inner domain.*
- *To live a life of excellence identify with your core values and live them as best you can.*
- *Adopt a growth mindset toward excellence, which is the springboard to success.*
- *To live a life of excellence is a call toward wholehearted living, irrespective of your comparisons to others.*
- *Success is a destination while excellence is an enduring journey of self-discovery and blinding detours.*
- *The person who succeeds in their goals, their vision and mastery of self is the one who follows through and sticks with it,* **no matter what life throws at them.**

- *Future events are only present moment possibilities.*
- *To be prepared means no matter the obstacles you encounter, they are placed in your path for your greatest growth.*
- *Vigilance is a state of being. It's a way of asserting your mental state, despite outward conditions.*
- *Persistence is a powerful force that can be harnessed toward success.*
- *Every time you face obstacles, you're invited to grow.*
- *Goal attainment is a byproduct of one's journey.*
- *Life becomes replete with the meaning you assign it. It is upheld by your passion toward your purpose.*
- *The journey becomes a continual process of refinement, leading you toward your ultimate victory—the accomplishment of your goal and the strength of character to match.*

Your Authentic Self Awaits

"The privilege of a lifetime is to become who you truly are."
—C.G. Jung

I opened the book outlining several principles to live by if we wish to awaken the Authentic Self. They are depicted below and form the basis of an integrated life, since this is who you are at the deepest level. When we connect with the core our being, we merge with the Truth of our spiritual self. This self is not obscured by labels or limiting beliefs about who it should be, because it knows how to survive in the world. This self is your true essence and because we dissociate from it, we lose our way. But you can never become lost when you are tied to universal intelligence. Point seven below states, "find time for silence" because without regular silence we are caught up in the outside world and get distracted by the external noise. Worse still, we move into our heads and listen to the stream of incessant thoughts which occupy space in our minds. I'm not suggesting we ignore our thoughts; rather our thoughts have little to offer us by way of who we are. They are labels, ideas, and impressions we pick up along the way during our life's journey. But just as a GPS device, they tell us no more of who we are if we are not connected to a satellite or use the wrong map.

- Accept Yourself
- Know Thyself

- Discard The False Self
- Don't Associate With Thoughts
- Surrender Addictions
- Stop Seeking Validation
- Find Time For Silence
- Connect With Your Heart And Mind
- Accept The Process Of Life
- Focus On Yourself First
- Relationships Are Vital Lessons
- Connect With Purpose

To reveal the Authentic Self, we must learn to let go of ideas instead of accumulate more. Consider a hoarder who buys collectibles without selling existing items. Soon enough his space is packed full of items and he cannot move around until he frees up additional space. Your mind is the same. It is so full of thoughts that it becomes a distorted representation of the nature of reality. I use "distorted" in the kindest possible sense to show it being obscured from seeing the truth. Reflect on the following tale:

A long time ago, there was a wise Zen master. People from far and near sought his counsel for his wisdom to become enlightened in the way of Zen. He seldom turned any away. One day an important man of command and obedience came to visit the master. "I have come today to ask you to teach me about Zen. Open my mind to enlightenment." The tone of the important man's voice was accustomed to getting his own way.

The Zen master smiled and said they should discuss the matter over a cup of tea. When the tea was served, the master poured the visitor a cup. He continued to pour until the tea overflowed the rim of the cup and spilled over onto the robes of the man. Finally, the visitor shouted, "Enough. You are spilling the tea all over. Can't you see the cup is full?" The master stopped pouring and smiled at his guest. "You are like this tea cup, so full that nothing more can be added. Come back when the cup and your mind are empty."

Like the important man visiting the wise Zen master, he cannot gain more information when his mind is full. Letting go of our stories, ideas, and beliefs is not easy because we fear we will lose our identity if we do so. If you believe that to be true, you have built an identity on shaky ground. You cannot form a true identity on unstable foundations, for that is equivalent to building a house on sand hoping it won't sink into the ground. That's why we must gradually abandon our perceptions of life to replace them with the truth. It was the late Dr. David Hawkins who stated in a Sedona Seminar in 2002, "There is one basic saying in Zen that one can rely on completely: Walk through all fear no matter what, committed to spiritual truth, no matter what."

It may take an entire lifetime to awaken the Authentic Self, which is concealed by the weight of past conditioning. However, it is better to live an authentic life than imprisoned as someone you pretend to be. In her book *The Top Five Regrets of the Dying: A Life Transformed by the Dearly Departing*, author Bronnie Ware states the following as the five regrets:

1. I wish I'd had the courage to live a life true to myself, not the life others expected of me.
2. I wish I hadn't worked so hard.
3. I wish I'd had the courage to express my feelings.
4. I wish I had stayed in touch with my friends.
5. I wish that I had let myself be happier.

The number one regret of the dying is to have lived a more authentic life and not live according to the wishes of others. Depending on your circumstances, you still have time to chart a new course while striving to live from the heart. The mind will lead you so far, while the heart with its infinite wisdom will direct you on a journey of self-discovery. Contained within this self-discovery is the journey to awaken you to your Authentic Self. It is author Paulo Coelho who affirms in *The Alchemist,* "Remember that wherever your heart is, there you will find your treasure." The heart is the seat of the soul and since your soul is infinite, it knows the best passage for your life's journey. As outlined earlier in the book, soulful living is an invitation to live beyond the material world and be led by your heart's wisdom. You will not be led astray if you follow your heart. I devoted several paragraphs to *Knowing The Language Of The Heart* in Chapter 7 to guide you on the language the heart communicates in.

I leave you with the knowing that heart-based or soulful living is the awakening of your Authentic Self. Once you awaken this loving-kindness within, you can never go back to living your former ways. Like a gradual awakening of the heart, you will experience life through the eyes of a child, because you now see life through an awakened mind instead of an overflowing cup. I wish you continued success along your life's journey. As you follow your heart, it will lead you to destinations and experiences infinitely orchestrated for your personal evolution.

To your continued health and happiness,
Tony Fahkry

About the Author

Tony is a leading self-empowerment expert speaker, author, and coach. His understanding and integration of mind and body concepts bridges the gap between self-empowerment and human behaviour.

Tony has developed a comprehensive self-empowerment program, The Power to Navigate Life. The program teaches participants how to achieve continued mental, emotional, and physical well-being using easy-to-follow principles. The book which bears the same name is testimony to the principles espoused in the program.

The book achieved local and international attention with Dr. Eldon Taylor NY Times Best Selling author contributing the foreword. Tony's follow-up book, *Reconstructing The Past To Create A Remarkable Future* gained the attention of international author, Dr. Joe Vitale from *The Secret* film who wrote the foreword.

Tony has achieved the highest authorship of Platinum Author for Ezine Articles with over two hundred and fifty articles to date. He writes for several leading personal and spiritual growth websites to include: *Thought Catalog, Niume, Scriggler, MOGUL, Niume, Medium, Pick The Brain,* SelfGrowth.com, StartsAtSixty.com, *Ezine Articles* and many more.

YOU MIGHT ALSO LIKE:

101 Essays That Will Change The Way You Think by Brianna Wiest

Tell the Truth, Let the Peace Fall Where it May by Bryan Reeves

Your Soul is a River by Nikita Gill

THOUGHT
CATALOG
Books

THOUGHT CATALOG

IT'S A WEBSITE.
www.thoughtcatalog.com

SOCIAL
facebook.com/thoughtcatalog
twitter.com/thoughtcatalog
tumblr.com/thoughtcatalog
instagram.com/thoughtcatalog

CORPORATE
www.thought.is

Printed in Great Britain
by Amazon

80454822R00185